ALIVE AND WELL
IN PAKISTAN

A. Khawoja
April 15, 09

ALIVE AND WELL IN PAKISTAN

A Human Journey in a Dangerous Time

ETHAN CASEY

First published in 2004 by Vision,
a division of Satin Publications Ltd.
101 Southwark Street
London SE1 0JF
UK
info@visionpaperbacks.co.uk
www.visionpaperbacks.co.uk
Publisher: Sheena Dewan

A catalogue record for this book is available from the British Library.

ISBN: 978-1-904132-48-6

2 4 6 8 10 9 7 5 3

Jacket photo: Sipa/Rex Features
Jacket and text design by ok?design
Printed and bound in the UK by Mackays of Chatham Ltd, Chatham, Kent.

CONTENTS

PAKISTAN AND KASHMIR

Skardu

KASHMIR

Kargil

Muzaffarabad

Peshawar

Srinagar

Islamabad

Line of Control

AFGHANISTAN

Rawalpindi

Lahore

Faisalabad

Amritsar

Quetta

Multan

Delhi

PAKISTAN

IRAN

INDIA

Hyderabad

Karachi

ARABIAN SEA

PROLOGUE

A TYPICAL FLIGHT
TO LAHORE

It was as if I was already in Pakistan. Flight PK758 was still at the gate at Heathrow, and I was in a bulkhead window seat. The aroma of lamb curry wafted across the aisle. Then the fight broke out.

A couple of rows behind me a tall man with a moustache was shouting, accusing another man of being drunk, while other passengers and flight attendants admonished and tried to calm him.

'Please, please!' cried a clean-shaven, mild-countenanced smaller man in elegant shalwar kameez and vest, spectacles and carefully tended greying hair.

'I am not going on this flight!' shouted the tall man.

'You've got a problem with him, deal with it in your own time,' remonstrated another man, in a British accent. 'I have urgent business. You are holding up four hundred people. You are now holding my business up. You are on the same plane as him. If you had any sense you'd realise that he's on the same plane as you, and you can deal with him when you get to Lahore. It's none of my fuckin' business.'

'Don't touch me!'

'There are two ways of dealing with this. Either you will sit down or, I promise you, I will call security and get you both off the fucking plane.'

'Call the fuckin' s'curity! Call the fuckin' s'curity!'

The benign-looking man leaned on the seat next to mine and confided, with a grin: 'This is a typical flight to Lahore.'

It seemed a good omen, somehow.

'What's it about?'

'The other bloke was piss drunk, in the seat behind you. And he was leaning over this fellow's seat, playing with his hair.'

'They didn't know each other?'

'They didn't know each other. I thought they were friends. So this guy punched the other guy. And then …' He gestured in the direction of the scene we had just witnessed.

The tall man disappeared.

'Where is he?' someone asked.

'In the toilet,' replied someone else.

'Good. Let's lock him in there.'

It must have been resolved somehow, because suddenly a female voice was giving safety instructions in English and Urdu, the crew were bustling and demonstrating, and the plane was easing toward the runway. Half an hour late, we were airborne.

I awoke to bright sunshine and a clear view of the brown, bare mountains of Afghanistan. The abrupt transition between worlds that air travel entails shocks the system. The air traveller cultivates non-attachment, chronically standing apart from the disorienting variety of people and places he encounters, at the same time craving inclusion and connection with them. I had not been in Asia in two and a half years, or in Pakistan in more than four. A great deal had happened in the meantime. One fine morning two years ago tomorrow, everything had seemed to change. Returning to Pakistan for a five-month stint was for me a way of keeping faith with my own experience, comparing notes with my younger self. Looking down on Afghanistan I felt how far away I had been, and for how long, from Asia, where events had real meaning and urgency and where I felt most alive.

'The difference between you and me,' my friend Tony Davis had said to me near the end of my five-year sojourn in Bangkok, 'is that I'm a Western man who belongs in Asia, and you're a Western man who just happens to be in Asia.' This stung, but it was true. Reluctantly I admitted that I needed to return to my own wellspring. But another five years later, I was again bored with the West and its trivial obsessions and meta-media. Asia, where I had cut my teeth as a journalist and crossed the shadow-line between youth and maturity, had become part of me. Maybe I belonged there after all.

Tony Davis and I had become friends in 1995, after he wrote a letter to the editor of the *Bangkok Post* accusing me of 'retailing silly conspiracy theories' in an article about Kashmir. I acknowledged the justice of some of his points, challenged others, and invited him for a beer. I came to know him as a great and under-appreciated authority on Afghanistan and Asian security issues, a hard-working role model, and a large-hearted and loyal friend. Tony wrote for *Asiaweek* magazine and *Jane's Defence Weekly*.

On my last visit to Asia, in early 2001, we had spent several days together in the far north of Thailand, near the Burma border, where there had recently been cross-border shelling. Tony's father, who had been in the British Army, had advised him not to join the military because the Empire was dying and the good old days were over. For Tony, being a journalist was the next best thing. After we visited a Thai Army camp where our visit must have been the most interesting thing to have happened to the soldiers in a while, Tony remarked to me: 'Soldiering is probably the profession with the most time spent sitting around with nothing to do. But journalism – or at least our kind of journalism – is a close second.'

For me, journalism had started out as the next best thing to Writing. As a teenager, I wanted to be William Faulkner. I fell into journalism, as the *Observer* foreign correspondent Gavin Young wrote about himself, 'as a drunken man falls into a pond.' Until inevitably becoming rich and famous, I needed to make a living, and I figured journalism was a way to make money while seeing the world and getting my name in print. Along the way, my perspective changed. I came to value above all the concrete sense of place, event and history-in-the-making that the practice of journalism gives me. Thus did Tony's words resonate when, sipping beer one evening on a hotel rooftop near the Thai-Burma border, he said: 'There's no substitute for the sniff on the ground.'

As the plane crossed Pakistan and descended toward Lahore, I read Michael Ignatieff's article 'Why Are We in Iraq? (And Liberia? And Afghanistan?)' in *The New York Times Magazine* and glumly and enviously pondered a culture of publishing that tempts writers to trade hard-earned authority for bylines over well-phrased policy recommendations in prestigious periodicals. Such writing has its uses, but after its best-by date it's of little more than antiquarian or novelty interest. When I read such articles I always wonder: what you mean 'we', paleface? I'm not in Afghanistan. I'm not in Iraq. I speak only for myself.

I saw no other Westerners on the plane or, for that matter, during my first several days in Lahore.

'Sir, you are transit passenger?' a man asked as I was getting a baggage trolley.

Startled, I said: 'No. I'm waiting for my bags.'

'Not going to Islamabad?'

'No.'

'You stay Lahore,' he confirmed. He seemed surprised.

'Yes.'

I sat on my trolley near the baggage conveyor; the bags were taking a long time to come out.

'Yes? May I help you?' This time it was a uniformed porter.

'No, thank you. I'm waiting for my bags.'

'Okay. I also am waiting your bag.' He laughed at his own joke.

4

At another conveyor stood several hundred soldiers in fatigues and blue berets. I was later told they had just returned from peace-keeping duties in Sierra Leone.

The next day, I marked the second anniversary of the attack on the World Trade Center by rereading Joan Didion's essay 'Fixed Opinions, or The Hinge of History,'* in which she wrote of 'repeated pieties that would come to seem in some ways as destructive as the event itself':

> The final allowable word on those who attacked us was to be that they were 'evildoers,' or 'wrongdoers,' peculiar constructions which served to suggest that those who used them were transmitting messages from some ultimate authority … We have come in this country to tolerate many such fixed opinions, or national pieties, each with its own baffles of invective and counterinvective, of euphemism and downright misstatement.

The day's issue of the Pakistani paper *The News* led with this:

> Asia stays alert on eve of 9/11 anniversary
> Violence-hit
> Sharon quits
> India early
>
> Trip called climax of ties;
> India to import lethal hardware from Jewish state;
> Tel Aviv to send telescope into space on Indian rocket

A cartoon showed Indian Prime Minister Vajpayee and Israeli Prime Minister Sharon shaking hands and smiling at each other, both

* *The New York Review of Books*, 16 January 2003

saying 'Anti Muslim' while President Musharraf of Pakistan, looking puzzled and bereft in the background, holds a sign saying 'Recognition of Israel', with a question mark in a thought bubble over his head.

In the second section were two pages of articles full of national pieties about Mohammed Ali Jinnah, the late Quaid-e-Azam ('Great Leader') of Pakistan, written in the tedious, verbose subcontinental style. I wondered why, until I saw the spectral founder's portrait at the top of the page, surrounded by the words:

DEATH ANNIVERSARY OF THE QUAID-I-AZAM

That evening, in the lounge of the guesthouse where I was being lodged, the PTV news dutifully reported commemorations at Jinnah's mausoleum in Karachi.

'Today is the day he died,' I commented to my dinner companion, a woman named Zarina Sadik. Pakistan's founder died on 11 September 1948.

'Is it the 11th?' she replied. After a pause to consult her mental calendar, she added: 'Yes, that's right.'

PART ONE

BEFORE

CHAPTER ONE

A DEPICTION OF SOMETHING TRUE

I had travelled a long road from Wisconsin to Pakistan. I grew up in the 1970s outside Milwaukee, in a town that was becoming a suburb, typical enough, idyllic yet stifling and self-satisfied, a medium-sized town outside a medium-sized, declining industrial city, in a medium-sized state in the middle of North America. I felt at home there but my parents, who were from Texas, made clear by their body language and tone of voice that we didn't belong there. Where, then, did I belong?

My father took me with him to Haiti in 1982, when I was sixteen, and transformed my awareness of the world and my place in it. To have seen Haiti is to know how artificial and stylised life is in suburban America, like a sitcom in endless reruns. Once I had pierced the membrane and escaped, there was no going back. In 1986 I whimsically decided to spend an academic year in Nepal, on a University of Wisconsin programme. It was a time of innocence. I explored the Kathmandu Valley and trekked to the base of Everest. I felt very far from home. I communicated with my family in the US via handwritten aerogrammes that took two weeks or more to arrive. Once, when I needed to reach my parents quickly, I went to the General Post Office and sent a telegram, for which I paid by the word. America was just where I wanted it: as far away as possible from me.

The books in the many bookshops in Kathmandu's tourist section were of exotic interest to me; most were in British editions I had never seen before. In America one didn't see V.S. Naipaul in Penguins, for instance. In any case I had never heard of Naipaul, so my obsession with him declared itself innocently. I bought and read *An Area of Darkness*, his first book on India, in an early Penguin edition with a soft-focus drawing of a *shikara*, a lake boat, on the Dal Lake on the cover. Next I read *India: A Wounded Civilization*, then *The Middle Passage* and *Among the Believers*, the collection *The Overcrowded Barracoon, Finding the Centre* and several novels. Soon I was reading no longer for the subject matter but for the author. I was sensing that, whatever he wrote about, this Naipaul guy wrote close to the bone.

It was this callow obsession with Naipaul that led me eventually to Pakistan, via Kashmir. Bored after only ten months editing wire stories in the *Bangkok Post*'s air-conditioned building, I quit the paper early in 1994 and went to India. In particular I went to Kashmir, because Naipaul had written vividly about it.

My first day in Delhi, a Sikh cycle-rickshaw driver told me I'd better check in with a 'government tourist office', at which he would be happy to stop en route to the hotel I had named. It turned out, after the young Kashmiri at the 'tourist office' made a phone call, that the hotel I had in mind was full. But there was this other place, just 300 rupees a night. As these things sometimes turn out, the Kashmiri and I quickly became good friends.

Where did I want to go? Agra? Jaipur? Rajasthan? He could help me. I really didn't know, I said. Right now I'd better rest. I would come back tomorrow. He pressed me: why not decide right now? No better time than the present! I'd better leave a deposit: sometimes these buses fill up, you know. I was to watch him put the same hard sell on many another helpless foreigner and, later, I took pleasure from secretly knowing I was on his side. I took even greater pleasure from peremptorily rejecting the ingratiating advances of the numberless other Kashmiris on Connaught Place and in Paharganj, where they sidled up with whispered promises of 'free information', as if that were something illicit.

'Hello. You want bus ticket train ticket flight ticket? You want go Kashmir?'

'*No!* Get away from me!'

Actually, yes, I said that first day: I did want to go to Kashmir. There was a particular place I wanted to stay. Not a houseboat. A hotel.

Might he inquire which hotel?

'Hotel Leeward.' I had a special reason for wanting to meet the proprietor, I said.

'Mister Butt.'

My skin crawled. He was *real!*

No one stays at hotels like the Leeward, explained my new friend; they were only for Indians. Foreign visitors stayed on houseboats. The houseboats were the whole reason people went to Kashmir. And he just happened to know an excellent one.

My awareness of the Kashmir insurgency had begun a few months earlier, when I learned of the siege of the Hazratbal mosque while scanning the wires at the *Bangkok Post*. Overnight on 16 October 1993 about 1,000 Indian Army soldiers had surrounded the most important Muslim religious site in the Vale of Kashmir – the heartland of the State of Jammu and Kashmir disputed since 1947 between India and Pakistan, described by the *New York Times* as 'a gentle swath of fields and forests carved by the Himalayas'. Indian government spokesmen told the *Times* man that about a hundred 'Muslim separatist guerrillas' had taken refuge inside the mosque with arms and ammunition.

One read the phrase often. Like 'Himalayan kingdom' in stories about Nepal, or 'poorest country in the Western hemisphere' for

Haiti, it covered a lot of ground – too much. Such phrases, propagated by reporters on deadline, approved by editors with limited space to spare and desired by readers wanting understanding without effort, were the opposite of poetic, leeching the complexity and subtlety out of a situation. The men inside the Hazratbal mosque certainly were Muslims, and separatists, and guerrillas. But there was more to say about them than that. As I began to learn, the Kashmir problem had a history, and no party to it was without blame, and its roots traced back to the partition of the subcontinent – which is to say, to the creation of Pakistan. The awkward truth was that the real issue was not the status of Kashmir but the existence of Pakistan.

The Indian government 'was likely to carry out a programme of stealing the holy relic of Prophet Mohammed (peace be upon him)', Mohammed Yusuf Sofi, aka General Idris, intelligence chief of the pro-independence Jammu and Kashmir Liberation Front (JKLF) and leader of the militants inside the mosque, later told me. The relic was a hair believed to be a whisker from the Prophet's beard, and it had been the subject of a similar Hazratbal crisis in 1963. Some colleagues had told General Idris that the area was being cordoned off, so he went to the mosque with the intention of protecting the whisker. 'The moment he enters into the mosque, he puts on his communications set and was trying to catch the signals of BSF [Border Security Forces],' his translator told me. 'Then he orders to the boys to take up positions, and be ready for any worst.'

The Indian government, he said, 'had this plan to paint this movement as a communal movement' and 'angering the masses so that they would break down the sanctity of the mosque'. JKLF deputy chief Altaf Qadri added that if the government's claim was valid that the army had to surround the mosque because militants were taking advantage of Friday prayer times to give political speeches, then the army 'should have come at the right time, when certain people were giving speeches. There was no gathering at all. The sole purpose was to steal the holy relic.'

General Idris was killed on 11 February 1995, near the Hazratbal mosque, by gunmen from Hizbul Mujahedin, a rival, pro-Pakistan group.

The siege lasted 32 days and deepened the bitterness, springing from what they considered broken promises, that had motivated many Kashmiris to take up arms against India in 1989. It ended with either a surrender or a negotiated settlement, depending on whom you believe, and it didn't really end until 6 August 1994, when the bunkers around the mosque were removed after the pro-Pakistan group Harkat ul-Ansar made a full lifting of the siege a condition of its allowing the annual Hindu pilgrimage to Amarnath to proceed in safety.

It was my first exposure to the dissonant perspectives and poisonous vocabularies partisans bring to matters of dispute in the subcontinent.

'Nothing brings out the Indian commitment to democracy and democratic values as strikingly as its handling of the seizure of Kashmir's holiest shrine Hazratbal by Pakistani-based terrorists in 1993,' wrote M.L. Kotru in *The Kashmir Story*, an Indian government document given to me in June 1995. 'It was a diabolical plan whose purpose was to tarnish India's image by trying to provoke Indian security forces to react and force their way into the Shrine. In the event the raising of a month-long cordon around the Shrine complex broke the will of the armed men inside and led them to surrender themselves to the security forces.'

'The Indians were clever in Hazratbal in reverting to a political process,' Sardar Abdul Qayyum Khan, prime minister of Azad ('Free') Kashmir, the portion of the state controlled by Pakistan, told me around the same time. The siege, he noted, had come less than a year after the December 1992 destruction of the Babri Mosque in Ayodhya by Hindu extremists and 'exposed Hindu fundamentalism. It highlighted throughout the world the Kashmir issue. All these things together gave a great boost to the freedom movement.'

Such matters were beyond my horizon at first. Truth be told, it was the lure of literary history that first enticed me to the Dal Lake. Until Hazratbal, my knowledge of Kashmir had been limited to what I had learned incidentally from a particular book.

'It was my eye that had changed,' writes Naipaul, and this happened eventually to me too. Through the alchemy of writing, Naipaul had both exorcised his own Indian illusions and conjured new ones for me. I had had to create my own virtual versions of his settings, as he writes in *The Enigma of Arrival* of having done, as a boy in Trinidad, to the settings of Dickens. The Dal Lake and Gulmarg and Amarnath were in my mind Naipaul's territory. His great gift to me as a reader was to have stimulated my curiosity enough that I wanted to see the world for myself. If ultimately I've gained a perspective different from his, it doesn't diminish my gratitude for the gift. The irony is that, having read Naipaul's work for the author, I came to decide that the subject matter is more important and interesting, and that I have as much claim to it as he does.

An Area of Darkness is not a shapely book. It is jerry-built from three ill-fitting parts: 90 pages of brilliant direct narration set in Kashmir, sandwiched between more general musings on India at large. But the book is a classic, and the Kashmir section is distinguished by a precision of depiction rarely equalled even elsewhere in Naipaul. Notably in evidence is his superb ear for spoken language; he captures the odd Kashmiri pronunciation *touriasm*, for instance (though nowhere in his account does the reader encounter the more common *tourist-es*). After all that has been lost beyond recovery since 1989, the greatest of the many virtues of Naipaul's book is simply that he witnessed and recorded Kashmir at a moment now irretrievable. And it's all there: the languor, naiveté and salesmanship of Kashmiris, and the futility of their situation; the Amarnath pilgrimage; the whisker from the Prophet's beard.

Naipaul had gone to Kashmir 'by the road built by the Indian army in 1947 at the time of the Pakistan invasion'. The North Indian plains became 'like an illness whose exact sensations it is impossible, after recovery, to recall'; the Valley was 'coolness and colour: the yellow mustard fields, the mountains, snow-capped, the milky blue sky in which we rediscovered the drama of clouds. It was men wrapped in brown blankets against the morning mist, and barefooted shepherd boys with caps and covered ears on steep wet rocky slopes.'

It became all these and more for me too, but my first arrival was by air. The view from the small plane as it descended was of mountains rising abruptly from an expansive floor. In the airport building I was made to fill out a form. Under OCCUPATION I wrote 'writer', thinking it was best to be above board. As I waited at the baggage conveyor a uniformed Indian soldier approached, wearing a look of mild alarm.

'Your occupation is writer?'

'Yes.'

'What magazine you work for?'

'I write books,' I said, hopefully. I hadn't yet written any.

His look changed to one of relief.

'You write "Books" here.'

Not everyone takes to Kashmiris, but I did. I was befriended during my time of discovery by an old man to whom I owe a great deal, whom I must call simply Haji. He was habitually gracious and hospitable, and well connected, with a strong personality; a presence.

I wish I felt free to describe him physically. He had seen a lot of history in his own valley, but the great adventure of his life had been the Haj, when he and his wife made the pilgrimage to Mecca. He delighted in telling me of all he had seen there, especially the truck-loads of ice donated by rich men that were thrown down into the immense crowds of pilgrims suffering under the Arabian sun. He had never seen that before, not in Kashmir!

He was a great lover of the hookah, or 'hubble-bubble', which he said was the English word. 'I think smoking is your very favourite thing to do,' I once said to him.

He grinned. 'Whenever I go on a trip,' he declared, 'wheresoever I may go, first thing I always take with me is' – he paused as he liked to do, for effect – 'my hubble-bubble.'

In his house were many birds, slightly larger than sparrows, with forked tails, constantly flying in and out the windows. As he sat in his front room one afternoon, puffing away on his hubble-bubble, a mother bird busied herself building a nest near the ceiling.

'You should look in that corridor there,' he said happily. 'There are *hundred* of birds.'

The growing baby birds flew in circles around the front room, completely unafraid, alighting on shelves, the alarm clock, the TV set.

'I think these are the young ones,' said Haji, 'because they don't know how to fly yet. And they lost their way.'

I asked why there were sheets of cardboard nailed near the ceiling in the corridor. Was it to help the birds build their nests?

'Because when they shit down,' he said matter-of-factly. 'No, they don't need cardboard for to build nest. They make very *strong* nest.'

'Do birds live in all houses here?'

'No-o. I think they live in only *few* houses. They are clever. They know where to live, where they are safe.'

Did the young birds return the following spring to the same house, after they had grown up, to make their own nests?

'They go away in month of September,' he said. 'No more birds. Then on second of March I see birds flying to window and then away. I wonder why. Then I realise, these are birds that live in my house summer before. I open window, they fly inside. They know their own house, they know their nest, everything.' He grinned, smugly. 'In Arabic we call them *abbaibil*. I forget the English name. All my relatives don't like them. Even my daughter-in-law does not like them because she has to clean the floor. But I say don't harm them.'

Haji reminded me a bit of a Haitian priest I had known who spoke in riddles and who, like Haji, radiated an indulgent patriarchal air and a seemingly ill-founded calm that was both alluring and slightly maddening. The difference was that Haji had a sense of humour. It had taken me time to see that the priest's enigmas were his surrogates for answers, carefully cultivated over a long lifetime of asking questions. Only after some time spent in Haji's company did it occur to me what the mysterious something was about them both: religious faith, or a personal certainty that there exist aspects of this world not governed by politics.

Unlike the priest, Haji was not reluctant to involve himself in politics, though on his own terms. 'Sel-ef-determination. That is my main objective,' he told me many times. Kashmiris had been promised a plebiscite, he pointed out, and besides, freedom was the birthright of every man. Simple as that. He would get his hands dirty on more particular matters when and only when necessary, but never would he compromise on his bedrock commitment or commit himself to any party or group, any of them. Why should he? All he wanted was self-determination. Once he told me the young president of the JKLF, Yaseen Malik, had asked him (as he quoted him), 'Haji, why you don't join politics? Why you don't belong some party?'

'I support only one party,' Haji had told him.

'Which party?' asked Yaseen Malik.

'Sel-ef-determination.' He grinned, in that way of his.

I spent a lot of time with Haji's servant, an unpretentious man who made a point of having nothing whatsoever to do with politics or militancy. Only three things mattered to him: his religion (he awoke each morning early to lead the call to prayer), his family, and his work. Once during my second visit, as he paddled us somewhere in his shikara, my companion asked if he had been to Delhi, assuming he had. He replied that he had been to Ladakh – the even more remote, Tibetan area of Jammu and Kashmir State – but never to Delhi, and frankly he didn't care to go: from what he had heard, it didn't sound very appealing. Too hot, too crowded, too polluted.

'There is only one place I want to go,' he said.

'Mecca,' I guessed.

'Mecca,' he confirmed. He didn't even smile; he was in the greatest earnest. When I returned the next year he had grown a full beard, in anticipation.

He possessed a wealth of knowledge about anything to do with Kashmir other than politics; as we glided along in the houseboat neighbourhood and on the open lake toward the island of Char Chinar and the Moghul Gardens, he would tell me things as he propelled us with his heart-shaped paddle. 'You see, this is both side engine,' he said, squatting at one end of the shikara rather than the other. 'Front and back. Two engine. One horsepower.'

'And you're the horse,' I said.

He laughed. 'Yeah.'

The Dal Lake had shrunk within his memory, because the population had grown, and more people had begun taking mud from the bottom to make new islands. More women wore the veil now than when he was young, and he was yet to be convinced that was a good thing. The lake rises each year with melting snow from April until June or July, he said, then goes down again in August. This year there had been very little snow, only 12 inches. There were more migratory birds, teal and others, as well as more bears and other wildlife; since 1989 people had had to turn in their registered hunting guns to the army. To him it seemed there were maybe three or four times as many birds now as before. 'We still had the king-fisher,' writes Naipaul in *An Area of Darkness*. 'But other birds appeared less frequently in the garden. We missed the hoopoe, with his long busy bill, his curved back and white wing stripes, his crest fanning out as he landed.' I came to know two kinds of kingfisher (they came in black-and-white and in colour), always poised to dive into the water from tree branches, water pipes or electric wires; a yellow sparrow; a coo-coo bird grey like a dove; hawks hovering proudly over the lake; a bird with a crest like a Mohawk haircut (was that the hoopoe?). And there were the plants and flowers: daisies, bright red poppies, cannabis growing wild on neglected hillsides and river banks, a sight that always delighted me wherever I encountered it in Asia (outside the Burmese embassy in Kathmandu, in the grass lining the sedate planned streets of Islamabad) for the sheer disdainful lawlessness of it.

Haji's servant showed me the Shalomar Road, built by the Moghuls on a narrow strip of land made from lake-bottom mud, crossing the lake all the way from the Moghul Gardens to near Hazratbal, destroyed early in 1990 by the Indian government. Only one small section had been left standing. I asked why.

He shrugged. 'The memory.'

Gently, always in vain, I tried to goad him into talking politics. 'Do you think Kashmir will ever be free?' I asked.

He was silent a moment. 'I don't think so.' That was all he had to say about that.

In the troubles there was a distinctive, Kashmiri sort of rhythm to the way things happened and were reported. Something happened more or less every day, it seemed; so many civilians killed, so said the rumours, so many soldiers, the government says this many died but everyone knew it was really this many. The government said this happened but really that happened. Two days after I arrived, militants attacked soldiers in three places outside Srinagar city, and a building and 20 vehicles were burned. Some said the militants had set the fires; others said the militants had escaped and the army had done it. It was not easy to know the truth.

The same evening, Haji told me there had been a bomb blast – the alliterative phrase slid easily off Kashmiri tongues – at the army cantonment area outside town. Three were confirmed dead; a militant group was taking credit. A building had burned, for which a different group was claiming credit. Haji's information was that there actually had been 40 killed, all army personnel. The BBC had broadcast the story.

I wanted a sense of scale. How many had to die before it was News?

'Is this big news?' I asked, maybe a little breathlessly.

'Yes,' said Haji. 'But BBC has already published it!'

The next morning, Haji came to the houseboat I was staying on with an update. The government – 'India' was his word – was officially admitting that a Major-General and 14 other army officers had been killed in the bomb blast. This meant that even more had actually died; official figures never overestimated. 'India' claimed the blast was accidental. But if so, why was the army tightening security around the cantonment? And a militant group had taken credit. It sounded to Haji as though an attack of embarrassing proportions had been perpetrated on the Indian military.

V.S. Naipaul and his English wife, Patricia, came to Kashmir in April 1962 and stayed long enough to join the annual Hindu pilgrimage to the ice lingam at Amarnath in August. He probably celebrated his thirtieth birthday in Kashmir, and here he wrote his short novel *Mr Stone and the Knights Companion*: on the last page of that book is the terse italic note *Srinagar, August 1962*.

The famed houseboats of the Dal Lake, he writes, 'lay on the lake in a white row against floating green islands, answering the snow on the surrounding mountains … In shikaras we were ferried over to the houseboats, where, mooring, and going up dainty steps, we found interiors beyond anything we had imagined: carpets and brassware and framed pictures, china and panelling and polished furniture of another age.'

But the houseboats' 'relics were still too movingly personal', so instead Naipaul found the Hotel Liward (so spelled), on an island in the lake, behind the rows of houseboats: 'a rough two-storeyed structure with ochre concrete walls, green and chocolate woodwork, and a roof of unpainted corrugated iron.'

Naipaul needs an adequate writing table and a reading lamp. Aziz, the hotel servant, shows him an 'old weathered table lying out on the lawn'.

'We paint,' he assures Naipaul. 'We fix.'

'It was then that I felt they were playing and that I had become part of their play,' remarks Naipaul. But he decides to stay, and thus begins a mutually ambivalent four-month struggle of wills and comedy of manners between guest and hosts, delicately and memorably narrated. 'Service was his world,' writes Naipaul of Aziz. 'It was his craft, his trade … I became as alert to Aziz's moods as he had been to mine. He had the power to infuriate me; his glumness could spoil a morning for me … I wished, above all, to be sure of his loyalty. And this was impossible, for I was not his employer. So in my relations with him, I alternated between bullying and bribing; and he handled both.'

The Liward's proprietor is M.S. Butt. 'Mr Butt he say,' Aziz tells Naipaul after proudly demonstrating the new flush toilet to him, 'this is not his hotel. This is your hotel.'

Naipaul returned to the Valley in April 1989, and he might have been better advised not to. A smarmy nostalgia pervades much of his cumbrously-titled 1990 book *India: A Million Mutinies Now*, notably the short, self-indulgent Kashmir section near the end. 'The road to the town was being improved,' he observes. 'It led past many big new houses; I hadn't seen that kind of private wealth in 1962.' Although he mentions in passing 'a secessionist Muslim group' that 'had been setting off bombs in public places', he seems shockingly oblivious to what is coming in Kashmir. Or perhaps, given his willfully elegiac mood, he prefers not to think about it.

Eagerly he returns to the Hotel Leeward, 'in that corrected spelling, according to its big signboard. Not the modest cottage and lake garden I had lived in, but an establishment dominant even in the new commercial clutter: solid, concrete-walled, many-winged, many-gabled ... With the steep pitched roof, the effect was Tibetan or Japanese.' There he has a sentimental reunion with Mr Butt and Aziz and meets Aziz's son Nazir, a 'small handsome young man' who is studying accountancy. Nazir, they tell him, 'had wanted to become a doctor. But they had talked him out of that. There was no business like the hotel business.'

Haji knew Mr Butt well, he told me when I asked; Haji seemed to know everyone. Mr Butt was ill; he had a prostate problem and a heart condition, and high blood pressure. He recently had had an operation on his prostate. Naipaul had remarked on Mr Butt's declining health in 1989; Aziz had told him he needed to stop smoking. 'But I am good, sir,' Mr Butt had assured Naipaul, shaking his hand firmly. Mr Butt was mainly a 'farmer', Haji told me, though it might have been more accurate to call him a landowner; Nazir had pointed out to Naipaul an orchard he owned outside Srinagar. The Leeward, Haji told me, was Mr Butt's 'side business'. Hotels like it had depended mostly on Indian tourists, not foreigners, and had done most of their business during August, when Hindus came for the Amarnath pilgrimage.

I asked Haji if he knew Aziz, who had worked for Mr Butt.

Abdul Aziz, he corrected me. Oh yes, he also knew Abdul Aziz well. He and Abdul Aziz had played together as children. Abdul Aziz was not more than two or three years younger than himself, he was sure; that would put Abdul Aziz in his early sixties, depending on Haji's own age (he gave me several figures on different occasions). Abdul Aziz and Mr Butt were brothers.

Brothers?

Yes, they were brothers, as Naipaul seemed never to have realised. Same father, different mothers. Mohammed Sidiq Bhat* and Abdul Aziz Bhat. Mr Butt, or Bhat, was about 14 years older. Mr Bhat's mother had died, his father had remarried, and Abdul Aziz was the son of the father's second wife.

I pressed Haji to introduce me to them and one morning, I in high excitement and he wondering what was the big deal, we went in his shikara to the Hotel Leeward. There it was as we rounded a bend among houseboats and trees, big and white with the Tibetan-looking pitched roof, the three-story new building of Naipaul's second visit, dominating its little lake neighbourhood.

'I don't think the Leeward will open again,' said Haji. 'Those hotels were only open when there was a rush, all these Indian tourist-es. That rush I don't think will come back.'

We docked and walked through a back yard to a room off a narrow corridor. The room was dark and unadorned. Lying on his side on a mattress on the floor beneath blankets, a cloth cap on his head for warmth, was Haji Mohammed Sidiq Bhat. Although he was lying down, he seemed very tall – Haji confirmed later that he was taller than I, taller than six feet – and very thin. He did not look well.

---

* 'Bhat' was 'definitely' the 'correct' spelling, Haji insisted, and wrote it out in Arabic script to prove it. If 'Bhat' was 'correct', that would explain why they had changed it. And around the Valley were a great many Bhats; it was one of a small number of very common surnames. But if 'Butt' was incorrect, it had not been Naipaul's mistake; that had been the spelling on the hotel's documents and signs in 1962, as is clear from *An Area of Darkness*.

Several men sat around in a companionable semicircle; there was a hookah, and the room was smoky. We sat down. Haji and a plump man wearing a fur cap exchanged words in Kashmiri. The plump man smiled.

'V.S. Naipaul,' he said.

'You see, they already know how you know about them!' cried Haji happily.

The plump man was Aziz, of whom Naipaul had written memorably. He seemed to enjoy the notoriety. Naipaul had arrived unannounced in 1989, he told me. He had not written ahead. But yes, he had recognised him immediately. Naipaul and his wife had stayed four and a half months in 1962, and in 1989 Naipaul had returned without his wife but with some other people and had stayed three or four days, at the Palace. Naipaul was an 'Anglo-Indian', and his wife was German or American or something like that.

Somebody went to fetch Aziz's son, Nazir. As we waited Aziz told me, unprompted, a story he had told Naipaul; apparently it was still on his mind. The Tourism Department had objected to Naipaul's portrayal in *An Area of Darkness* of laundry hung out to dry from windows and spread out on the lawn. 'You don't *understand* the book,' Aziz had told them. Nazir now ran the medical supply shop on the corner of the island. After some minutes he came and sat down and asked me a few polite questions: did I like Kashmir? What had I seen? Then it was decided that he would show me the hotel. When we got up to leave, Mr Bhat, who had not spoken and did not seem fully lucid, smiled, sat up, and shook my hand firmly. Then, at my behest, Mr Bhat, Aziz and Nazir sat together for a photograph.

Aziz was jolly, the kind of man one could like instantly. He shook my hand heartily again in the corridor. 'You send photo,' he said. 'And write in your book.'

With Nazir I walked through the empty hotel, to a room on the second floor with a double view of the lake and the mountains, like the view Naipaul had enjoyed.

'Mr Naipaul loved the scenery,' remembered Nazir.

He was a quiet, diffident young man, self-contained, seemingly shy. I asked if he had read about himself in *India: A Million Mutinies Now*. Naipaul had sent them a copy, he said (he didn't say if he had read it), but someone had borrowed it and not returned it. He said this casually, without resentment or any other feeling, simply as a fact. Sometimes these seemed the two emotional possibilities for Kashmiris: fierce anger – even hysteria – or else complete indifference.

Naipaul had written that Nazir was studying accountancy. 'Accountancy is good for doing any business, isn't it?' I remarked. He smiled. 'Yes,' he agreed. 'It is needful whatever you do. Very needful.' Naipaul had been mistaken to write that he had never been outside the Valley. Nazir told me he had gone yearly to Delhi and Bombay to solicit business from travel agents. But not since 1989.

I asked about the awkward moment at the end of Naipaul's visit, when Naipaul had offered him money for having shown him around. He hadn't wanted money, he insisted, a little fiercely as though he really earnestly wanted to make the point. He had spent time with Naipaul for 'friendship'.

Haji then gave a sermonette on Kashmiri hospitality. 'Not like you stay in hotel in Delhi or Bombay, where they take your money and forget about you,' he said with casual, customary disgust. 'If you stayed Hotel Leeward, Mr Butt would send you Christmas card. And he would make *you* send *him* Christmas card.'

'I respect him like my father,' said Nazir, still speaking of Naipaul.

He pointed across the courtyard at a window near the sitting room where Naipaul had bought a Kashmiri shawl from Mr Bhat's friend Mr Sharif. He wanted me to see the bullet hole made on 20 June 1990, by Indian troops responding to a rocket attack by militants.

'I don't think Mr Butt will be alive when you come back,' said Haji later, as we floated away in the shikara.

Although they were little more than politely hospitable and I made no lasting connection, meeting Mr Butt and Aziz and Aziz's son helped me to see them as what they are: human beings with lives and worries of their own, outside any book. Paradoxically, I gained a new appreciation for what Naipaul had done. No longer was *An Area of Darkness* mere literature; now, to me, it was a depiction of something true, a true story.

In May I returned to Kashmir; the place had got under my skin. A friend had joined me from Bangkok, and we planned to go trekking. Haji insisted, with proprietorial pride, that it was not easily forgivable to visit Kashmir without going trekking. The day we arrived was the eve of the Muslim festival Eid, and Haji had bought four handsome tall goats for the occasion. ('Not like the ordinary short-haired goat were these,' writes Margaret Cotter Morison in *A Lonely Summer in Kashmir*, a travelogue published in 1904, 'but big, high-standing animals, with long sweeping hair, some broad, some pearly grey, some black.')

'Actually, we have to honour the goat,' he explained. 'Because the prophet, he was spose to sacrifice his son, and God came and told him sacrifice goat instead.'

It sounded like a story I had heard before.

'Abraham?' I ventured.

'Abraham,' he confirmed. 'And so we have to wash the goat. And then tomorrow' – he grinned – 'we kill him.'

We went again to see Mr Bhat and Aziz. Aziz greeted me in the corridor with a warm smile and a handshake, then he parted the curtain and we went in to the same green-painted room, with the same near-antique radio in the corner. Mr Bhat was sitting up, drawing on his hookah. He wore the same knit hat, but he obviously was doing much better.

He reached for my hand. 'Hello, sir,' he said. 'How are you, sir?'

'I hope you are well, sir,' I replied.

I sat down beside the mattress. There were no visitors this time, but a handsome boy three or four years old sat nearby on the floor. Peremptorily, Mr Bhat called to him. The boy took hold of the hookah, filled it with water – surely it was very heavy for him, and the coals were burning on top – and carried it effortfully the six feet or so to where Haji was sitting. Haji smoked happily.

'Who does the boy belong to?' I asked.

Aziz said something to Haji.

'He is Nazir's son,' said Haji.

'Already he had intimations of the world outside,' Naipaul had written of Nazir. 'Already, through that monthly exchange of letters with a foreign girl, there had come to him the idea of the possibility – always in Allah's hands – of a foreign marriage.'

Naipaul had hoped Nazir's horizons would broaden, that he would leave the Valley. 'New ways of seeing and feeling were going to come to him, and he wasn't going to be part of the valley in the way he was now,' he had written. But the prediction, wishful even at the time, rang badly false now. And here, now, was Nazir's handsome son.

Mr Bhat, smiling, handed me a piece of round Kashmiri bread. 'Kashmiri roti,' he said. I took it and thanked him. Aziz poured tea.

'Good bread?' asked Mr Bhat.

'Very good.'

We waited some time for Nazir; he was attending to customers. I gave Aziz a copy of the photo I had taken in April. After a while we went over to the hotel's office, where I asked Nazir and Aziz some questions.

'God knows,' said Nazir when I asked when the hotel might reopen. 'We can't say anything. If the situation will be okay, then we hope that the tourist-es will come again.'

Yes, he said, most of the Leeward's guests had been Indians. The hotel had opened in 1962 and closed in 1989. The situation in the Valley had worsened in September 1989, and business had plunged then and never recovered. 'Yeah, it was a successful hotel before 1989,' said Nazir. 'I was supposed to take the management. Touriasm was most important, because in this valley 90 per cent of the people were standing on touriasm. Before '89, this was the only business, this hotel.' Now the family's only business was the medical shop. *Hartals*, strikes, did not affect it; the shop always stayed open. Medical businesses and vegetable merchants usually were not affected by hartals.

'Medical and vegetable,' interjected Haji helpfully.

Nazir had no plans to leave the Valley. The family's savings were gone. The medical shop made only three or four thousand rupees a day.

Aziz walked Haji and me to the end of the wooden pier at the front of the hotel, where our shikara was waiting. 'Not anywhere road,' he observed. 'Whole side is water.' He gestured happily at the tall, copiously blooming rosebushes that flanked the path.

'No work,' he said, beaming. 'No work!'

He was justly proud: in Kashmir in spring and summer, the roses' abundance and beauty were amazing. Among the kingfishers, the shikaras, the floating vegetable market, the mullahs' haunting calls to prayer – among all the wondrous things on the Dal Lake, the roses were the most impressive.

Aziz steadied the shikara with his foot and held out his hand to help me in. 'Thank you,' he said. I waved goodbye, and we glided away.

'You see, all this is destroyed,' said Haji, pointing out the Leeward's wooden pier, its steps rotted and in disrepair. 'It is almost like a ruin.'

CHAPTER TWO

VESTIGES AND RUINS

I had first arrived in Kashmir thinking of it, too reverently, as a Potemkin stage set where a portion of a Great Writer's life had been enacted. That dusty yellow building with the bunker in front next to the bus yard was the Tourist Reception Centre, the very one mentioned by Naipaul! Right behind the Boulevard was Shankaracharya Hill – *the* Shankaracharya Hill, the one in the book! 'One can go up there' as Naipaul had done, Haji told me, unimpressed by my interest, 'but it might not be safe. The Indian Army might be there, or sometimes the militants hide themsel-eves there.' Vestiges and ruins remained scattered around Srinagar and the Dal Lake and hill stations such as Pahalgam. In Srinagar still stood the charred hulls of buildings – a school, a cinema, houses – burned in fires and battles and bomb blasts since 1989. Houseboats, given fanciful names like Moon Valley Super Deluxe and Michael Jackson, rotted in the water. Handsome shawls and exquisite wool and silk carpets gathered dust in merchants' houses. 'There are certain things that can't be rebuilt,' a houseboat owner said to me. 'There are certain things that won't be back with us. They are gone for good.'

But old habits die hard, and the supreme Kashmiri craft remained a uniquely pushy tradition of salesmanship. In Kashmir I often had the feeling of improvising a role in someone else's play, learning the lines only as I went along. I was a tourist, therefore I must do the things tourists do, such as go trekking and buy handicrafts.

This has been true for at least a century. Margaret Cotter Morison wrote in 1904: 'The perpetual swarm of merchants round one's boat thrusting themselves and their goods in at the window repeating their never ceasing cry of: "Only see, lady, only see; don't buy, Mem-sahib" – these are suggestive of Srinagar, and only Srinagar, for their like is seen in no other part of the earth.'

'Looking is free,' protests the shikara merchant when you insist you don't want whatever he's selling.

'Cigarette! Choc-lette! Bisk-ette!' cries the sundries-shikara man. 'You want cigarette, sir? Cashew nut? Apple juice?'

'You know Mick Jagger?' asks the lady selling honey. 'Rock singer. Very famous. He came my shop. He-lio Iglesias came my shop.'

'You want a hat?' inquires the leather-goods man.

'No thank you.'

'Cheaper prices.'

'No thank you.'

'And what about a passport bag?'

'No thank you.'

'Cheaper prices.'

'No thank you.'

'Any ladies' gloves you want?'

'No thank you.'

'Cheaper prices.'

'Really. No thank you.'

'Good day,' he says quite suddenly, and paddles off toward a cluster of shikaras bearing a group of fresh tourists from Taiwan ('Taiwanis', the Kashmiris call them).

'You want some nice *thanka*?' says the thanka man as his shikara sidles up to yours. 'Tibetan thanka.'

'No thank you. Nothing.'

'Some jewellery?'

'Nothing!'

A pause ensues.

'What for you coming to Kashmir? Only for eating rice? I am already rice man, but you are rice man too.'

Vestiges of the tourist's Kashmir existed cheek by jowl with the place's hard new realities, as I learned when I went to Pahalgam for a week's trek toward the Kolahoi glacier with Haji's laconic younger son. 'Two days ago 20 people died in Kashmir,' he said suddenly, after our car had stopped at a town for supplies.

'Killed by the army?' I asked.

'Killed,' he said. 'By the army.'

'Militants or' – the right word eluded me – 'people?'

'Civilians. In a village. Not in the city.'

It was the time of year when the shepherds lead their flocks uphill, to the high meadows. After we began to climb, we had to crawl along for minutes at a time behind a flock, until our driver could force a way through.

'Where are the sheep going?' I asked Haji's son.

'They are going to Pahalgam for the trekking,' he said, deadpan.

We stayed the night at Aroo, a meadow that climbs the right side of the valley just off the road, where a week later two Brits would be kidnapped. (They were released unharmed after two weeks.) I awoke early next morning and stepped out of the tent several times to watch the sun's progress down the western slope as it rose in the east. I felt appropriately insignificant among these mountains, but I also felt the profound, uncomplicated peace of mind and spirit that one feels only when truly at home: the birds, the wildflowers in the high meadows, the alpine scents, the sound of running water and the thin chill air evoked a place in southern Colorado where I had spent some of the happiest times in my childhood.

From Aroo we hiked to Lidderwat, a larger and even more beautiful meadow bisected by a river and hemmed in on the west by sheer cliffs. At Lidderwat springtime was in full flush, but only a couple of hours' walk further were snow bridges over the stream and a frozen lake. The snow melted furiously, swelling the rivers; the sound was a pleasant, constant background roar. It was the beginning of June; by August, autumn would be at hand.

That afternoon I learned that some militants were staying in the small cabins at one edge of the meadow at Lidderwat. The man who told me said they would be happy to talk to me and that their leader was a famous commander of Hizbul Mujahedin, the biggest pro-Pakistan militant group. So after sundown I found myself stealing through the dark meadow in the rain, knocking on a door, waiting for an all-clear, then shaking hands with half a dozen armed, fierce-looking bearded men.

The famous commander was Amir Khan, district commander of the Islamabad district for Hizbul Mujahedin. (There is a town in Kashmir called Islamabad, not to be confused with the capital of Pakistan.) With him was Sharif ud-Din, battalion commander of the Siddiqi Akbar Battalion. We talked for an hour by lantern, then they and their men posed for a few photographs. They were cordial and obliging, and seemed frank enough despite clearly hewing to a party line. Amir Khan told me government forces had recently burned his house, which had stood in a village near Pahalgam called Liver. This didn't really matter, though, he said; he didn't live in his house any more.

'I came in militancy in 1990,' he told me through a translator. 'I belonged to Jamaat-i-Islami of J & K. When India became independent from British, there was some status disputed. In disputed status was Kashmir also. According to UN resolution and leaders of India, they promised to people that we will give independence to Kashmir. From that time they have not given independence to Kashmir.'

I asked if he would be satisfied with elections.

'We have had many elections, from 1972 to 1986,' he said.

I asked what, precisely, he was fighting for.

'We want here Islamic regime based on principles of Quran, which alone can lead mankind to happiness and prosperity,' he said. 'And we want to have independence from India.'

Would he accept independence without an Islamic regime?

'No. Because it is not according to our Holy Quran.'

But what about Ladakh, whose people were Tibetan Buddhists, and Hindu-majority Jammu? How could these parts of the present Jammu and Kashmir State fit into an Islamic state?

'If they do not want to become part of Pakistan, we will also fight against them.'

'We have started the militancy there, in Ladakh,' volunteered Sharif ud-Din.

I asked Amir Khan what he had done before he joined the freedom movement. He had been a businessman, he said, selling apples and walnuts. 'And we have also land.'

From where did his fighters get weapons and ammunition?

'We get from other countries, and also we disarm Indian troops.'

I asked which countries in particular supplied him with arms. Politely, he declined to answer.

Pakistan, perhaps?

'We only get aid from Azad Kashmir, not from Pakistan.' This was a fine distinction: Azad, or 'Free', Kashmir is the ostensibly autonomous portion of Jammu and Kashmir State controlled by Pakistan.

Why did these other countries arm his group?

'Because they are also Muslims. They have tried to help us.'

Did these Muslims from other countries want to help Hizbul establish an Islamic government in Kashmir?

'Yes,' he acknowledged readily. 'Only for this purpose they are helping us. The Western countries also are helping us.'

A touching faith in the United Nations and/or America was a theme I heard expounded almost daily. 'We Kashmiris, first thing we bleeve in, we bleeve in God,' a friend had told me. 'After that, we bleeve that if America takes an interest in our problem, it will be solved. America can do anything. When America wants to solve Kashmir problem, he can do it.'

I asked Amir Khan why in the world the United States might be interested in helping Kashmir against India.

'Because independence is our basic right,' he said. 'Therefore they help us in this matter.'

Why was Kashmir of such interest to Pakistan, in particular?

'Because Pakistan is also a Muslim country. And according to the resolution of the UNO, Kashmiri people get right if you want India or Pakistan.' India, he alleged, wanted only 'the forests of Kashmir, the natural beauty of Kashmir,' not its people.

'And in so many states of India, there are freedom fighters against India,' interjected Sharif ud-Din, the battalion commander. 'India thinks if we give independence to Kashmir ... Pakistan wants people of Kashmir, not land of Kashmir. All the people of Kashmir wants to go to Pakistan.'

Was it true, as I had heard, that support for militancy had declined?

'It is not fact,' said Amir Khan. 'This is also propaganda of India.'

But did not some militants extort money from civilians?

'It is also fact,' he admitted. 'But they are not with organisations. They are taking advantage. We also collect money, but not by force. Not pressurefully, but peacefully.'

Did most Kashmiris want an Islamic regime, then?

'Yes.'

I asked what was the group's attitude toward foreign tourists.

'We do not prohibit the touriasm to Kashmir,' said Sharif ud-Din.

What about foreign mercenaries?

'Afghani mujahedin came here to fight against India,' said Sharif ud-Din, 'because Kashmiris also fought against Russia in Afghanistan. We also help them, so they also help us.' In Kashmir now, he said, there were 'thousands' of Afghans, Sudanese, Arabs, and Iranians, seeking martyrdom in the jihad. 'They do not move freely,' he said. 'They are under our command.' The foreigners brought with them money and American, Russian and Australian weapons. New recruits 'in thousands' were being trained in Afghanistan, in Azad Kashmir, and here, in what they called Occupied Kashmir.

Did the freedom fighters expect their movement to succeed?

'Why not?' said Amir Khan. 'Every country has had success when they fight for their basic rights.' And besides: 'We are believing in Allah.'

One day during my first visit I was sitting in the outer yard of the Jamia Masjid, reading and waiting for Haji, who was inside praying, when two fully veiled women approached me.

'Please come here,' said one of the women.

Baffled and not a little uneasy, I followed her through a market and around the corner of the mosque. I found myself being made to sit on one of several canvas cots with half a dozen women, all completely draped in black *burkah*, not even their eyes visible. Children stood nearby, gazing at me frankly. I tried to ask what was going on.

'I English no speak,' replied the woman who had brought me.

But what was I doing here? I stayed a few minutes, then thought I had better leave. People began to leave the mosque; prayers were finished.

'Um, I think I need to go,' I said and stood up.

'You wait. Two minutes.'

I waited, and soon learned why I was there. It was a blood drive:

women lay down, fully veiled, on the cots and rolled up their sleeves to give blood. Indian hospitals would not treat Kashmiri militants, a woman who spoke English told me. So the people gave blood. They had wanted me to see that they were giving blood for the militants.

Another day, a Friday, Haji took me with him to an important large field called the Idgah, where he would be among a large crowd offering prayers. It would be the first time Eid prayers had been offered there since the insurgency began. Haji went ahead to meet some friends and pray with them, and I settled on the grass to watch. Within moments, a cluster of young men gathered around me.

'… or we could go under UNO,' said one. 'Better to be with America than with bloody India. Mr Bill Kill-inton is very powerful. He can do what he wants.'

'As our messenger, kindly take a message to the people of your country,' said his friend. 'The people are confident that Mr Bill Kill-inton will do something for us.'

'We have seen Bofors tanks here,' said another. 'I can identify, because they have the Swedish sign on them.' These Swedish tanks, he said, were mostly in remote areas, where India was afraid Pakistan might attack across the Line of Control.

They were angry at local and Indian journalists. BBC correspondent Satish Jacob recently had come to Kashmir and filed a story showing people playing cricket, as if everything were fine and dandy. 'He hasn't been to Baramulla, he hasn't been to Sopor,' said one of the young men. 'He hasn't spoken to public. The most tense area, Sopor.'

The huge field was nearly half covered with skullcapped men lined up evenly beside and behind each other, bowing in unison. I had never seen anything like it, not with my own eyes. I had seen Muslims praying in such numbers on television – but we've all seen everything on television.

After prayers Haji found me and extricated me from the boys. He

warned me not to talk too much to strangers; it was impossible to
know who might be an agent for whom. Mixed in was the usual
Kashmiri ulterior motive: Kashmiris could be very possessive about
their guests, 'their' tourists. It could get a bit stifling. He took me to
the Martyrs' Cemetery at the far end of the field and showed me the
rows of marked graves. I was still new to the scale of it, the horror
of the things that happened daily, the grief. 'What Indian Army do
is, they capture a boy,' explained Haji. 'They put him in car or van,
they drive him little further, where no people are. They take him out
of car and tell him to run. Boy thinks, 'I am being release-ed.' He
runs. Army shoot him.' He paused.

I looked up. His habitual ironic grin was gone. His eyes were wet.

'But I don't think he will succeed,' he said, falteringly. 'I don't
think India will succeed in Kashmir.'

To make a short cut, Haji and I climbed a chain-link fence, and I
watched with horrified admiration as this diabetic sexagenarian
jumped ten feet to the ground. Around us, men and boys streamed
away in groups, chanting:

'Azaadi! Azaadi! Azaadi!'

Freedom!

I spent a lot of time on the ground in Kashmir with Kashmiris, then
later stepped back and looked at it again from afar. And I listened
not only to Kashmiris' stories, but also to their opinions and to what
they said they wanted. Maybe because of my own provincial background, I've never appreciated the presumption that the naïve and
wishful perspectives of people from small, neglected places should
be considered less valid than those of people who hold power –
unless it's true that might makes right.

Mufti Baha-ud-Din Farooqi was a former chief justice of the
High Court in Jammu and Kashmir State who had served 40 years,
but resigned after Indian Prime Minister Indira Gandhi tried to

humiliate him with a transfer to Sikkim for refusing to be corrupted by her agents. 'So far as Kashmir is concerned, every one of them is an Indira Gandhi,' he told me. 'They nearly converted it virtually into a colony. Restrictions and limitations imposed by the constitution did not matter with them. And things have come to a pass where even the constitutional safeguards that are available to other states in India are not available to Kashmir.' Kashmir had been under special President's Rule without interruption since 19 January 1990, the date of the second coming of the notorious Governor Jagmohan. 'Here they continue it with impunity, and they don't even bother to amend the constitution. You have all the constitutions, all the laws, and they can say that those are available to the people in Kashmir. And yet people are being killed like cattle. Genocide is going on here. The situation is worse than in Bosnia.'

He noted the three options Kashmiris theoretically had before them: remaining with India, joining Pakistan, or becoming independent. 'For us, all three options are an evil,' he said. 'So we have to make a choice that is least harmful. India we have tried for 45 years.'

Professor Abdul Ghani, a leader of the umbrella political grouping called the All Parties Hurriyat Conference, was a prickly, intense man who chain-smoked in the subcontinental way, inhaling from his cupped fist. The founder of Pakistan, Mohammed Ali Jinnah, had been to his house. When he told me this, his retainers and colleagues nodded gravely.

'When you are big, you do not need any excuse,' he said. 'You simply display your wanton strength and annex. The people would vote for Pakistan. No two opinions about it.'

I asked about the third option.

'But the question is: is independent Kashmir a practicable idea?' he said. 'I don't think so. Even as an independent state, you have relations with either India or Pakistan.' Like many others,

Professor Ghani took for granted that it was not possible to have good relations with both. 'We are surrounded by big, giant countries,' he pointed out. 'The big fish can eat up the small fish any moment, like the big India fish ate the small Sikkim fish with impunity. You cannot establish peace unless you resolve the dispute in Jammu and Kashmir. They have fought three wars over Jammu and Kashmir, and they are preparing for yet another. Unless peace is established, no economic activity can be pushed ahead, anywhere in South Asia.'

Like many Kashmiris, he was profoundly contemptuous of India and confident, not to say smug, that it would meet its comeuppance. 'The forces of history are more powerful than even the atomic weapons. The Russians could not stop the forces of history. India will break. As sure as I am talking to you. India is a crowd. It's a hell of a job to keep a crowd together. India must leave Kashmir and preserve India.'

Ninety-year-old Mohammed Iqbal Chapri, who had owned houseboats during many years of boom time and had been a leader of an association of houseboat owners, spoke in full sentences, like a lecturer. His eyes were pale, glazed over, like a blind man's. 'I have seen so many imprisonments,' he told me when I visited him with Haji. 'At the present moment it is claimed by India that Kashmir is an integral part of India. That has never been proved. I deny it, right to the bottom. We thought of ourselves as Kashmiri. We thought, because one of the parties was leaving that signed the agreement of 1846, naturally we would become independent.'

He took the very long view. 'I know that when Alexander the Great invaded India, 300 years before Christianity, Kashmir was an independent state. I believe in independence. But I have got some attachment for Pakistan. I am a free man. But I must be thankful to Pakistan that in 1947 Pakistan has always contributed a lot in our favour. But that does not mean that he has bought us.' I enjoyed listening to Mr Chapri and was sorry to learn, when I returned the next year, that he had died.

'We are hungry for peace,' a young Kashmiri told me. 'But at the same time we want to live with honour.' The Kashmir problem was 'not a law and order problem,' another insisted. 'It is the deserved rights that we want. No Kashmiri will bleeve any Indian, ever again.' Said the human rights activist Jalil Andrabi: 'We thought that if people of Romania can go out on the streets and get rid of a dictator, why can't we go out on the streets in Kashmir?'

'I am happy in a way,' a businessman told me, 'because it has given us a lot. It has given us hell, but it has given us a lot as well. God gives you exams in your life. He gives you hard times, he gives you good times. Each and every person must accept the reality. There are limitations. We have to think about the future of our country, the future of our children. We don't want to become another Afghanistan. My son, he was three when militancy started. Now he is almost in his eighth year. So good years are passing by, they are not coming back.'

In most of what you and I read, 'Kashmir' is less a place name than shorthand for an abstract obsession of outsiders. Like 'Vietnam' in its time, the word pushes buttons.

An Indian woman I met at a party in Bombay flinched visibly when I told her I was a journalist and interested in Kashmir. 'You're going to attack India,' she said, then launched into an impassioned rendition of an Indian version of the domino theory: if Kashmir 'goes', she said, Punjab will 'go' next, then Nagaland, then every other state and minority with a grievance. If India were to fall apart, then what many had been calling a nation could turn out to have been only a deceptively vivid mass illusion. Surely this must be a frightening prospect to the many educated Indians who had staked their self-respect on loyalty to the modern, post-colonial, secular entity they called India. The illusion must be maintained at all costs. (This was the mid-1990s, before the Nehruvian secular ideal fell out of fashion in India.)

In Bangkok a few months earlier I had met Clyde Edwin Pettit, who changed my way of reading the newspapers. Ed came to Bangkok every year around the same time and was obsessed with making a documentary about post-war Vietnam. He had the special gift of seeing through the lies and fictions we tell ourselves, and the curse of being unable not to see through them. Like many deeply insightful people, he was also deeply lonely; I was good company for him because I was genuinely interested in hearing his well-polished stories. I soaked them in as we sipped whiskey together in his hotel room.

Ed was from Arkansas and had worked as an aide to US Senator Carl Hayden, had done radio journalism in Vietnam during the war, had written an influential letter from Bangkok in January 1966, was author of *The Experts: 100 Years of Blunder in Indo-China* (alternately subtitled *The Book That Proves There Are None*), and had known Bill Clinton when Clinton was 19 years old. One of Clinton's duties had been to push a cart down the corridors of the Senate office building where he worked. According to Ed, whenever he passed anyone coming the other way, young Bill would stop, stick out his hand, and say, 'Hi. My name's Bill Clinton.'

Ed told me what his advice had been to American draftees: 'Don't go to Canada or Sweden. Go to Vietnam. Be part of the action and passion of your time. Do whatever you can to discreetly fuck up the war effort, so long as you do nothing to put any of your countrymen in jeopardy.'

Telling a Washington anecdote, he would pause to add, 'He's one of my dearest friends, you know, but he's white trash.'

'White trash?'

'You know: corporate attorneys, lobbyists, undersecretaries, journalists, Hill staffers – white trash. Some of my best friends are white trash.'

On religion, he was equally jaundiced. 'He belongs to one of these cults. You know.'

'No, I don't know. What kind of cult?'

'One of these cults. You know. He's a' – his face registered a practiced grimace, and his voice fell to a whisper – 'a Methodist. Unfortunately, many of my friends belong to cults.'

He gave me a copy of the letter he had written to Senator J. William Fulbright, Democrat of Arkansas and chairman of the Senate Foreign Relations Committee, on 13 January 1966, 'on a borrowed German typewriter, on morphine and alcohol,' while recovering from a bad accident in Bangkok. To Ed's alarm, Fulbright had caused the letter to be published in the *Congressional Record*, spawning headlines such as 'Fulbright Reveals Note From Vietnam Saying US Losing' and 'Arkansan Doubts Viet Nam Victory'.

'It wrote itself, from notes and what I had seen,' Ed told me. 'It just poured out all night long. It was addressed to Lee Williams – the man who hired me and Bill Clinton – and Senator Fulbright. Lee was one of my two closest male friends and remains so to this day. Fulbright at that time was getting sometimes a couple of thousand letters a day, sometimes much more than that after a speech. So Lee carried it in to him, and it electrified him – as he has testified repeatedly. Senator Fulbright had led us into the war with the Gulf of Tonkin Resolution. There were only two votes against that: Wayne Morse of Oregon and Ernest Gruening of Alaska; there should be statues to them everywhere. There really should be a statue to Fulbright, because he had much more eminence, and had the courage, the manhood, the good citizenship, to say – hundreds of times, in private conversations and on television – "I was a fool. I was lied to about the Gulf of Tonkin," and to admit his mistake and then lead the main thrust of the antiwar movement. Slowly the idea was forming in me, as a contrarian, that it made no sense. If you hear something a hundred times, you're inclined to believe it. If you hear it a thousand times you begin to wonder: am I mad, or is the rest of the world crazy? I made the perilous assumption that it was the rest of the world.'

Having talked 'intensively to over 200 people from colonels to privates, journalists and businessmen, Vietnamese, and English and French colonials' in Saigon, Ed asserted in the letter that it was 'vitally incumbent that we speak and speak with sincerity' to the Vietnamese:

> I question both our original involvement and the deepening of our commitment ... I am very frightened. I could talk about bright spots; there are many. I do not think they override the stark, terrifying realities of a stalemate, at best, purchased at inconceivable cost and coupled with humiliating setbacks and losses. Then always, and I do not say this lightly, there is the unlikely but ever-present possibility of catastrophe. The road from Valley Forge to Vietnam has been a long one, and the analogy is more than alliterative: there are some similarities, only this time we are the British and they are barefoot ... I would rather America err on the side of being overly generous than on the side of military miscalculation of inconceivable cost. For what, the world might well ask should we win the gamble, have we won?

'You would hear constantly, "Napalm will win the war for us,"' Ed told me. 'Fucking napalm was the greatest thing ever to come down the pike, you woulda thought. It was always *something* was winning the war. It was always "these *little* gooks," with the emphasis on how diminutive the people were – and are – not perceiving that that was an advantage. They were always surrendering in six months.'

The second time I saw him, Ed pressed on me a copy of his

book *The Experts* with a fulsome inscription. 'Read nothing but the foreword,' he instructed me. 'Then read the book from the front through Dien Bien Phu. Most people pick it up and flip through it randomly looking for Top Secret reports. Or they look in the index to find themselves. But the whole point is that you're supposed to read it straight through, from front to back.'

The Experts consists of 439 pages of nothing but direct quotations from politicians, professors, and press pundits, all purporting to understand what was happening or to know what was going to happen in Vietnam, arranged chronologically. Published by Lyle Stuart in 1975, it amounts to a narrative of mounting horror and increasingly tortuous self-delusion. 'I bragged for years on radio and television that there were about 30 Top Secret papers that I stole or borrowed from senators and Xeroxed,' Ed told me. 'I wanted to be arrested or interrogated, and I never could be. You can't ever be busted in the US when you want to be.'

Vietnam had taught him that 'all governments are bad'. Or, as he puts it in the foreword: 'The Vietnam War is a textbook example of history's lessons: that there is a tendency in all political systems for public servants to metamorphose into public masters, surfeited with unchecked power and privilege and increasingly overpaid to misgovern.' The book was about 'our own credulity and the inexplicable tendency in all of us to believe what we are told and to follow those whose ambitions are to lead,' he wrote. 'It is about our forgetfulness of the history of our species – the record that there is no morality among nations and the only law is the law of the jungle.'

'There's a disease going around these days that no one has noticed,' Ed told me. 'I was the first to diagnose it. I call it mass Alzheimer's. Nobody remembers anything!'

Born in 1965, the year US combat troops first went to Vietnam, I had grown up in what I viscerally felt to be a fallen world, aware that there existed something big and ugly that the older people around me were pointedly not talking about – or at least, not talking about to me. Ed taught me the history other Americans wanted to forget.

I read *The Experts* on a houseboat on the Dal Lake and was bursting with what I had learned from it, when I was invited to write an opinion article for *The Times of India*. In my piece, published 7 August 1994, I wrote:

> Whenever I read cant in Indian publications about 'restarting the political process' in Kashmir, I am reminded of the American pipe dream of winning Vietnamese 'hearts and minds'. When I am told Kashmir is 'an integral part of India', I recall the stridency of American claims that South Vietnam was a sovereign country. When Indian politicians and headline writers refer pointedly to 'Pak-trained' militants, I think of the US insistence that North Vietnam, with support from 'Red China', was fighting a 'war of aggression' against 'sovereign' South Vietnam.
>
> When I hear references to 'Islamic fundamentalism' in Kashmir, I am reminded of the US-fostered spectre of communism. Just as surely as communism existed, so undoubtedly 'Islamic fundamentalism' exists, perhaps even in Kashmir. Yet what is achieved, beyond a spurious feeling a self-righteousness, flogging it endlessly? Would it not be better to examine and work to undermine its root causes? Two such causes are Hindu fundamentalism and, less noted but not less important, secular fundamentalism. 'If you are a believer in Islam, you will be called a fundamentalist and a terrorist,' a Kashmiri once told me.

The parallels I had gleaned were not fanciful or idiosyncratic. 'Look at the Vietnam pacification campaign. This is a pacification campaign all over again,' the Pakistani newspaper editor Najam

Sethi told me. Jalil Andrabi, the Kashmiri lawyer and human rights activist, asked me: 'Why can't 700,000 Indian troops defeat 10,000 militants, if the movement is not indigenous? This is do or die for us. We know we will be wiped out as a nation if we surrender.' Two French journalists I met in Srinagar in 1994 came back from a day trip, babbling excitedly about the sensation they had felt walking with Indian soldiers, the road flanked by trees and rice paddies, sure that at any moment they would be ambushed by militants. 'It was *juste* like Vietnam!' they cried, high on the blend of joy and dread that motivates many journalists.

I relayed the story to a young Kashmiri friend. 'They told me where they were walking, it was just like Vietnam,' I said.

'Ah, yes,' he said.

After a long pause he asked: 'Vietnam is in what country?'

'Vietnam is a country,' I said. 'Near Thailand. In the '60s, when you and I were born, America fought a big war there. They sent five lakhs of American boys there to fight the Communists.' In the subcontinent, a lakh is 100,000.

'Yes, Communists.' ('Communists don't bleeve in God,' Haji had said to me, gravely.) 'Which countries fought in that war?'

'It was a civil war – some Vietnamese fighting against other Vietnamese. The Communists controlled the northern part of Vietnam. Actually, they weren't only Communists; first they fought for independence from France. Just like England ruled India, France ruled Vietnam. The Vietnamese kicked out the French. Then the strongest group in Vietnam was the Communists, sort of. America didn't like that, so they sent five lakhs of American boys to fight them.'

'And they beat the Communists?'

'No. America lost.'

'America lost?!'

'America spent so much money on bombs and airplanes, the war became very expensive. And half a lakh of American boys died in Vietnam. Many American people got fed up and came out on the streets, just like here during the Hazratbal siege. Lakhs of people went out on the streets.'

'Yes, I understand,' he said thoughtfully.

'They said, 'Why should we spend so much money and send our boys so far away to die?' Vietnam is thousands of kilometres away from America.'

'Bring our boys back. How did it end?'

'Finally, too many American people were too fed up, and the government decided to quit, and they left Vietnam.'

'And the Communists ruled Vietnam.'

'They still do.'

CHAPTER THREE

THROUGH THE
LOOKING-GLASS

Kashmir was like a child being fought over by divorced parents.

'Pakistan will remain incomplete without Kashmir,' declared Prime Minister Benazir Bhutto on 14 August 1994, in a speech marking Pakistan's independence day. Kashmir, she said, represented 'an unfinished agenda' of Partition. Pakistan was prepared to negotiate with India on the basis of a plebiscite in Kashmir.

'The Pakistan zone of Kashmir should be with Kashmir,' retorted Indian Prime Minister P.V. Narasimha Rao the next day, India's independence day, in a speech outside Delhi's Red Fort. 'That is our only unfinished task. You can never take away our Kashmir. No one can. We will not rest until we stop this interference. Kashmir will always be with India. We will crush this terrorism.'

The rhetoric and behaviour of politicians on both sides suggested that Kashmir was a pawn or proxy in a struggle that was really about something else. I realised that in order to understand Kashmir, I would need to visit Pakistan.

I first went there in February 1995, overland from Delhi via Amritsar and the border crossing at Attari-Wagah, to Lahore. Two Pakistani Christians there, sentenced to death for alleged blasphemy against the Quran, were about to be acquitted on appeal by the High Court. This was a top international story at the time.

I checked into the Salvation Army hostel on Fatima Jinnah Road and asked the Christian manager which way was downtown.

'Brother, there will be trouble downtown today,' he said. 'Why don't you rest here today, then go downtown tomorrow?'

'I'm a journalist,' I said.

In that case, he said, downtown was that direction.

On the Mall, a demonstration was in progress. It was a Friday. Outside the mosque at Regal Chowk were several hundred men, mostly young, chanting slogans and listening to bearded imams. Above the crowd on sticks loomed larger-than-life photos of the Ayatollah Khomeini. An American flag was burned. The air was tense, and many journalists milled about. Armed police stood ready nearby, and when the crowd began to march up the Mall toward the Punjab Assembly building, the police followed. I stood aside, but several young men approached me and aggressively asked if I was a journalist.

Yes, I said.

Would I kindly write in my newspaper that a certain Member of the National Assembly was 'the worst enemy of Islam' and 'the production of the red light area'?

I said I would.

There was no violence until some of the demonstrators vandalised some traffic lights. Suddenly, the police charged across the intersection, truncheons flying, beating those demonstrators they could get their hands on and quickly dispersing the rest. I saw one man being dragged across the asphalt by his collar. A few minutes later, in front of the mosque, another group began hurling rocks and clods of dirt at the police. The cops charged again, fired tear gas and fired into the air.

It was my first day in Pakistan, my first riot, and my first experience of tear gas. Later I learned that neither the two Shia groups I had seen clash with the police, nor the other two groups demonstrating that day, were on the street to protest the acquittal of the Christians. The religious parties were chronically at odds with the Western-leaning government of Benazir Bhutto, several of their leaders had been arrested in recent days, and the situation was further complicated by tensions between Benazir and the chief minister of Punjab province. No matter, decided most of the foreign reporters who had been on hand, or their editors; it would take too many words to explain all that.

I was to be told many times that most Pakistanis opposed the extremist religious parties. They had failed to make much of a showing in elections, but the religious parties' strength lay in their ability and willingness to take to the streets. Also, in a country founded on religious identity, to oppose religious parties too strongly could be unwise for a politician like Benazir who was seen as pro-Western.

'Some self-appointed spokesmen for the "ideology of Pakistan" are delighted that the two alleged blasphemers have been sentenced to death,' editorialised the Lahore-based weekly *The Friday Times*. 'Such people do not care about the requirements of due process or justice, they do not care about minority rights, they do not care about the disastrous consequences of the immoderate image Pakistan presents to the world outside.'

'This thing is becoming dangerous,' *Friday Times* editor Najam Sethi told me in his office. Since the time of military dictator Zia ul Haq (1977–88), he said, governments had tried to appease the religious extremists with minor political concessions, to no avail. 'Instead of being appeased, they now want more. Five years from now it may be too late.' The federal government should summon the political courage to crack down on certain groups as examples to the rest. 'If they provoke violence, they must pay for it. There is no reason why we should treat them with kid gloves.'

Fortuitously, the Salvation Army was a hub of the local

Christian community. Through its staff I arranged to interview the man who had volunteered to serve as bodyguard during the trial for the two defendants, 14-year-old Salamat Masih and his uncle Rehmat, and the Church of Pakistan bishop. 'After this case we have disappeared from our offices, and I am not personally in the home,' Younis Rahi, president of the Pakistan Christian National Party, told me. He and PCNP General Secretary Joseph Francis had been the Masihs' volunteer bodyguards. Of the 9 February verdict by the lower court, in which the Masihs had been sentenced to death despite a near-total lack of evidence, he said: 'We were absolutely satisfied with our case. But the sessions judge, I think, was under pressure from outside. You can't believe, we was all weeping there. Salamat is a very brave boy. He was not weeping. But Rehmat was weeping.'

Recent similar blasphemy trials had 'definitely made the Christians more politically aware,' Bishop Samuel Azaria told me. The law had 'made the minorities very fearful and insecure. General Zia ul Haq has created all these problems for Pakistan. And I'm sorry to say that General Zia's major support came from the West. All these religious laws have been introduced by General Zia ul Haq, and we are now reaping the fruits of these laws.'

After the April 1994 murder of blasphemy defendant Manzoor Masih, Younis Rahi's relatives in Canada had asked him to emigrate, but he had refused. 'We want to live in Pakistan,' he said. 'We are Pakistani. If I leave, if Joseph Francis leaves, who will fight this case? We are not worried on the bullets, because we bleeve on Jesus Christ. We are all the time ready to face any problem.'

A few days later I was in Rawalpindi, the military city near which Islamabad had been built in the 1960s, when two American employees of the US consulate in Karachi were killed by a gunman as they rode to work in a van, and my editor at the *South China*

Morning Post phoned from Hong Kong to ask if I could go to Karachi. Two days later two dozen people were killed by a bomb outside a mosque, and the next day I was on a train 30 long, hot hours south, through the lawless hinterland of Sindh province. The trip gave me a sense I would not otherwise have gained for how far away Karachi is from Pakistan's other cities, and introduced me to its tragedy.

I consulted my Lonely Planet guidebook before I went. 'I came close to being abducted on one of Karachi's main streets by a man claiming to be a member of the police, but managed to run away despite the risk of being shot,' the author had written. 'There have been explosions and sporadic incidents of gunfire in the streets … Riots and strikes are also commonplace. No part of town visited by foreigners is immune.' The guidebook had been printed in April 1993, before things got really bad.

Karachi's complex plight boiled down to a bloated, multi-ethnic population and too few jobs to go around. The original Mohajirs, or refugees from India, had come from places like Bombay and Delhi and Lucknow and were better educated than the local Sindhis. But Zulfiqar Ali Bhutto was a Sindhi, and when he came to power in the 1970s he had found it convenient to promote Sindhi interests, instituting ethnic quotas for government jobs and university placements that favoured rural Sindhis over Mohajirs and made Sindhi the province's sole official language.

So the growing population of Urdu-speaking Mohajirs found themselves too well educated, too ill provided for and being used as pawns by national politicians. Their grievances had merit. Unfortunately, the man able to articulate them was Altaf Hussein, a former taxi driver turned power-hungry and unscrupulous demagogue, described to me as 'almost Hitlerian' in his ability to whip up crowds. The organisation he founded, the Mohajir National Movement or MQM, burst onto the scene in 1984 and made its first big splash with a rally held in 1986. The Afghan war meanwhile flooded Karachi, and the rest of Pakistan, with secondhand American and Russian weapons. In the early 1990s the army occupied the city but failed to control it and, humiliated, withdrew at the end of November 1994. The army-sponsored splinter group, the so-called MQM (Haqiqi), degenerated quickly into little more than a criminal gang hostile to the original MQM. And sectarian tension between Sunni and Shia Muslims, not previously a factor, suddenly manifested itself. As of my visit, in March 1995, perhaps as many as 1,500 people had died by violence in Karachi since the start of 1994.

'What is your country?' is a question one encounters often in the subcontinent.

'England,' I said my first day in Karachi, when a well-dressed young man asked, as I sat on a kerb looking around.

'Do you know about Karachi's situation?' he called to me, with evident concern.

'Yes, thank you.'

'Yet you are so confident.'

I didn't feel as confident as I may have looked. I walked over to him; we shook hands; he offered me a cigarette. I took one and told him my real nationality.

'You should never tell anyone here that you are from America,' he advised me gravely.

I asked who was to blame for the unrelenting shootings and mosque bombings. Most Karachiites blamed America, India and the Jews, he said. People in Pakistan admired Germany, by the way, because it was a powerful country, a rich and efficient country. And besides, he added with a chuckle, 'They killed the Jews!'

I must have looked shocked, because he quickly added, 'Oh! You are not a Jew, are you?'

'No, I'm not.'

He was relieved. 'If you were a Jew I would not have said that. Because we have to be hospitable to our guests.'

I asked what solution he saw for Karachi.

'Some kind of revolution,' he said, half-heartedly. 'Some kind of new gummint. Perhaps.'

'New national government?'

'Yes. But then we will have to watch what that new gummint does.'

I visited the offices of *Newsline*, one of Pakistan's two English monthlies, where a young employee was kept busy poring over all the daily papers, adding up the reported deaths, and I arranged to interview two officials of the US consulate, colleagues of the two who had been killed. Both were cordial and seemed to be going out of their way to be helpful to me, though they obviously were exhausted and strung out. The killing of the Americans seemed to me not anti-American in any comprehensible sense, rather a kind of semi-conscious ratcheting up of the atmosphere of pervasive terror, the message being that in Karachi not even Americans were safe. The officials agreed. Nor, they said, was any of it connected to religious extremism, nor had any evidence whatsoever been unearthed of any connection between the Americans' deaths and the recent extradition from Pakistan of Ramzi Yousef, an Iraqi who was the US government's main suspect in the 1993 bombing of the World Trade Center.

'There's been a remarkable degree of restraint,' argued one of the officials during our long conversation. When mosques of one of the two Muslim sects had been attacked, worshippers from a nearby mosque belonging to the rival sect had rushed to aid the wounded. He had been posted in other Muslim countries. 'In some countries a rumour is enough to get mobs into the streets,' he said. And anyway, 'If a Muslim robs a bank, that's not Islamic terrorism, that's just a bank robbery.' Of the rumoured Ramzi Yousef connection, the other official said: 'Frankly, I wish it were that. I can't figure out who gained and who gained what.'

Conjecture that the Indian intelligence services might be fanning the flames in Karachi was general. It was a clear case of tit for tat, people said; if you were India, and Pakistan was arming and training separatist guerrillas in Kashmir, as everybody knew Pakistan was doing, what would you do? They cited as evidence the sudden, unprecedented rise in Shia-Sunni strife in Karachi, which previously had been restricted to the Punjab. The people who said these things – journalists, government officials, 'ordinary people' – assumed an Indian hand in Karachi as a matter of course, but with more sadness than rancour. What else could India be expected to do? And the target was too tempting: the border between Sindh and India's Rajasthan state was porous.

Characteristically, Pakistanis reserved their greatest ire for themselves. Where had they gone wrong? How and why had they failed to live up to the national ideal – which was, after all, to be Islamic in the best and most rigorous sense, since otherwise the country had no reason to exist? Theories and expressions of outrage abounded in opinion-making circles. In a 7 March speech the president, Farooq Ahmed Khan Leghari, blamed illiteracy for sectarianism and terrorism. 'We have made religion a plaything,' he said. 'Imambargahs and mosques are being attacked and we are branding each other kafirs [unbelievers] owing to ignorance.'

'The spate of attacks on mosques in Karachi and the cold-blooded killing of the faithfuls are signs of the moral sickness that Pakistan is suffering from,' wrote Khaled Al-Maeena in the newspaper *The Nation*. It was 'degrading' that in a country founded on Islam, 'armed guards are needed to protect the worshippers.' The claims of an 'Indian hand' in Karachi were irrelevant, even if true. 'While external hands may have fanned some of the flames, the blame lies squarely on those who actively were engaged in and encouraged sectarianism in Pakistan. Pakistan has enough enemies within; it doesn't need an enemy from without.'

My first visit to Pakistan achieved its main goal – a sense of what the Kashmir problem looked like from the other side – and a great deal more. Over two eventful, dusty months I conceived a genuine liking for this improbable, hyper-political country that wore its many grave problems on its national sleeve. 'Pakistan's strange origins have given it a tendency to national self-analysis which initially attracted me to the place,' writes Emma Duncan in *Breaking the Curfew*, her excellent account of the transition from the Zia dictatorship to the civilian government of Benazir Bhutto in the late 1980s. 'A country based on an idea has an ideal, however confused that may be; at least, different people in it will have some sort of ideal that the place is supposed to be living up to.' As an American, I appreciated the pathos of a country trying, and usually failing, to live up to an ideal.

'To a political journalist, a politicised country is thrilling,' writes Duncan. And a politicised Islamic country was a canary in the mine-shaft, at a time when many were beginning to see Islam as the latest global menace. In Pakistan, political speech and posturing were usually framed in terms of more-Islamic-than-thou; politicians and political writers sometimes cited, literally, chapter and verse of the Quran to refute each other. In Pakistan I began to see Islam as a complicated grid of religious traditions and political, moral and social ideas, contingent on their history and sometimes only obscurely related to each other. How this was anything but strictly analogous to Christianity or Indian secularism or 'the American way of life', I failed to see.

Pakistanis were hospitable to a fault and would go out of their way to help a guest. When I got on the wrong train out of Karachi, heading back north, a young man got off the train with me at Hyder-abad, found a railway official, asked when and on what platform my train would arrive, explained what I needed to do and, when I thanked him profusely, put his hand over his heart and said simply: 'It is my duty. You are our guest.'

I also liked Pakistan for attracting a tougher and more interesting breed of foreign visitor than India. Any old backpacker can go to India, but it takes an extra measure of nerve and imagination to visit Pakistan. Pakistan is the India of Kipling and the Great Game and the romance of 19th-century empire. This could be difficult to grasp, since India was still named India and Pakistan wasn't. 'Although India has acquired a monopoly on imperial nostalgia, at the time it was the area that is now Pakistan which stirred the British imagination and won their respect,' writes Duncan. The point is vividly demonstrated in John Keay's two marvellous books on the explorers who tramped through the Punjab and the passes and glaciers of the western Himalaya around the time of the Empire's zenith.

But my most vivid impression of Pakistan was that going there was like stepping through a looking-glass. The press officer at the US consulate in Karachi agreed; his last posting had been in Berlin, and Pakistan and India struck him as having the same kind of morbid fascination with each other as the two Germanys. To travel overland from Amritsar to Lahore was eerie. The people on both sides were Punjabis: husky, hearty people recognisably of the same stock. Only after one had travelled in Pakistan did one get an inkling of the true size and importance of the greater Punjab, which stretches nearly from Simla to Peshawar. In Amritsar the automobiles were Ambassadors; in Lahore they were Japanese brands. Everything was exactly the same, only different.

The bisected Punjab is a microcosm of what has been done to the subcontinent as a whole, and it's impossible truly to understand the depth of the wound the civilisation has suffered without visiting Pakistan. Before I went there the proprietor of my hotel in Delhi, a relative of the Indian capital's Hindu-nationalist governor, asked me a favour. He wouldn't have me go out of my way, but if I happened to get to Faisalabad, formerly Lyallpur, in the Pakistani Punjab, would I try to find the family of the man who had been his father's employer? He and his brother had not yet been born, but their father, a Punjabi Hindu, had been an accountant at a certain firm near the grain market in Lyallpur. When partition came, his Muslim boss had given him money and food to help the family on their journey. He, the son, fondly hoped that someday he might go to Faisalabad and meet the family of the man who had done his father such a great kindness.

I did go out of my way and, improbably, after a quest through the maze-like new and old grain markets and with some help and luck, I found the family. The patriarch had died only a few years earlier at age 107, but his son and grandson served me coffee and biscuits in their company's plush offices. They had prospered and now owned one of Pakistan's largest soap manufacturing firms. Back in Delhi, my friend beamed with pleasure when I gave him their card and telephone number. If a referendum were held today, he declared, most people in both countries would vote to reunite: 'If East Germany and West Germany can get back together, why India and Pakistan can't get back together?'

Back in Rawalpindi, a tall blond Dane named Peter Johansen, a graduate student writing a dissertation on the Pathans, invited me to go with him to Peshawar. He insisted that it was impossible to appreciate Pakistan fully without seeing the North-West Frontier Province. In Rawalpindi, Islamabad and Lahore one met only Punjabis, but the Pathans were much more fun. They were fiercely independent and congenitally hostile to all authority, suspicious not only of all non-Pathan entities such as the British Raj and the government of Pakistan, but also of each other in shifting combinations. There were varieties of Pathans, and if you asked a Pathan to identify himself ethnically, he would name his tribe, saying for example 'I am an Afridi.' The assorted Pathans of Pakistan and Afghanistan were the largest population in the world still living according to tribal ways, said Peter. They were 'tribesmen first, Muslims second'; they had a sly twinkle in their eyes and an ineradicable love of freedom in their hearts. 'They seem invincible in a way,' said Peter. 'They maintain an ironic distance to things.'

I knew Pathans only from books, as the 'tribal marauders' who had invaded Kashmir in October 1947. 'Those people are just a wild people,' a Kashmiri friend had told me. 'They don't have any sense of humour. They became addict to violence and fighting. Afghanis are born on weapons, from the beginning. But Kashmiris don't have that history.'

With relish, Peter read to me from a letter a British officer, Sir John Maffey, had written to the Viceroy in 1922. 'The tribesmen, active in mind and body, lead appallingly dull lives in their barren hills,' Maffey had written. 'They fidget the triggers of their rifles till their fingers itch.' He listed for the Viceroy the reasons he believed Pathans enjoyed warfare, such as 'a) It is a holy war against the Infidel', 'b) The few who will be killed will go to paradise' and 'd) There will be loot of rifles, ammunition, and stores.'

'In fact all's well that ends well,' he concluded. 'And if anybody doubts this, I should like him to see the flash in Pathan eyes, and hear the frenzy of the drums echoing on the rocks when over the camp fire the Afridis sing their ballad of '97. Through it all … we remain always the enemy, the infidel power that tries to take from them their God-granted slag-heap of mountain trash. But without avail. To Allah the praise.'

Peter approvingly told me that the Pathan-dominated frontier was 'kind of a grey zone in the country. It's technically a part of Pakistan, but they have their own way of doing things.' It was there that the connections among Karachi, Kashmir and Kalashnikovs became clearer to me. Peter told me about a town outside Peshawar called Darra Adam Khayl, where AK-47s and other weapons were made. Weapons manufacture had been Darra's sole industry since British times, and the town had prospered during the Afghan war against the Soviet Union. The British had encouraged weapons manufacture, because agriculture was difficult and few other industries could be made to thrive. In recent years Darra's factories had learned to copy Chinese, Russian and American weapons, and their copies were inferior only in the quality of materials. With Afghanistan still far from peaceful and Kashmir and Karachi in flames, there still was a ready market for Darra's wares. I had to see this place for myself. Peter and I secured permits to make a day trip into the tribal area.

Darra consisted of little more than a single street lined with small factories and shops amply stocked with Kalashnikovs, rocket launchers, handguns, knives, pen guns (a tempting little James Bond-type item; but to buy one was to invite the shop owner to snitch on you to the police, who would search you on the bus back to Peshawar), brass knuckles and antique British rifles. The geography of the place, dusty bluffs beside a wind-swept plain, and the physical bleakness and gold-rush atmosphere of the town itself, reinforced the Wild West impression. Customers stepped into the street to test their purchases, shooting live rounds into the air.

At one shop, Peter stopped to look at a handsome black Chinese-made pistol.

'You this Denmark?' the shop owner inquired politely.

'No!' replied Peter, both amused and horrified. 'Police big problem.' The shop owner shook his head in disgust and disbelief. What kind of place was this Denmark, where a man wasn't free to carry his own pistol wherever he went?

'You must be right at home here,' Peter teased me, 'as an American.'

Darra was a living, thriving mockery of the policy proposals of well-meaning liberals in offices in Islamabad, such as one Sher Khan, who had written in *The Nation* of 22 March 1995: 'There is a compelling, urgent need to TOTALLY BAN the possession of automatic assault and military weapons like the AK-47 altogether by non-military/paramilitary personnel without exception. Once the ban is imposed, any civilian carrying or possessing an AK-47, M-16, MP-5, Uzi etc, can be easily identified and hauled up there and then, without going into the semantics of its being licensed or otherwise. Then, perhaps we may yet see some peace and quiet in this land.' Fat chance, could be the only response of one who had seen Darra. People everywhere in Pakistan had taken to shooting off AK-47s instead of firecrackers at weddings. Everywhere you looked in Karachi, you saw gun shops and armed guards.

Peter and I split the 250 rupees it cost to shoot 30 live rounds at a mountainside from an AK-47 and took photos of each other in Rambo poses. We were disappointed that all our self-appointed guide/guard offered us to shoot at was an empty mountain. And what about that man walking along the ridge, we asked. Shouldn't we wait until he was out of the way? Don't worry, said our guide, just go ahead and shoot.

'No problem, no problem,' he chuckled. 'Tribal area. No gummint!'

Before I left Pakistan in April, I had to visit Azad Kashmir.

'Kashmir is beautiful, sir,' said the man on the bus to Muzaffarabad. 'And Occupied Kashmir is' – words briefly failed him – 'paradise on earth.'

The looking-glass sensation became stronger as we rode toward the capital of Azad Kashmir, during British times just a town on the road from Rawalpindi to Srinagar and the site of the Maharaja's penal colony. I had not been to Kashmir in nearly a year, and I felt nostalgic. The deep valleys we rode past and the climbing and falling road evoked the Kashmir I knew, though less spectacular, less breathtaking. Muzaffarabad was attractive but not stunning, a dull town stretching up a long valley, just above the confluence of the Jhelum and Neelum rivers. The Jhelum was the very same that flowed through Srinagar. Up the Neelum to the north a snow-capped peak loomed into view, but here in the valley a kind of palm tree grew.

A government official I interviewed told me something hard to credit: that until 1989, it had been possible for Kashmiris from Azad Kashmir to visit the Valley, albeit by a circuitous route. It had been necessary first to go to Islamabad, to apply for a visa. Then one had to go to Lahore, six hours further south, and cross the border at Wagah. Then south from Amritsar to Delhi, *then* by bus from Delhi to Srinagar, itself a 24-hour trip. From Muzaffarabad to Srinagar direct used to take six hours, I was told.

I was visiting Azad Kashmir at one of those periodic moments of heightened tension, at once alarming and tediously familiar, almost routine, even ritual. 'We are at the brink of war,' Sardar Abdul Qayyum Khan, prime minister of Azad Kashmir, had said a few days earlier, on 5 April. 'We are sitting on a powder keg and it can blast off at any time.' Indian troops had stepped up their apparently routine firing across the Line of Control, up the Neelum valley from Muzaffarabad. If you read far enough down in the Reuters story, you would have had to conclude that there existed little more than the usual cause for alarm. But 'at the brink of war' sounded pretty serious to me.

Well, actually, Qayyum told me when I asked, 'It's a war-like situation already. And the proxy war is already going on. It has de-escalated to some extent, but the substantive position has not changed.

Some invisible hand seems to be holding the two sides back.'

I had secured an interview with the so-called prime minister of the ostensibly kind-of independent entity known as Azad Kashmir with less than 24 hours' notice. In Kathmandu you could ask almost anyone you passed on the street for the prime minister's home telephone number. Here it was even easier: you just strolled down the road to the complex of government buildings (too new and imposing for such a small place) and inquired with any of the many functionaries whiling away the day in their offices. You might be detained for an hour or two to smoke and drink tea and talk politics, but your new friend would gladly arrange an interview or direct you to the man who could.

I felt slightly naughty being there and tried half-heartedly to be clandestine, since technically I should have secured clearance to visit Azad Kashmir through the proper channels in Islamabad. But there was no problem: they welcomed journalists here, effusively. Too effusively: they knew they had the upper hand morally over India, and they milked it. Daniel Lak, the BBC bureau chief in Islamabad, had warned me about Azad Kashmir's public relations machine. It was so smooth, and his access to information so dependent on official sources, that he had been unable to file a story.

At 9.30 one morning I was ushered into an anteroom at Prime Minister House, on a hill above the town. The house was spacious and well appointed, the drill well rehearsed: a well-practiced policy was in force regarding the treatment of journalists. On the other side of the Line of Control, the danger was only physical. Here the danger was of being co-opted. It was easy to think: gosh, I like these people.

Qayyum sat at the head of a long hardwood table. I sat to his left. Attentive retainers sat on both sides. One manned a video camera. A man brought breakfast on a tray and filled my delicate glass with orange juice. The cutlery was heavy, and the napkin was the kind you feel guilty wiping your hands on. I drank the juice but ate less than I would have liked; it wasn't practical to eat and take notes at the same time. I was being taken off my guard, but the stakes were not high: I would have been handed a party line regardless.

Qayyum was grey-bearded, patriarchal, effortlessly gracious, inoffensively condescending. I asked about the prospect of elections in the Valley, which at the time were planned for that July. 'How can you have elections with 600,000 people [Indian soldiers] sitting there with arms in every nook and corner?' he had told Reuters. 'Who in the world would accept the result of that election?'

'I don't think they [Kashmiris] will participate,' he told me. 'How can they, after all that has been done to them?' The planned elections were 'just to appease the international opinion. It is window-dressing for the West.' In 1987, Kashmiris had rejected fraudulent polls; India had a lot to answer for. At any rate, India surely could hold polls only in Hindu-majority areas such as Jammu. 'I don't think they will hold elections. You see, the Indians can never hold an election that is credible. The resistance movement in Kashmir will perhaps step up, but gunrunning is not the cause. It is the consequence.'

Elections were no substitute for a plebiscite, he said. The army should be withdrawn; candidates should not be made to swear allegiance to the Indian constitution; any polls should be supervised by the United Nations. 'But India with their massive propaganda machine, they are capable of persuading people in the West. They claim Kashmir to be an integral part, but they don't accept the Kashmiris.' Kashmiris were 'naturally affiliated with Pakistan,' he claimed, by culture, trade, geography, the flow of rivers, and religion. 'The entire trade over the centuries has been by this route.'

I asked about the nuclear issue. 'The principle, the concept of a deterrent is essential for Pakistan,' he said. 'This is the only country where there is a clear-cut danger of use of nuclear weapons anywhere in the world.'

What about a partition of Jammu and Kashmir State?

'I personally would not like to agree to a partition of the state,' said Qayyum. 'It should not be imposed from outside. And I am also sure that given a choice, they [Kashmiris] would like to live together. As a last resort, they might like the idea of a trusteeship. The tension that is building up is more important than the solution.' He suggested a three-stage programme for negotiations: first, steps should be taken to 'de-escalate' the level of tension. Second, Kashmiris from both sides of the Line of Control should be allowed to talk to each other, perhaps in Nepal, which was more or less neutral ground. Finally, the several parties should get down to 'brass tacks'.

I asked about the Afghan connection. And was he allowing or encouraging smuggling of arms and/or militants across the Line of Control from Afghanistan?

'Immediately at the end of the Afghan war, I was contacted by almost all the leaders of the Afghan movement,' he said. But he had not encouraged Afghans to join the jihad in Kashmir. 'Any activity on that level might reduce the possibility of a political solution.' Individuals crossed over individually, he said; he couldn't really stop that, could he? ('The boys come and go,' he had told Reuters. 'We don't stop their movement.') But Afghanistan was relevant in another way: 'The very pattern is that of the Afghan war.'

He made the predictable accusation that the Indian forces in Kashmir were corrupt. 'The Indian Army is reported to be selling weapons.' He remembered meeting some Gurkhas, from Nepal, during the fighting in 1947–48. He didn't find them very impressive as warriors, contrary to their reputation. He asked them why. 'You are fighting for your country,' they had told him. 'What are we fighting for?'

There were times when it seemed everyone was waiting for America to do something. 'I think you Americans also are bogged down,' suggested Qayyum. 'Because you took on the responsibility of leading the world.' He thought this was proving more than we could chew. 'America is the only positive force in the world. If they fail, the world is doomed to destruction.'

I thought of all this man must have seen, all he had been through, all the petty political battles he had fought with his own Kashmiri allies and with Pakistanis (he had been on bad terms with Benazir Bhutto during her first term as prime minister). I thought of how far he had come since 1947.

'There's no going back,' he said. 'Absolutely no going back.'

The same day Professor Iqbal Mirza, director general of public relations for the Azad Kashmir government, honoured my request to visit a refugee camp. Another official drove me six kilometres north of town, past the decaying 17th-century Red Fort, to Kamsur refugee camp. Further along the road was impassable, because of sniping by Indian forces at the Line of Control.

The camp was a forlorn cluster of khaki tents strung down several levels of the side of the valley. Moments after we pulled up, I knew exactly what Daniel Lak had meant when he said he had left Azad Kashmir with no story worth filing. My mere presence prompted 200 men to sit on mats facing a row of chairs. They seemed to have nothing better to do, anyway. I was seated on one of the chairs, given a cigarette and a smudgy carbon copy of a page full of statistics ('BASIC DATA REGARDING REFUGEES FROM INDIAN HELD PART OF STATE OF JAMMU AND KASHMIR UP TO 28-2-95 ... 4. In case of a death of a person Rs. 1000/- as burial expencess [sic]'). And I immediately became both audience and show as an official pointed at maps and graphs on an easel (the refugees were given an initial grant of six hundred to a thousand rupees, he said, pointing; this camp held 350 families, more than a thousand people; the subsistence allowance was 20 rupees per day per person; etc), and selected refugees were made to stand and tell me their stories.

'I welcome to you behalf the refugees in this camp,' began the first man's laboured but well-rehearsed tale of woe. I dutifully took notes, seeking an opening to ask a relevant or incisive question. In April 1990, at 'start of reign of terror', Indian Army soldiers had come to the man's village, on the other side of the Line of Control. They had demanded that the village's youths be handed over. The villagers had 'denied' them. The soldiers made all the people come out of their houses and arrested 35 youths. They killed the youths and raped the women. 'They gang-rape with women.'

I asked why this was done.

'First of all, the Kashmiri population all is Muslim,' he said. 'They are doing this as punishment for people.' But 'no single *jawan* [soldier] has been arrested. None of those jawans, none of them has been executed.' The man had been in this camp since 1992.

The official who had brought me to the camp was a soft-spoken, gentle man. In my hotel room, where I gave him tea, he politely, diffidently asked me to take my copy of a book titled *Muhammad and the Koran* off the floor, to show reverence, for his sake, for 'our Prophet' and 'our Holy Quran'. He took me to another hotel for lunch, in obedience to standing instructions. It was not necessary, I said; I really did want to be alone.

'It is my duty,' he insisted. 'You are our guest.'

Azad Kashmir made me think again of Germany. I had visited Germany in the summer of 1990, after the revolution but before reunification. On 31 May I had crossed the border in a car. 'One year ago,' said the West German giving me a ride, 'to go to ze German Democratic Republic you needed a visa. Until May 25 you needed a passport, not just your identification card.' A month later

I alighted from a subway at an East Berlin stop open that day for the first time since 1961, and saw my East German friend's eyes light up in delight and wonder.

I was in Lahore, about to return through the looking-glass to India, when I learned about the bombing in Oklahoma City. The widespread initial assumption was that it must have been done by Islamic fundamentalists. Back in Delhi, my Kashmiri friend exclaimed: 'There was bomb blast in America!' He was surprised, but what struck me was that he was only mildly surprised, that there would be a bomb blast in America, of all places.

I had come to know that bomb blasts happen all the time around the subcontinent. Now they happened in America too. This was why I had left Wisconsin: to learn that the serene small-town world I had come from was of a piece with the world at large.

Oddly, I found my new awareness comforting. The previous November's congressional elections already had shown the truth of the ominous obverse of Norman Mailer's assertion, in 1962, that 'so long as there is a cold war, there are no politics of consequence in America.' The chickens were coming home to roost.

CHAPTER FOUR

SCENARIOS AND LOSSES

I returned to Kashmir a third time, by bus, in June 1995. I had changed, but the Valley had not: I felt the familiar, ineffably sad sensation I had felt too many times before, in Kathmandu, in Haiti, in Milwaukee, of coming home to a place I was only passing through. There was the Valley stretched before me, green and yellow and sky blue, as we came down into it from the Pir Panjal range. There in turn were the mountains immutable as ever in the distance as we rode along the straight, flat National Highway toward the town, poplars and rice fields on either side. At last we were in Srinagar, and I was in first a motor rickshaw, then a shikara, then finally on a houseboat among the friends I felt I now knew so well. It was almost as though a long year dense with work and adventure and loss had not intervened.

Haji and his servant welcomed me effusively with hugs and protestations of having waited anxiously for me to return. The houseboat had the pleasant dry woody smell I remembered. There were new cushions on the balcony and new upholstery on the couches in the front room. This particular family had not suffered too badly this past year. The birds that had nested inside Haji's house were gone: the womenfolk had objected to the mess and Haji's son had prevailed on him to keep them out for the sake of domestic tranquillity. I didn't feel a need to visit Mr Bhat and Aziz again, but was glad to hear that Mr Bhat's health had greatly improved. The mullahs still moaned their haunting prayers at dusk, and the sunset across the lake was as unbearably beautiful as before.

I had been in Kathmandu in May when two fires swept through the Kashmiri town of Charar-e-Sharief, destroying many houses and shops along with the mausoleum of the Sufi saint Sheikh Noor-ud-din Wali, ending a two-month siege by the Indian Army of militants holed up in the shrine.

'The government of Pakistan condemns this act of sacrilege, which is an affront to the conscience of Muslims the world over,' said Pakistan's Foreign Affairs Ministry in a statement. The way the siege had ended was a 'challenge from India', said JKLF chief Yaseen Malik. 'The shrine was the symbol of the very identity of the Kashmiri people. We'll take positive steps to counter this challenge.'

A leader editorial in *The Times of India* called the destruction of the shrine an 'avoidable tragedy' and argued that the 'terrorists' had 'refused to avail of the safe passage offered by the government. This was clear enough indication of their intention to do the worst and should have served as a warning to the security forces to be prepared for the deplorable sacrilege which has now taken place. The intention of the militants was obviously to make it difficult for the government to hold elections in the state while at the same time furthering their own sectarian objectives.'

I had followed the siege desultorily while in Pakistan, but to glean the truth from newspapers was impossible. Now, the 15th-century shrine of Sheikh Noor-ud-din Wali, along with the unique relics and religious manuscripts it had housed, had to be counted among the world's irretrievable losses.

Before returning to Kashmir I had gone to see Ram Mohan Rao, representative of the Jammu and Kashmir State government in

Delhi. He gave me tea and a manila envelope full of reports, statistics and polemics alleging Pakistani sponsorship of terrorism.

'An elected government would be better suited to tackle the problem of alienation than a bureaucratic government,' he told me. 'A bureaucracy doesn't consider itself to be answerable to the people.' Kashmiris were ready to vote now, he suggested. 'The Kashmiri is afraid now that he will become another Afghanistan. It's not impossible, with this jihad thing.' And Kashmiris were becoming disillusioned with Pakistan. 'They have been watching what has happened in Pakistan over the last year and a half, where the people who fought for Pakistan – the Muslims of north India – still are treated like refugees.' This was a reference to Karachi, and an artful one. Elections probably would be held in Kashmir later that year, though nothing was firm at this point. With regret, he said the plan had been to hold elections before the end of President's Rule on 18 July, 'but unfortunately the burning of Charar-e-Sharief gave a little larger-than-life picture' to the situation. 'The assessment of the political leaders who visited the place was that it would be insensitive to rush through elections.'

Kashmir was 'a business' for Pakistani journalists, officials, and military officers, he claimed, and there was a lot of money coming in from the Muslim world. Pakistan used the summer months to infiltrate more militants into Kashmir while the mountain passes were open; Indian intelligence reports said some four to five thousand militants and foreign mercenaries were in readiness at present. More than 250 BSF and Army soldiers had been court-martialled for 'excesses' in the line of duty, he claimed. I asked for documentation of this. He didn't have any on hand, he said; but I should be assured the records were public and obtainable.

I asked the bottom-line question: what was the solution? Whenever I asked this question, I felt an irrational hope that someone might surprise me with an original idea.

'I think the government is conscious that there is a desire among a sizeable portion of the people that they want to manage their own affairs,' said Ram Mohan Rao. 'Without arousing controversy at the Centre', the prime minister could 'arrive at a kind of consensus' and at the same time 'meet the desires of the Kashmiri people, to the extent possible within our system.'

At any rate, he added in a jocular tone, what was this thing *azaadi* anyway? The Kashmiris didn't really know what they wanted. They needed only a facsimile of freedom, a semblance of autonomy, and they would behave themselves. 'It's a question of a child wanting a toy,' he said with a smile. 'Once you get a toy, you throw it aside.'

Back in Kashmir, my first project was to see the aftermath at Charar-e-Sharief. Haji hired a man named Ali Mohammed to drive us there, and on we bumped in his Ambassador through dusty red-brick villages and past verdant rice fields and clumps of tall narrow poplar, the snowcapped Himalaya in the distance.

Ali Mohammed had driven me once before in his Ambassador, on a day trip to Pahalgam. I met several Ali Mohammeds in Kashmir, and Naipaul writes about one in *An Area of Darkness*, 'a small man of about forty with a cadaverous face made still more so by ill-fitting dentures' whose 'job was to entice tourists to the hotel' by hanging around twice a day outside the Tourist Reception Centre. Every morning at breakfast, Ali Mohammed would squat before the charcoal brazier in the hotel dining-room, 'his back to us, utterly absorbed, turning over slices of bread with his fingers. A dedicated toastmaker he appeared, but he was in reality listening to the fifteen-minute programme of Kashmiri devotional songs that follows the news in English on Radio Kashmir. In the curve of his back there could be sensed a small but distinct anxiety: the toast might be required too soon, we might turn to another station, or he might be called away to other duties.' In *India: A Million Mutinies Now*, on his return visit in 1989, Naipaul writes only that Ali Mohammed 'had gone away'.

My driver was a small, gaunt man with the usual Kashmiri hook nose, a small moustache and white stubble, and grey hair slicked behind his ears like a Mafia don. What seemed his chronic nervousness was tempered by what might have been an ironic kind of happiness. 'It was hard to tell with Ali,' writes Naipaul. 'He always looked slightly stunned whenever he was addressed directly.' In *India: A Million Mutinies Now* he calls him 'blunt-featured and earnest'.

On the three-hour drive to Pahalgam we had ridden in silence for some time, until I summoned the courage to ask: 'Are you the Ali Mohammed that Mr Naipaul wrote about?'

He smiled, still looking straight ahead through the windshield. 'Yes, sir,' he said, and seemed genuinely happy to have been recognised.

After a pause I asked, 'So what was he like?'

He said nothing.

'Mr Naipaul. What was he like?'

'It is their wish,' he mumbled.

'Excuse me?'

He was embarrassed, I think. It was hard to tell with Ali. 'It is their wish,' he repeated. 'They want I say nothing about Mr Naipaul.'

The road out of Srinagar that day had been congested with trucks and jeeps brimming with soldiers, some facing rearwards, rifles casually aimed through our windshield. Ali stopped so I could tour the ruined ancient temple at Awantipur, which I dutifully did: built in the 9th century; destroyed in the 14th by either the King of Persia or an earthquake; excavated by the British in 1923. Beside the ruin was a new mosque, built 'five–six years ago' according to the man who attached himself to me. There had been a government programme to restore the temple, but that had stopped when the insurgency began.

Ali Mohammed had driven me past mountains on both sides of the road, the range to our right a distant unbroken line of snow-covered peaks, past fields of bright yellow mustard alternating with the famous but less spectacular saffron. Past Awantipur were rice paddies and more mustard; sheep, goats and horses grazed among the crops. Ali had stopped again at a village called Sangam, to show me the cottage industry of cricket bats, stacked beside the road, made from willow, for sale in India and abroad. Willows and poplars lined the road here, and the road remained well asphalted until we turned left toward Pahalgam. Just before the turn was a place where one month earlier, said Ali, Indian soldiers had killed 42 people at once, as they came out of their mosque after Friday prayers.

Beyond Islamabad, the Valley's red-brick second-largest town, beyond a Sikh village, beyond the pool home to holy fish, beyond the mud huts and high garden walls of gypsies was Pahalgam, bracingly chilly at 8,000 feet, where Ali Mohammed and I had tea in the town and ate lunch beside the river, then I enjoyed the scenery while he prayed in a meadow beside his parked Ambassador.

On the drive back, I had quizzed Ali. He told me he had been 12 years old in 1947, which made him 59 now, and 27 (not 40) in 1962 when Naipaul had known him. His business now was driving, he said. He paid the same taxes to the government as he had before the troubles began. The government-owned bank had assured him they would reduce the interest on his loan, but had not done so. 'But they give me no concession. Indian didn't give us any hel-ep. And they told lot: "I will give taxi drivers, houseboat owners, shikara-wallahs." But up till now they have given nothing. Even single penny they didn't give us. Before '89 we got plenty money, we didn't care for that. Everybody has got a hope, sir, that tourist season will be better. But nowadays I think it will be worse.' Educated people were working in menial jobs now. His own two sons were doing all right, both working for a Swedish company that was building a hydroelectric dam. One was a driver; the other worked in the mess.

* * *

A year later, driving to Charar-e-Sharif to witness the aftermath of the fires, Haji and Ali Mohammed were in a joking mood. 'One newspaperman was caught by army in city,' said Haji over his shoulder to me from the front seat. 'They said what are you doing here? He said press. They said, Oh! You are *dhobi*, laundry man.'

I laughed appreciatively.

'These milit'ry people, all are illit'rate!' cried Ali Mohammed happily.

On the long winding road up the hill to Charar-e-Sharief, we were made to stop at a Border Security Force checkpoint. The soldiers played good-cop bad-cop, or maybe they weren't playing: the young enlisted man grinned cheerfully at me, happy to meet a foreigner, and his officer was suitably stern. Ali Mohammed had secreted my notebook in the glove box. The officer looked down on me through the rear window, expectantly. I knew what he wanted, but I wasn't going to give it to him until he asked. A moment passed.

'Yes?'

'Passport.'

I handed it to him.

He glanced through my visa stamps. 'You have been to Pakistan?'

'Yes, I have been to Pakistan.' The passport he was holding contained two Pakistani visas, each with the word JOURNALIST handwritten in all caps.

He paused, then handed back my passport.

Haji asked if I had a spare piece of paper. At his bidding, on the back of a copy of my editor's letter of introduction, I scribbled PRESS in large letters. Ali Mohammed propped it against the inside of the windshield with a twig, and we drove on.

At a village further on we were stopped, and two men got in. 'We are glad to hel-ep you from each and every quarter,' said a third man through the window. 'But do the duty of your profession, and place the *facts* before the public.'

They lost no time giving me their version of the facts. Immediately after the fires, they told me, it had been announced that 30 crores, 300 million rupees, would be granted in relief or compensation, 15 crores each from the State and Central governments. In addition one lakh, 100,000 rupees, per family was to come from the Prime Minister's Fund. But all that had been received was 10,000 rupees and five blankets per family in 'ex gratia' relief (whatever that was), and this given only to influential families, at the beginning of June. There had been nothing since. Government-controlled Radio Kashmir had reported in mid-June that the 'second phase' of the compensation programme had begun, but that was a lie. There were cases where several families shared a house, but relief was to have been granted per house; this would leave many families with less than 40,000 rupees with which to rebuild their lives. 'It is impossible to construct two rooms and a bathroom at present for 40,000 rupees.' Local engineers and press reports had estimated total damage to the town at 240 crores, 2.4 billion rupees.

Exactly what had happened at Charar-e-Sharief, who had set the fires, whether and how – and why – the militants inside the mosque (said to be a pro-Pakistan bunch led by one Mast Gul) had been allowed to escape, even whether militants had been there at all, was a web of mystery. The siege had begun on 7 March and ended on 8 May when, as one of my local informants alleged, 'The town was gutted by the army.' This was a very different telling from the one in the Indian press. There had been three fires, said residents: one on the night of 8–9 May, that destroyed much of the town; one on the night of 10–11 May, in which the shrine of Sheikh Noor-ud-din Wali and the nearby mosque had burned down; and a third during the day on 11 May. The local people gave me names of civilians they said had died in the first fire: Ali Mohammed Kumar, 60, a potter; Bashir Ahmed Mir, 50, a carpet weaver; Mohammed Akbar Bhat, 35 or 40 years old, a *chowkidar* or watchman; Mrs Khadiji, 50. Haji had been keen to tell me what François Musseau, of the Paris daily *Libération*, had told him: that all the corpses he had seen immediately after the fire had looked to him like Kashmiris – not, say, Pakistani Punjabis or Pathans.

Gulam Mohammed Baba, general secretary of the Alamdar Shopkeepers' Association, was ready with numbers: 360 shops had been gutted, 70 looted by Indian Army soldiers, 20 potters had lost their places of business, 84 willow worker units had been lost. Only about 20 or 30 shops had not been destroyed, he said. There was a shopkeepers' strike on that day, the second since the fire. All the shops still standing were closed. GIVE COMPENSATION FOR OUR BURNED AND LOOTED SHOPS, read the banner in Urdu on a fence and the signboard over the main street. Business had been slow lately anyway. 'All the shopkeepers are idle, from siege time to this time,' he said.

Charar-e-Sharief had been famous not only for the shrine of Kashmir's most revered Sufi missionary, but for a longstanding cottage industry in pottery and 'winter wives', the fire pots Kashmiris use to keep warm in winter. 'This town was famous in whole of Kashmir because there were so many fire-pot makers,' one local man said.

'That is traditional *heater* here,' said his friend, with a grin. He meant it as a self-deprecatory joke. I duly smiled.

'They were solely dependent on the shrine,' explained Haji. 'It is from the generations, from 700 years back. Every day 20, 30, 40 buses used to come here. There were no hotels here. Only houses. People used to stay in house, tomorrow they would leave, and give two-three hundred rupees.'

Indian public opinion took little care to distinguish between militants and so-called fundamentalists or, similarly, between separatists who fought with guns and ordinary Kashmiris, most of whom quietly despised India. 'If the two bulls fight,' said Haji, 'the poor landlord lost his crop. The bull should pay! Gummint says the militants were inside the shrine. They should *prove* whether militants were here or not.'

We went further up the hill to see what was left of the shrine. It had been reduced to a stone foundation perhaps five metres square, now covered with a cloth tent, in a kind of stone courtyard. To the left, about a dozen yards away, was what was left of the mosque. A few charred beams could be seen, but much of the rubble had been cleared away by local people, bricks and beams piled neatly on the stone floor. On the hillside beyond were the red-brick remnants of at least 100 houses, stretching fully across my field of vision. The banality of it all: it was hard to summon outrage or even melancholy; I felt only that here in front of me was the way things were *now*. As of 1 July, the world as it was prior to 10 May exists only in memory.

The army had threatened the people to make them vacate the town, alleged Ghulam Nebi Kaw, president of the Shopkeepers' Association. The army claimed the soldiers had stayed two to five kilometres away from the town during the siege. But that was 'absolutely fake and false'. Everyone in the town had seen that they had been right there, on that hillside; and did I think that hillside was two to five kilometres away? I agreed that it was not. 'And see the violations of human rights that they did not allow foodstuffs or lifesaving drugs or any kind of materials to come into the town.' Fifteen people had died, he said, five militants and ten civilians, including 'a lame lady of 70 years old'. On 8 May the government had announced that the army controlled the town and that the mosque and shrine were safe. Then, on the night of 10–11 May, the mosque and shrine had burned to the ground. 'Then who put fire on the mosque and the shrine? Then it is *clear* who gutted the shrine and mosque!'

But why? I asked.

'They are not in a position to elect here, to make a gummint,' said Ghulam Nebi Kaw. 'They want to give an impression to other countries and the world that militants have gutted the shrine. Their main thing was that they were trying to involve the Pakistan in militancy in Charar-e-Sharief.'

'Nobody has guts to stand,' added Haji, meaning stand in elections. 'This is their excuse, the shrine is burn-ed.'

Eagerly, the crowd of men showed me several mortar shells, about six inches long, and small parachutes stamped PARA SYSTEM FOR SHELLS 51 MM and O.P.F. KANPUR. Kanpur, the men said, was a city in Andhra Pradesh in central India, where there was an ordnance-producing factory. The shells had been dropped from 'heli-crafters', and the gunpowder in them was ignited during the firing that followed from both sides.

Clearly enough, the shells and parachutes were Indian. But they could have been stolen or bought from Indian forces and planted. I still don't know the truth. What Kashmir taught me, more than anything, was to accept ambiguity – political, moral, above all factual – as a fact of life.

A number of relics connected to the life of Sheikh Noor-ud-din Wali had been housed in the shrine. I had wondered to Haji what had become of these. He was quite sure they had been removed to a safe place during the siege. Now we learned that this was wrong. These relics – a 'thing to carry vessels on head' believed to have belonged to the Prophet's daughter Fatima; a walking stick belonging to Hazrat Owais Karani that had been a masterpiece of carving in glass; items of clothing belonging to Sheikh Noor-ud-din Wali and Sheikh Said Ali Aali, Emperor of Balaq – had burned. Outside the shrine, charred and on its side, lay the fireproof locker in which they had been stored, its heavy door open and twisted. The locker had been guaranteed safe for 24 hours, the men said. But the fire had burned for 48 hours. The relics had been destroyed.

The shrine, built during the period Kashmir was ruled from Afghanistan, had been the most important and revered Sufi shrine in all Kashmir. Kashmiris manage to be at once devout Muslims and fervent idolators, descendents of their Hindu ancestors, and Charar-e-Sharief and its relics had been almost as near to their hearts as the Prophet's whisker at Hazratbal. 'Every prime minister of India used to come to this place, to visit this shrine,' said Haji. 'One crore people were visiting this shrine every year, from all over Jammu and Kashmir State. *Many* thing Sheikh Noor-ud-din gave to Kashmir. He was the *great* man of Kashmir. The Kashmiris are indebted to these saints, for the reason that they have Islamise-ed this whole region. "My grandfather was Hindu," Sheikh Noor-ud-din used to say, "and I am his grandson." Therefore Hindus used to come pray here. They pray their way, we pray our way.'

'God is one,' the saint had said, in Haji's translation. 'He has millions of names. Not a single leaf of the tree or the vegetable is without the name of God. Everybody takes the name of God in their own way.' The local men nodded in pious agreement.

On the way from Srinagar, we had been stopped and checked by soldiers of the BSF. On the way back we were stopped by their enemies. Several young men were standing around casually on the shoulder of the road and in the ditch. Ali Mohammed stopped the car, and two of them came up to my window.

'Which press you are from?' one asked me.

'I am from the *South China Morning Post*, the newspaper in Hong Kong,' I said.

'You have complete your work?'

'Yes, I believe I have completed my work.'

He paused, as though trying to remember his next line.

'Now you can go,' he said.

'Militants?' I asked Haji as we drove off.

'Militants,' he said.

One day, waiting to interview JKLF leader Yaseen Malik, I found myself seated next to Jalil Andrabi, whom I had interviewed the year before. Andrabi was what is too glibly called a 'human rights activist'. He was a likeable and impressive young lawyer who, with colleagues in the Kashmir Bar Association, travelled to remote villages, painstakingly documented atrocities committed by Indian forces, and filed usually fruitless writs in the High Court. It broke one's heart to think of the effort they put into raw documentation, the naming of persons and putting on record of events that otherwise would have been forgotten by all but the obscure sufferers themselves. Typical was the thick document titled 'Report on Human Rights Violations in Kashmir State from 1-1-94 to 20-3-94, Report VIII', which included this characteristic passage: 'Forces during crackdown operations killed two persons, namely Mohd Ashraf and Mohd Yaseen of district Islamabad on Jan 6, 1994.'

Andrabi struck me as extraordinarily intelligent, informed and thoughtful. He exercised his professional skills in the service of what to him was a moral compulsion.

'What we believe is, that human rights are guaranteed to every human being who is born on earth,' he had told me. 'India also recognises this right, under Article 21 of the Constitution of India.'

Talking of this and that as we waited, we differed politely on the United States' position in the Kashmir dispute. I thought Washington was purposely sending conflicting and confusing messages, in order to preserve its own freedom of action for its own benefit. He chose not to believe this, because it was a pessimistic idea and he preferred to be an optimist.

Well, I rejoined, what had the US done lately for the cause of truth and right in, say, Burma? He responded by telling me a startling piece of news – which is how I learned that Aung San Suu Kyi had been released from house arrest.

Later the same day I went to Andrabi's office, on the dingy upper floor of a dusty building, because he wanted to give me some documents. He was dictating a High Court writ to a clerk when I arrived. When I returned the next day for yet more documents, he gave me a Pepsi and prevailed on me to stay for a few minutes. I asked why he did what he did. He felt compelled to do it, he said; it had to be done; truth and justice had to be served, however ineffectually. Otherwise, he could not have lived with himself.

I felt too tired to take notes – I was leaving the next morning and had many things on my mind – and among the many things I regret is that I felt too distracted and rushed to stay longer with Jalil Andrabi that day. You never know when might be the last time you'll see someone. His words brought to mind the American writer Wendell Berry, who has written: 'Protest that endures, I think, is moved by a hope far more modest than that of public success: namely, the hope of preserving qualities in one's own heart and spirit that would be destroyed by acquiescence.'

Jalil Andrabi was kidnapped in murky circumstances on 8 March 1996. Later that month his body was found floating in the River Jhelum, its eyes gouged out. I was in Bangkok when I heard the report of his death on CNN.

On the eve of the Fourth of July 1995, Haji and I talked for a long time. We discussed Islam, the Quran and the Bible, religion in general, and the coming end of the world. We considered, among other things, the possibility that the authors of writings claimed to be prophetic, such as Nostradamus and the author of the Book of Revelation, might just have been on to something. He told me that Muslims, like Christians, believe Jesus will come again. Jesus? I asked. Not Mohammed?

No, Jesus, he said.

Why Jesus? Wasn't that a little strange?

He didn't see what was so strange, and he didn't really understand why it should be Jesus that Muslims expected to return. Nor did he feel any need to understand. It was right there in black and white, in the Holy Quran.

He sat calmly, knees drawn up, smoking his hubble-bubble. I told him about the explosion and shots I had heard earlier in the day. Yes, he had heard them too, he said. There was a certain part of the old city where clashes were occurring daily now.

'I don't think they can stop these militants,' he said.

I pondered for a moment how no war or rebellion that I could think of seemed ever to have ushered in a permanently better state of affairs. I considered how I might express this to Haji. 'Two hundred years ago,' I said, 'we had a revolution in my country.'

He drew on his hubble-bubble.

'Who was there?' he asked. 'British?'

'Yes, British.'

He nodded sagely as though to say it figured. 'British ruled almost *whole* of world,' he observed. 'Almost *whole* of world.'

'We kicked 'em out,' I added.

It was an almost physical pleasure to be back in this remarkable man's presence. His very mannerisms gave me a kind of joy, a mélange of affection, respect, familiarity and comfort. Be involved and be aware, was his message to me, write, try to change the world, but don't let it get you down. The preponderance of evidence to the contrary, something better may well be in store for us. At any rate, one day you too probably will be 71 years old. Pace yourself.

I watched him light his hubble-bubble, as I had seen him do dozens of times before. He would pick glowing coals out of his winter wife with the tongs that hung on a chain from the hookah, blowing carefully on them as he did so. He would lay the coals lovingly, one by one, atop the tobacco or whatever it was in the bowl of the hubble-bubble. (On at least one occasion, to judge from the scent and the effect on me, it must have been something other than tobacco.) Then, with a practised gesture, he would set the bowl back in place on the end of the stem that rose from the water chamber. Then he would smoke.

'Last fourteen hundred years there have been no amendments to Quran,' he said. 'There's no way.' This, he noted with high disdain, was in marked contrast to the Indian constitution. The Quran had been translated into many languages, but its proper language was Arabic. A great deal was lost in translation, he said, and besides, almighty Allah had given the Quran to Prophet Mohammed (peace be upon him) in Arabic, not in English or any other language. But that was unfortunate for people who can't read Arabic, he observed generously.

'I can only read the Quran in English,' I said.

He had had a Quran in English, he said, but he had given it to a guest some years before, a Russian who expressed great interest in Islam. It was forbidden to take religious books into the Soviet Union, but the Russian said he would find a way. Haji had happened to see the man again in a group of Russians at a hotel in Delhi. To Haji's satisfaction, the Russian had indeed succeeded in smuggling the Quran into Russia.

'Restrictions make men clever,' observed Haji.

He drew on his hubble-bubble.

'So maybe restrictions are good things,' I suggested.

'Well, some of these boys, they smuggle drugs,' he said. 'Gummint puts restrictions, but boys, they find ways.'

'Some people smuggle drugs, some people smuggle the Quran.'

'Some people smuggle drugs,' he agreed. 'Some people smuggle the Quran.'

We talked again the next evening, more down to earth. 'And now we don't trust any gummint, anybody,' he concluded a political disquisition. 'We want that the United Nations should command the elections. We don't even trust America. He may be corrupted by

Indian gummint.' He drew on his hubble-bubble. 'History never ends,' he remarked.

'We want it to end,' I said.

'We want it to end,' he agreed. 'But it will not.'

Our conversations always went like this, with long pauses between sometimes unconnected items or observations, punctuated by the hubbly-bubbly noise of the water as he inhaled.

'I can tell you, if there is this pill-biscite or anything like that, I can tell you that people will vote JKLF,' he said in a tone of finality. 'People prefer independence. Not Pakistan.'

The next morning, Haji relayed to me the news he had heard on the BBC: several Westerners had been kidnapped, apparently near Aroo, where the two Brits had been kidnapped the previous June, and where I had interviewed the Hizbul Mujahedin militants. Details were sketchy; it might be six, four or ten. Nationalities unknown. The previous year's incident had ended happily enough; as Haji had put it to me, the BBC had squawked, the Voice of America had squawked, Kashmir had got a little attention in the outside world, the hostages had been released.

This time the local papers were little help, only giving the misspelled names of the hostages. *The Kashmir Times* reported that 'nine foreigners including some women' were 'intercepted by the gunmen. After preliminary questioning five of them including the women were allowed to go but four were kept hostages and whisked away to some unknown destination.' The *Greater Kashmir* cited police sources as saying 'a new militant outfit Al-Faran' had claimed responsibility. Two days later, officials had yet to establish contact with the kidnappers, and *The Times of India* was saying that security forces had 'conducted an aerial survey' of the area around Pahalgam.

Exactly where had the kidnappings taken place? How many hostages were there? What countries were they from? Who exactly were these kidnappers, anyway? Nobody believed anybody else; there was too little common ground between those who accepted the Indian government's vision of the way things should be and the large majority of Kashmiris, who already had been asked to believe too many lies. The situation was ripe for self-serving and paranoid speculation.

'We have never heard of this group before,' a Hurriyat leader told the *Mirror of Kashmir.* 'Those who have indulged in abduction of the guests cannot be the friends of our movement.'

'Maybe it is the work of gummint agents to defame militants on international level,' suggested another Hurriyat leader.

'Before this kidnapping, Al-Faran was nowhere in the scene,' Yaseen Malik told me. 'We cannot rule out Indian agents.'

To judge by the coverage the topic immediately began getting in the Indian papers, an official line had been tacitly handed down, and there was no shortage of writers willing to disseminate it. Reading the Indian press on Kashmir was like reading a novel published in installments, in which certain things were simply taken for granted, not even explained on first mention, so that even the assiduous reader began to wonder: have I missed something? Take for example the theoretical, possible, speculative involvement of Harkat-ul-Ansar, the group that had claimed credit for the previous summer's kidnappings, slipped in casually as an established fact in a *Times of India* analysis on 8 July. 'There is a growing feeling in official circles here that the abduction of four foreign tourists by militants belonging to the Pakistan-based Harkat-ul-Ansar, is not a ploy merely to seek the release of their imprisoned colleagues but also to assert their group's supremacy in the Kashmir Valley,' wrote Sunil Narula.

I interviewed an American woman who had been robbed in the same incident in which the four had been kidnapped. Haji knew the owner of the houseboat she was staying on; I had left a note asking if she would meet me, and she surprised me by showing up. She was 23 years old, Puerto Rican, from New York. She was easily one of the most beautiful women I had ever seen, and she was talkative and opinionated; almost the first thing she told me was that she and all her friends hated journalists. Not to worry, I assured her; I wasn't like all the other journalists.

She came with the man who had been her guide on her trek. She had been trekking alone, camping the night of 4 July at Lidderwat, to the right side of the bridge that crosses the river. It was early evening, about six o'clock, and she was in her tent reading, when two armed men arrived and spoke to her guide. The guide came into her tent, told her they were being robbed, urged her to stay calm, and coached her in what to say. The men hung around for quite some time, while the woman observed them. Her guide brought her food. Then she saw two men – she called them militants – crossing the bridge with three foreigners and two other militants behind. Soon after, a man arrived who seemed to be a commander. The woman had had to show her passport to the first two militants, and now she had to show it again. The commander told the guide to take away her food. The woman asked if she could put on a sweater and some shoes; the commander said that was all right. The guide came to the kitchen tent, where the woman was, and told her the men had taken both her valuable cameras, a drawing pen and some film and 25 rupees (less than a dollar). They said they would return these at Aroo, but she never saw any of her stolen belongings again. Then the militants left.

This is all the woman said she saw that evening; the other tourists were staying elsewhere in the meadow at Lidderwat. She heard that evening that people had been kidnapped – three Englishmen and one American, or maybe two English and two Americans; she and the guide were not sure. A Canadian had been spared because he was ill, and no women had been kidnapped or raped. The woman and her guide stayed that night where they were, then went down to Pahalgam the next day.

The kidnappers spoke 'pure Urdu', the guide told me, which to his mind meant they were neither Kashmiris, who would have spoken Kashmiri, nor Pushtu-speaking Afghans. He thought they might have been from Doda or Kishtwar in southern Jammu and Kashmir State. There were 30 or 35 men, including no more than one or two Afghans. Most had long hair, and the commander had a long beard.

Aspects of the robbers' behaviour led the guide to suspect they were not Muslims. They asked him which direction was Mecca, he said. This was odd, since it was evening and anyone could see where the sun was setting. They asked to borrow a prayer rug, which as any Muslim knew is not prescribed: any clean, dry surface, such as the grass of the meadow, is perfectly acceptable. And besides, if prayer rugs were so important to them, why didn't they carry their own? A Muslim prayer rug rolls or folds up into a small bundle easily carried in a pack or bag. Also, the men prayed sometime between 6 and 6.30; prayer times, unlike the use of a rug, are strictly prescribed, and they prayed too early in the evening.

Haji had his own suspicions. The whole thing stank to high heaven, if you asked him. There were said to be no fewer than 40,000 Indian troops around Pahalgam and Lidderwat, and there were only a few roads into the area, and the mountains were difficult to traverse. 'Didn't they know there were 30–35 militants in Lidderwat?' he said. And the kidnappers were said to be demanding the release of 15 or so jailed militant leaders – but the names given were from a wide gamut of different militant groups, many hostile to each other. 'How strange this is. So how these people can grow like mushrooms now? Where they came from? And why in July? Who not in May, April, March?' He answered his own question: 'Because *yatra* has started.'

He meant the Amarnath pilgrimage. Haji's theory was that agents of the Indian government had perpetrated the kidnappings, with two objects in mind. First, they wanted to clear the area around Pahalgam of foreign tourists, so local pony-wallahs normally not eager to do business with Indians would be desperate to hire their ponies to the tens of thousands of Hindu pilgrims who walked to the cave to see the ice lingam every August. Second, the Indian government would be happy to discredit the Kashmiri separatist movement in general.

It was this incident and the scenarios that I allowed myself to spin from it that led Tony Davis to accuse me of 'retailing silly conspiracy theories' in his letter to the *Bangkok Post*. But too much journalism either willingly or inadvertently enables the state to mystify events and monopolise interpretation. 'The best way to forestall the development of a scenario is to keep your events episodic,' writes Norman Mailer in *Oswald's Tale*. On the other hand, and I think this was Tony's point, speculation is the lazy journalist's short cut. Scenarios that are plausible are built not from guesses but from facts, painstakingly gleaned one by one.

On 8 July the BBC confirmed the day's rumour, that a German had been kidnapped the night before near Pahalgam. Haji told me the official report of the day's toll was 28 killed, mostly civilians. This was the official figure, he stressed. The real figure had to be higher, as always. And people were saying that Governor Krishna Rao might be about to be sacked. Prime Minister Narasimha Rao was 'giving hell' to him about the kidnappings, Haji guessed.

'Any news about the German?' I asked him the next morning.

'No,' he said. 'Only BBC confirm-ed last night, it is true.'

'I sure hope I don't get kidnapped,' I said.

'No, no. You won't get kidnap.'

'You could kidnap me,' I kidded him, 'and get a lot of publicity.'

He smiled, enjoying the image. 'Yes. I could kidnap you.'

That afternoon I went to Lal Chowk to buy a newspaper and an electric plug. On the way back I lingered several hours at the Ice-Fern coffee house on the Boulevard, trading rumours and impressions with two Australians. When I got back to the houseboat, I learned what I should have realised ahead of time: that Haji had been worried about me.

I sat down to talk with him. I had been thinking a lot about the coming end of my trip. I had been away from what passed for home for nearly five months. 'I have a lot of work to do after I get back to Bangkok,' I said.

He grinned. 'I was thinking yesterday,' he said. 'If Ethan gets kidnap, I will go to the militant group and say, "Here are his books and papers. He needs these. At least let him have his books and papers."'

I laughed; he had my number. 'At least I wouldn't be bored,' I said.

'At least you wouldn't be bored,' he agreed, and drew on his hubble-bubble.

At the end of *An Area of Darkness*, Naipaul writes of India 'slipping away' from him. Having returned to Kashmir, seeing it once again, knowing in the gut that life and death had been going on in my absence, I tried and failed to retrieve my earlier two visits from personal memory. Where does the time go? I need no literary critic to explain to me the meaning of Naipaul's final sentence: 'I felt it as something true which I could never adequately express and never seize again.'

One evening, I sat alone for a while on a wooden pier and watched the world go by on the Dal Lake between me and the typically stunning sunset. It came to me to what an extent my experience of Kashmir had hinged on the kindness and friendship of one particular family. Haji's citified elder son was back from Delhi, preparing to take a rare group of clients on a long trek, and other young relatives were about. Suddenly, I found myself on the verge of tears. But I challenged myself not to indulge in the sadness of leaving a place, pleasurable though I knew that to be. 'Tears were running down his cheeks,' writes Naipaul of his 1962 parting with Aziz. 'Even at that moment I could not be sure that he had ever been mine.' It was a Kashmiri trait, I now knew, to be finally inaccessible. I was to have a disturbing similar experience the morning I bade farewell to Haji. I wanted to say something that would last, that would insure my attachment to him through the next separation. He was polite as ever but distracted, perhaps thinking of his own worries.

I would move on, I realised that evening on the pier, and life and death would go on in Kashmir as before. This was their life; it was only a slice of my varied, attenuated experience. I had no right to claim Kashmir, to feel sure that it was mine. I was not suffering and dying; I was not losing my livelihood. On the contrary, as a journalist I was literally making money from other people's suffering. And in more important ways, I had been given more than I deserved or felt I could repay. Maybe the best I could do was to say, with a faith truer and more confident than I could have mustered a year earlier: we'll meet again, *inshallah*.

CHAPTER FIVE

A FANTASTIC TIME
TO BE ALIVE

From Kashmir I returned to the hardscrabble life of a freelance journalist in Bangkok. I went to Burma during the period of false hope after Aung San Suu Kyi's release from house arrest, to Indonesia when street protests signalled an end to the Suharto regime, to Bangladesh to cover an election. I had the good fortune to be in Cambodia during the July 1997 coup d'etat. 'Well, you've survived your first coup,' Gavin Young said to me afterwards in Bangkok, enjoying his own avuncular wit. 'Every young man must have his first coup.'

I learned that among foreign correspondents there exists a caste system, with salaried and fully-expensed staffers at the top and free-lancers at the bottom, and that an individual reporter is like a Third World country whose economy depends on exporting primary commodities. I had gone freelance precisely in order to be free, and I learned the price of freedom. A staff correspondent enjoys whatever deference his or her employer's reputation commands; a freelancer has to earn respect story by story. And in the news biz, few really care how deep or subtle your insights are or how well you use language. They care more whether you're in a country they happen to be noticing at the moment. By 1997 I was broke, embittered and drained. Feeling defeated, I resolved to leave Asia and journalism behind.

But my experience of both taught me some truths: that the world is of a piece; that to understand it is a more urgent task than to judge or change it; that an action or stance can be at once morally wrong and politically right, or vice versa. And, reporting for newspapers with limited space and attention spans, I learned the discipline and value of explaining something irreducibly complex to uninformed readers far away, in chunks of digestible size.

I saw Ed Pettit, author of *The Experts* and of the January 1966 letter to Senator Fulbright, for the last time in Bangkok in December 1997. He already looked haggard in his final illness. At what I rightly feared would be our last meeting, I asked Ed for his take on the Asian currency crisis.

'Don't make any bets about the future of the world economy,' were his last oracular words to me. 'All I know is that the next five years is going to be the goddamnedest merry-go-round, the goddamnedest Ferris wheel. It's going to be a *fantastic* time to be alive.'

Not a moment too soon, I met a woman in England who helped me knit back together my frayed soul. But now in my thirties, and haunted by a sense that my adult life so far had gone to waste, I needed an income and had disqualified myself from most conventional careers. So, in 1999, I cobbled together a few gigs and made two month-long trips to Pakistan.

I stayed in Islamabad with my friend Scott Anger, who was the bureau chief for Voice of America radio. With Scott and his Pakistani deputy Ayaz Gul I went to Peshawar and to a town called Timurgharah, in a valley in the scenic foothills of the Frontier, where there was snow on the ground in January and where a local politician told us, 'We have nothing to do with Pakistani laws.' In dispute was Prime Minister Nawaz Sharif's attempt to impose *shariah* or Islamic law nationwide. Out here they already had shariah, thank you very much, and they didn't trust or respect the central government any more than they had during British rule. The region had joined Pakistan only in 1960; before that it had been ruled by a *nawab* or prince, with land disputes and everything else governed by shariah. Until 1965, Afghan currency rather than Pakistani rupees had been in use here. The politician pointed out to us that Nawaz Sharif had no beard and lived in a big house. 'He doesn't follow Islam,' he claimed. Local people also had a scornful saying about Jamaat-i-Islami, the largest of the Islamist political parties: 'Jamaat doesn't want Islam; they want Islamabad.'

Pakistani Christians, who made up less than five percent of the country's population, were mainly descendants of low-caste Hindu converts and still held much the same niche in society. Muslims called them 'sweepers', and this was what you often saw them doing, usually in the morning, stooping humbly to sweep the road clean in Lahore or Islamabad, their brooms rasping across the asphalt. Christians knew their place, and were made to remember it. In Islamabad there was a slum called French Colony, where most of the city's Christians lived; even though they held no title to their houses and had been illegally squatting in them for decades, the government wouldn't regularise their situation, though nor could it remove them: who would keep the capital's streets clean?

One Christian who stood out as exceptional was Cecil Chaudhry, a retired Air Force officer revered for his exploits as a fighter pilot in two wars against India. He was white-haired and moustachioed, genial and astute. The situation of Christians in Pakistan was inherently political, he insisted. 'You can't isolate the two,' he told me, 'because the plight of the Christians in Pakistan stems out of the political system.' He had decided to make use of his status as a national hero. 'I thought I should get maximum mileage out of that,' he said candidly.

He had resolved to resign from the Air Force when he was superseded for promotion, and the day he was superseded, he resigned. He told me this not in bitterness but as a matter of fact. His father had been a pioneering photojournalist for the *Pakistan Times* newspaper; he himself was now headmaster of St Anthony's School, attached to the Roman Catholic cathedral in Lahore. He also acted as general secretary of the National Christian Action Forum, a grouping of mainstream churches and Christian political representatives formed after the 6 May 1998 suicide of the Roman Catholic Bishop of Faisalabad, John Joseph.

Christians' complaints at the time were focused on a law promulgated by the dictator Zia ul Haq making it a capital offence to insult the Prophet Mohammed, and on the system of 'separate electorates' for religious minorities. Zia 'brought about tremendous changes in the constitution,' Chaudhry told me. He called separate electorates, in which religious minorities such as Christians and Hindus could vote only for members of their own communities, 'religious apartheid'.

'Whenever the majority of these blasphemy cases have taken place, no member of parliament stuck his neck out for us,' he said. 'Right now, if a poor Christian living in interior Sindh has a problem, he doesn't know whom to go to. If there were a joint electoral system, even if these laws existed, there would be very little chance of their being misused. Whenever a government fails to misguide the masses, they have taken refuge in Islam. Zia came to power in 1977 on the shoulders of the religious parties. In order to perpetuate his power, he flirted with the mullahs. In a country where there is such great religious intolerance, to take recourse to Islam actually does more damage to the country.'

Bishop John Joseph had taken his own life in dramatic fashion, shooting himself in the head at the entrance gate of the same courthouse in Faisalabad where the death sentence had been pronounced under the blasphemy law against a 25-year-old Christian named Ayub Masih. On 12 May the Lahore High Court had overturned the sentence, as it had done with the teenage boy Salamat Masih in

1995, but that was little comfort. As another Christian told me, 'The lower court judges are too afraid to give decisions based on merit.' John Joseph had killed himself after saying Mass on 6 May, the anniversary of the day in 1986 that the law had been passed mandating the death penalty for blasphemy.

Cecil Chaudhry had worked closely with Bishop John Joseph. 'He always said, "There will come a time when to get our rights in this country, we will have to start sacrificing lives,"' he told me. '"And I will be the first to sacrifice my life." In the bishop's frame of mind, the time had come when this law needed the attention of the world at large, and especially of Pakistanis.'

I asked how he felt about the bishop's decision, given that Catholics consider suicide a mortal sin.

'Suicide to my mind is a very technical term,' he replied. 'The philosophy behind that is what makes it a mortal sin or not. If I take my life out of desperation because of my own personal problems, that to me is a sin. But if you offer your life as a form of protest for your community, that to me is a sacrifice. I know that for this full week or more, he was fasting and praying.'

Three salutary changes had resulted immediately from the bishop's suicide, said Chaudhry. 'Number one, it opened the mouths and uncapped the pens of progressive Muslims. Those same chaps who were our silent supporters suddenly found strength. The minorities combined together. The Hindus joined us, the Sikhs joined us, and soon after we had a joint minorities conference in Lahore. And the third change was that it shook up the government for the first time, and they began talking in terms of looking into the blasphemy law. But then along came the Indian nuclear explosion [on 11 and 13 May 1998], and attention was diverted.'

In Pakistan, something was always diverting attention. In the spring and summer of 1999 it was the confrontation with India over Kargil, when Pakistani soldiers disguised as militants crossed the Line of Control into Indian-held territory, nearly igniting a full-scale war. I had an opportunity to visit the Line of Control, escorted by a major from Inter-Services Public Relations, in one of the last groups of journalists taken up as the conflict wound down, after Nawaz Sharif's humiliating snap visit to Washington to resolve the crisis in early July. I was the only foreign journalist in the group.

I flew from Islamabad to Skardu, with a glorious view of the mountain Nanga Parbat out the airplane window. From Skardu we rode several hours by jeep up a bone-jarring road that had been hacked and blasted out of a vertical cliff face by the Pakistan Army. '*So* many people died building this road,' Major Yahya told me. The starkness was relieved by a high, noisy waterfall that created a dramatic splash of green life by the roadside, and by villages of small stone houses and clusters of apricot trees. The trees' owners had a tradition of allowing travellers to pick and eat the fruit. The small apricots were ripe and plentiful, but Major Yahya warned me to eat only three or four.

'Don't eat more than that, or you'll get cramps in your stomach!' he said. 'That's what happened to Anita Pratap from CNN.'

Also along for the ride was Khalid Masood Khan, a columnist based in the city of Multan in Punjab province for the Urdu-language daily *Khabrain*, which I later learned had a reputation for scurrilousness and inaccuracy. He was staunchly patriotic.

'The people of Pakistan feel that this was a golden chance for us to equalise with India,' he told me. 'Common people are not aware of the economic problem we are facing globally. But people are really feeling that Europe has double standards for Muslims. We are unable to sell the truth. This is horrible. All Pakistanis are involved in our hearts with Kashmir liberation struggle. And the army comes from us. They did not come from some other planet. They are our brothers. But the Pakistan Army is very organised. They are obeying the commanders. And the commanders are obeying the gummint. The army will obey the gummint. But not with their hearts.'

Major Yahya showed us the wreckage of an Indian fighter jet that he claimed had crossed into Pakistani airspace, and we stayed overnight at a place called Bunji, where a colonel supervised a gun position and a few men. Indian soldiers on the other side of the ridge opposite shot artillery rounds up and over at us, and the Pakistanis fired back. It was rather perfunctory and desultory by this point and, especially given that both sides were firing blind, it would be a matter of luck whether we were hit. I prevailed on the colonel to play ping-pong and tried to draw him out. He was friendly and indulgent, but disciplined in his replies.

'Maybe they are trying to damage our positions before negotiations,' he guessed. 'Of course there will be casualties. We accept that these things happen.'

I was hoping for some suggestion of how army men felt about the prime minister's sudden climb-down in Washington for the sake of economic relief. 'We have to support whatever will be good for the nation,' was all he would say.

The army had launched the Kargil adventure behind Nawaz Sharif's back, but as far as I could tell Nawaz was also digging his own grave. The political atmosphere was extremely tense during both my 1999 visits. Nawaz, in his second stint as prime minister, had alternated in office with his arch-rival Benazir Bhutto. In 1988 she had come in as the darling of liberals and the West, in a moment of hope following the death of Zia. Benazir had squandered the credibility and goodwill many had been eager to offer her as the daughter of Zulfikar Ali Bhutto, the controversial but immensely charismatic populist foreign minister, president and prime minister of the 1960s and 1970s. Z.A. Bhutto had been overthrown in 1977 by Zia, his own army chief, and hanged in 1979 on what many considered a trumped-up murder conviction. The 1980s were a dark decade for many Pakistanis. Zia did 'untold damage', the editor and human rights activist Aziz Siddiqui told me. 'All of it has not yet come out. Nawaz Sharif is a product of it.'

The United States under Reagan supported Zia, who helped them train and supply the resistance that eventually forced the Soviet Union to withdraw from Afghanistan. The assumption is pervasive in Pakistan that Zia outlived his usefulness to the US and that the plane crash in which he died was a CIA-sponsored assassination.

Throughout the 1990s, neither Benazir nor Nawaz had earned distinction as a national leader. Nawaz was arrogant, perhaps none too bright, and a protégé of Zia. Benazir was arrogant, vulnerable for being relatively liberal and a woman, and beholden to the military establishment that had grudgingly allowed her to take office with a weak mandate. Their rivalry was implacable and often petty, and Benazir had been forced from office in November 1996 amid corruption allegations against her husband, Asif Ali Zardari, nick-named 'Mr Ten Percent'. Two months before that, her estranged brother Murtaza had been killed in a gun battle with Karachi police. Murtaza had lived in exile for 17 years, leading Al-Zulfikar, a terrorist group dedicated to overthrowing or assassinating Zia. He had returned in 1993, only to be arrested on arrival by the government now led by his sister – 'yet another farcical episode in the comic opera of Pakistan politics', Murtaza's onetime associate Raja Anwar calls it in *The Terrorist Prince: The Life and Death of Murtaza Bhutto*.

I had interviewed Murtaza for the *South China Morning Post* in March 1995 at 70 Clifton, Karachi – the Bhutto family home, bris-tling with armed men the day I was there – marking the launch of his own faction of the Pakistan People's Party to rival Benazir. He heaped scorn on her and felt that, as Z.A. Bhutto's son, he should have been his political heir. But nothing much came of his chal-lenge to her and, less than two years later, he was dead and she was out of office again.

Succeeding Benazir for the second time in 1997, Nawaz aggressively attacked the country's most important institutions, including the press, the judiciary, and the National Assembly, in order to weaken potential rivals. Armed goons loyal to him had physically attacked the Supreme Court; he had weakened the powers of the president and promulgated a law requiring Members of the National Assembly to vote *en bloc* with their parties (essentially guaranteeing passage of any legislation he favoured); he was threatening to punish the Jang Group, the country's largest media conglomerate, for tax evasion. And, in October 1998, he had dismissed the army chief.

'He seems to be accumulating all of this power, but he's not using any of this power to deal with the country's problems,' Maleeha Lodhi, then editor of the English-language daily *The News*, complained to me in her office in Rawalpindi. Nawaz found himself reduced to using the army to perform a census and read meters for Wapda, the state electricity company. 'This prime minister has amassed more powers to himself and is still weaker than any other in history,' a Western diplomat told me. 'Having amassed in a formal sense all the powers to himself, to deal with the really hard issues he turns to the army. Pakistan is proving that it's not cut out for parliamentary democracy.'

'What is happening now is precisely how a tiger becomes a man-eater,' Cecil Chaudhry warned me. 'It's obvious. This is how all our martial laws have happened. It's not as though there's Bonapartism in the army. It's failure of civilians. One institution after another is being destroyed or desecrated. He's opening up too many fronts for himself. The writing is there on the wall, the way the army is being involved.' The new army chief, he added in a tone of respect, 'is a soldier.' This was General Pervez Musharraf, whom the world soon would get to know better.

'The only way you could get rid of Nawaz Sharif is through an army coup,' Najam Sethi told me in February 1999. 'Otherwise you have to wait three years until the next election. And I can tell you that Nawaz is not going to agree to hold a fair election.' Aziz Siddiqui said that, however influential they might be, the armed forces 'cannot come in by the front door' to rule Pakistan overtly again. 'That seems to be out now.' Still, he added: 'If you rule out military coups, what is the alternative?'

In May, after giving a provocative speech in India, Najam Sethi was abducted by goons loyal to Nawaz Sharif and imprisoned for three weeks until domestic and foreign pressure, including an editorial in *The Economist* (for which he writes), forced his release. When I saw him in Lahore in July, he showed me where his abductors had dragged him out of his ground-floor bedroom and along the path outside. He was still fighting court cases; the government was coming after him on taxes and trying to get him declared a non-Muslim.

I liked Najam Sethi and was always glad to sit at his feet and learn about Pakistani politics. He had been kind to me during my first visit in 1995, and he was deft at explaining the Pakistani elite's perspective to the West and vice versa. He and his wife, Jugnu Mohsin, had founded *The Friday Times* in the immediate wake of Zia's death, sensing a window of opportunity. Their timing had been good, and *The Friday Times* quickly developed into an institution, required reading for the elite and for foreigners like myself. Sethi had been close – some said too close – to Benazir Bhutto, but when her first government had been dismissed he had tainted his credentials as a non-partisan journalist by accepting a position in a caretaker cabinet. But *The Friday Times* was a lively, refreshing change from the cloying earnestness and indifferent grammar and punctuation that made reading most other English-language periodicals in Pakistan a kind of self-torture. Sethi's great virtue, his impeccable English, was reflected in his paper, which featured a weekly front-page editorial written by him and

mixed commentary on high politics and world affairs with horo-
scopes, travel features, goings on about town and book reviews.

Sethi was tall and well built, physically imposing, with a dashing
moustache, tailored suits and usually a cigarette in one hand. He
tended to dramatise the fatigue and dangers he faced, but even that
made him somehow the more likeable. In any event the dangers
were real, and it was true that he often had dark rings under his eyes.

'It's so nasty that I'm getting acutely frustrated and angry,' he told
me near the end of one of our meetings in July 1999. He was
hurriedly typing a press statement about the court cases pending
against him, as I jotted down my contact details. 'We *have* to win,' he
said, with a wry grin. 'The good guys have to win – right, Ethan?'

The army ousted Nawaz Sharif in a spine-tingling but bloodless and
thoroughly unsurprising coup on 12 October 1999, after he reck-
lessly tried to dismiss the army chief for the second time in 12
months. The liberal West wrung its hands and imposed sanctions.
My experience of the coup in Cambodia had taught me that coups
happen when something has to give. For better or worse the armed
forces are a bedrock institution of any state, and power abhors a
vacuum. After its coup Pakistan under Musharraf limped along,
doing what it always does: making the best of a bad situation.

I was in England one afternoon not quite two years later, when I
heard a plane had crashed into one of the towers of the World
Trade Center in New York. I turned on the BBC. As I watched, the
phone rang.

It was my neighbour Syd. Syd was in his late seventies. He had
been in the RAF in France and Belgium during the war, and in India
just after. He had worked as a reporter for *The Daily Telegraph* and
other British papers, interviewing celebrities and doorstepping
politicians. He had once sailed to New York on the *QE II* for a story.
He had also worked as press officer at EMI Records, where he had

known the Beatles before they were famous. He hadn't been impressed with them then – they had put their feet on his desk – and he still wasn't. 'Two of those guys wrote a few pretty good songs, like "Yesterday",' he said. His tastes ran more to Frank Sinatra and old-fashioned jazz. He had been a bandleader himself and had a framed Silver Disc of his band's hit 'Hawaiian Wedding Song' on the wall of his downstairs toilet. I enjoyed spending evenings at his place, sipping gin and tonic or red wine and watching videos of Sinatra or Count Basie in concert.

I was glued to the BBC – and, as I could hear, so was Syd.

'Isn't it terrible?' he said. 'This has got to be one of the biggest tragedies you or I will ever see. Who would ever have expected this?'

We talked for several minutes, sharing the moment. I could hear through the phone the same voices that narrated what I was seeing on the television in front of me. 'It's terrible,' said Syd. 'Dreadful.' Then he said:

'But for any journalist – what an incredible story!'

PART TWO

AFTER

CHAPTER SIX

A REDISCOVERY

When I arrived in Lahore to stay for five months in September 2003, I was put up in a guesthouse run by a young couple, Abdul Shakoor and Nusrat. Shakoor was thin and bearded, happy-go-lucky and childlike. Nusrat was fair-complexioned, tall and slim, conservative in habits and views, and far more intelligent than her husband. I learned to consult her if a problem required analysis or insight. They had a 19-month-old girl. Nusrat had relatives in Bradford, the city in the north of England known for its large Asian population, where there had been race riots in the summer of 2002. When they saw me working on my laptop they asked if I could use it to phone her relatives.

I said I would happily email them. No, they said. Her relatives didn't have email. I said I was very sorry, but I didn't think I could make phone calls from my laptop.

'No problem, no problem,' Shakoor assured me. 'We go PCO.' A PCO is a public call office, the sort of storefront outfit I used in India and Pakistan in the mid-1990s to call home and fax stories to editors.

Later they returned and showed me a phone card: $5 for 175 minutes to the UK or 148 minutes to the US, through the Internet. The card interested me. 'In England this card no,' I explained.

Nusrat's face brightened with understanding. 'This card no available England,' she said.

'Yes, no available England.'

'In Pakistan *banned*,' said Shakoor. 'Black!'

The toddler crawled up on my bed and cheerily plopped down beside me. She had a pronounced hook nose and a mischievous, intelligent face. I asked Shakoor her name.

'Hafsa,' he said, and spelled it.

'Hafsa is very beautiful,' I said.

'She is mother very beautiful,' he said, indicating his wife. 'Baby beautiful.'

'She is also very happy.'

'Yes,' he said, beaming. 'Very happy.'

A couple of incidents reminded me of the delicacy of my position. A paying guest in a place like Pakistan can be vulnerable to the expectations and requirements of his hosts, without being equipped with all the circumstantial and cultural information needed to know when not to ask too much, or indeed how much is too much. One evening I was sitting on my bed, when I heard a knock. The door opened; it was Nusrat. Seeing that I was wearing shorts, she recoiled, shielding her face. 'No, it's all right,' I said, distressed as well as annoyed that this might mean I would have to wear long trousers even in my own room. But it wasn't all right; she handed me a bottle of water from behind the door and scuttled away.

On my first Saturday evening there, Shakoor asked what time I wanted breakfast the next morning. I told him 7.30, because I had made an appointment for tennis at nine. He looked at me, seeming a bit put out.

'Early,' he ventured. 'Weekend.'

'What time do you want?' I tried. But he would have none of it. I was the boss, whether I liked it or not.

'You decide.'

'Seven-thirty,' I repeated, trying to sound both decisive and flexible.

'Okay,' he said, with a tilt of his head that suggested both acquiescence and resentment.

When he brought me breakfast, he looked tired. I asked if he had slept well.

'Late,' he said. 'We go out of side. Visit relatives. Come home 2.30.' Did I hear reproach in his tone or see it in his glance?

I had been invited to Lahore to teach a class called International Journalism at a new university launched by the Beaconhouse School System, a private company run by the wife of Pakistan's foreign minister. Isa Daudpota, a Pakistani intellectual I knew previously only online, had written to me a few months earlier, asking if I knew anyone who might want to spend a semester teaching at Beaconhouse National University. I had said I might be interested myself, and here I was.

Returning to Pakistan was at once a rediscovery and a fresh adventure. This five-month stint would be a chance to build on what I already knew, to come to see Pakistan more nearly whole, as well as a spell in a kind of radio silence, away from the white noise of the West. England was a highly evolved organism, with an amoeba-like ability to absorb and tame – render safe and bland, anglicise – any threat or influence from outside. America was a sitcom in endless reruns. In Pakistan, history-in-the-making was in your face every day from the moment you woke, and nothing was ever settled or certain. It could drive you nuts or paranoid, it could suck out of you every ounce of physical and emotional energy, but it was never dull.

Until the semester started, two weeks after my arrival, I had time on my hands. Isa Daudpota walked me over the road to the Lahore Gymkhana and introduced me to Rashid Rehman, a journalist and the brother of my boss, Mrs Navid Shahzad. She had asked him to sponsor my guest membership in the Gymkhana Tennis Club. The university was a single building for now, next door to a Shell petrol station near the T intersection where Zafar Ali Road meets the Upper Mall. The guesthouse was in a neighbourhood on the other side of the Mall, about ten minutes' walk away. The Gymkhana was across Zafar Ali Road and around the corner, also walking distance. Zafar Ali Road was a boulevard, with an open sewage canal in the median shaded by trees and foliage.

Isa and I found Rashid Rehman on the grass courts, where he was training with a coach. Rashid was in his fifties and had a severe mien accentuated by a close-cropped white beard. He wore a sweatband and shorts that exposed impressively lean legs. No one in Pakistan wears shorts on the street, but behind the Gymkhana walls it was permissible. We shook hands and exchanged pleasantries, and I thanked him for sponsoring me. He explained the system and introduced me to the coach, Mohammed Tariq. 'He's a good boy,' said Rashid by way of recommendation. It was through Tariq that I was to arrange whatever I wanted to do at the Gymkhana.

Tariq was in his mid-thirties, stylish in a big, sporty, Punjabi way, with a dashing moustache and confident manner. The effect was lessened somewhat when he removed his baseball cap and you saw he was bald. We met at nine the next morning for a session on the hard courts.

'It's hot,' I remarked.

'Not hot,' he said. 'Normal.'

Within a few minutes my t-shirt was soaked. Tariq fed me balls and praised my forehand. 'Not too bad,' was his assessment when we sat down. A uniformed waiter brought me a glass of fresh lime with ice and black pepper, which sounds weird but tastes great.

Tariq had worked for four years as a coach in Dubai, where it was even hotter than here. His brother coached in the US. Tariq himself would have liked to go to the US or the UK, but 'visa is problem'. The water in Dubai had been bad; he said it was the bad water there that had made him go bald. We discovered a shared vocabulary of tennis lingo. We discussed Martina Navratilova: her work ethic, the size of her thighs. 'Not woman. Like man,' said Tariq admiringly. He told me the Gymkhana had the best grass courts in Pakistan. His brother had gone five sets, and held a match point, in a Davis Cup match on these very courts against the Thai player Paradorn Srichaphan. Paradorn had since beaten Andre Agassi in the second round at Wimbledon in 2002 and become the first Asian-born player in the world top ten.

We negotiated. In Asia, everything is negotiable. Tariq could get me a concession on the membership, he suggested, because the club secretary was his friend. A month should cost 3,000 rupees, about $50 or £30, but he could get mine down to 1,500 or maybe lower. Then he brought up the matter of his coaching fee.

'How much?' I asked.

'Hundred dollars?' He looked at me sidelong and grinned hopefully. I demurred. Quickly he came down to 3,000 rupees per month: 2,400 for him and 600 for the ball boy, a listless teenager in a baseball cap and green t-shirt.

I didn't really want to hire Tariq by the month, but I had the impression it was expected of me. Tennis coaches tend to be hustlers; so do Pakistanis. This guy was a Pakistani tennis coach. But journalists are hustlers too. I knew that if I scratched his back, he would scratch mine.

Within a week Tariq had sold me a new set of strings, three grips, two wristbands, and two Wilson logo shock absorbers, and he was softening me up to buy shoes and a new racket. He started by instructing me to buy two cans of Slazenger balls for 350 rupees per can. The price was reasonable but not especially low; I assumed they would have been imported and paid for with hard currency. He told me with authority that my strings were too loose, and that he would restring them.

'How much?'

He made a dismissive gesture with his hand, suggesting either that it was free because I was his friend, or that my question was vulgar.

At the end of our hour, he took my racket as if the matter had been settled. It was then that he told me it would cost 400 rupees. This was still a lot less than it would have cost me in England.

The next morning we worked on my backhand. 'Little little *inshallah* better,' he said, meaning not that it was better but that it would get better, *inshallah*. Our third session was in the afternoon, on grass. The grass courts were off limits in the morning, before the dew evaporated. I noticed that the set of three grass courts where I had met Rashid Rehman were now closed, and that the other three next to them had been mown, rolled and set up with nets. Tariq told me they moved the courts every week, to rest the grass. He said my forehand was much better today. I liked the tight new orange strings.

Around four o'clock the middle-aged gents started arriving. They came every day, mostly the same men, some with grown sons, some on visits back from America or England. They were a gregarious bunch and at first I liked them all. After I got to know them, I liked some of them and disliked others.

Doubles on the Gymkhana grass courts was a longstanding daily habit and social ritual for these men, and they were gracious enough to include me. First, though, I had to be introduced to the big man. This was Khwaja Tariq Rahim, former governor of Punjab province and friend of Farooq Ahmed Leghari, who had been Pakistan's president. As Tariq the coach pointed out to me, Tariq Rahim had an excellent, strong serve and was a good player and quite athletic, despite being in his sixties and a bit portly. When not playing tennis, he could be seen nearby lifting weights or running laps around the idle courts.

Tariq went with me over to the first court and introduced me to him.

'Rashid Rehman told me you would be coming,' he said as we shook hands. 'Welcome. Any friend of Rashid's is a friend of mine.'

I heard a sound like a small explosion and started. I looked up and saw a small plane flying overhead.

Tariq the coach laughed. 'That is maybe a wedding,' he said, meaning the firecrackers. He gestured up at the plane. 'You look like 11 September. But today is 16 September!' He laughed at his own joke. 'Okay, Ethan. See you tomorrow 2.30. I go to prayer.'

I watched for a while, until I was invited to help form a doubles foursome on the middle court. My partner's father had been Pakistan's top player and had played an exhibition against American great Ham Richardson. 'Beat him something like 6–1 6–2,' said the man who told me the story. 'He took the next plane out of Lahore!'

This man's name was Azhar Noon. He was one of the opposing pair, and I sat with him after our set (they won 6–3, but I held serve). He bought me a Coke, in a glass bottle with a straw, as Cokes are always drunk in the subcontinent.

'You're in business?' I asked.

'I'm retired from business,' he said. 'Nowadays I play tennis and look after my grandchildren.'

'I'm sure you've earned the time to do those things.'

He liked that. 'Yes, I've earned the time.'

'What business were you in?'

'I actually set up the first bottling plant for Pepsi in Lahore, in the early '80s.'

I remarked that that had been well before Coke and Pepsi were in India. When I first visited India in 1994, the Western soft drinks were just arriving. A friend in Lucknow had been amazed at his first sight of a Pepsi dispensing machine.

'Yes, before that they had their own aerated drinks, like Thumbs Up,' said Azhar Noon.

I told him that when I had lived in Nepal in the mid-'80s, Coke had seemed well established and, if memory served, Pepsi was just beginning to appear.

'Yes,' he agreed. 'The chap who was country manager was going there to set up a bottling plant, and that would have been right around that time.'

They all apologised for the humidity and said the weather would be comfortable starting a month from now, in mid-October, and that summer in Lahore was insufferably hot. Azhar Noon said all this too.

'Do you go away in the summer?' I asked him.

'Yes. I have a place in the mountains, north of Islamabad.'

'The Brits sure got it right, with the hill stations,' I joked, rather feebly.

He didn't get it. 'Yes, the Brits got a lot of things right,' he said. 'You have to admire the Brits. I went to Cambridge University. Two generations of my family went to Cambridge before me, so I went to Cambridge. When it came time for my son to go, he didn't do very well on his A-levels. I felt a bit embarrassed writing to my tutor, but he was very kind. He said that on the basis of his A-levels my son was not really up to snuff, but given the family connection they could consider admitting him.

'But when I told my son, he said, "Sorry, Dad, I'm not interested." He wanted to go to America. He went to Indiana University and studied business, then he went to San Francisco University and got an MBA. Now he's a banker, with American Express in London.'

'That sounds like a story with a happy ending,' I suggested.

'Yes.'

'If you had a son of university age now, would you send him to America?'

'Maybe not, because of the present situation,' he acknowledged, wistfully.

After our second doubles set was suspended on account of darkness, an affable, talkative man named Omar Qayyum bought me a glass of fresh lime with black pepper. Omar was in his early fifties, tall and fit, with a small moustache. We sat in the deepening dusk, and I became conscious of the pleasure I was feeling in the moment: crows circling trees nearby, the amplified call to prayer, fresh lime with black pepper, dusk, firecrackers.

I explained what brought me to Lahore.

'We thought perhaps you were with the embassy,' said Omar. 'Embassy people used to play here, like that political officer. And that lady –'

'Missus ...' ventured one of the other men.

'No, she was not a Missus, she was a Miss,' Omar corrected him. 'What was her name? Anyway, nowadays the embassy people don't come here, because they don't want to expose themselves.'

I returned the next evening. I began to learn that there was an unofficial but strict pecking order among the three courts. One tall, thin man with a bandaged knee made an excellent return of serve as I waited to cross the first court. 'Excuse me,' I said as I crossed after the point. 'Nice return.'

'Thank you,' he said, but the look he gave me said: 'Who are you?'

A loud dispute erupted in Urdu or Punjabi. Tariq Rahim, the big man, put an end to it by shouting louder than anyone else. No one except me seemed to consider it startling or unusual, and play resumed. I reflected that men's tennis is all about who's the alpha male, which is one reason businessmen and politicians like to play it.

I played with the same partner, Khwaja Khoram, this time against a retired army major and a film producer. When the producer, Sajjad Gul, sat down citing a heart problem, he was replaced by a mild-seeming white-haired man named Salim, with whom Khoram had a history of acrimony. Khoram's tendency to query opponents' line calls annoyed everyone. When I was about to serve at 2–5 down, he suddenly threatened to quit, claiming it was getting too dark to see on our side of the court. This would have been less of an issue if we had been changing ends after every two games, but that wasn't done here. As the dusk deepened, he stood helping himself to drinking water and stating his case.

'Okay, we play, but drinks off,' he said. This invited jeering from Major-sahib and Salim. The deal was that the losers bought a round of Cokes or fresh limes. After much verbal jousting we resumed, I promptly dropped serve, and we sat down.

Dusk at the Gymkhana was a reward for the effort one had just required of one's aging body. The gents relaxed in lawn chairs and bantered about each other's foibles as the ball boys took down the nets. The atmosphere was haunting, and the crows evoked the bats I used to see stirring at dusk from trees near the palace in Kathmandu. When I returned there in 1994, after seven years and a revolution, I had felt a joy born of returning perspective, like unfolding a map that has lain in a drawer. All experience is evanescent yet leaves a residue on a personality. So long as we're away from a place we've known, it retains an aspect of 'home'. The moment we return it becomes alien again, more or less accessible in concrete ways. Yet we remember: I was here seven years ago, at this street corner; the bats hung upside-down in those same trees. The policemen – different men then, perhaps – directed traffic with those same stylish gestures, in those same two-toned blue uniforms. Home is still there, now muffled beneath new layers of experience and change.

I explained again to various polite questioners what brought me here, and that my guest membership was courtesy of Rashid Rehman. They were all courteous and welcoming in a hearty way.

Omar asked what my plans were for celebrating Christmas.

'I'll celebrate Quaid-e-Azam's birthday,' I joked. Mohammed Ali Jinnah was born on 25 December 1876. Omar chuckled but hastened to reassure me.

'I'm sure you will be able to celebrate Christmas,' he said. 'We have Christians. We have, uh, minority groups.'

* * *

My fellow inmate at the guesthouse, Zarina Sadik, was a Malaysian who had married a Pakistani against her family's better judgment, survived the horrific Bangladesh War of 1971 and lived most of her adult life in Pakistan. Her father, an officer in the colonial police in British-era Malaya, had often been away fighting the insurgent Communists. She was one of 11 siblings; her mother had been from Ireland. The stories she told of her childhood made it sound like a romantic colonial adventure; one of her playmates was currently on Malaysia's rotating throne.

She had recently been home to visit family. 'I've never seen so many Arabs in Malaysia,' she remarked. 'They're all coming this direction for holidays, instead of going to the West. My sister says, "We're getting overrun by the Ninja Turtles." You know, with the faces covered, even at the poolside.'

The Beaconhouse School System rented the guesthouse for its staff who came to Lahore from elsewhere in Pakistan for meetings. It was dreary and sparsely furnished and had no natural light, but for me the guesthouse was useful because interesting people were usually coming and going. Most of these were women, and socially and politically connected: wives of generals and diplomats, with senior positions in Beaconhouse. Most were good company, the food was better when they were around and some gave me scuttle-butt and contacts.

Zarina Sadik was one of these women, but like me she was here for an extended stay. She had been based in Islamabad as head of Beaconhouse's Northern Region, but had taken on a special assignment that required her to work at the head office in Lahore. She had a house in Islamabad where she lived with both her sons, their wives and her seven-year-old grandson, but she was looking for a house to rent in Lahore. This was proving tortuous because there was a bubble in property prices, and she was having trouble finding a large enough house that she and her sons could afford.

'The market has gotten outrageously expensive, especially for houses,' she told me. 'Four-five years ago I could get a four-bedroom house on about 500 square yards for about 25,000 rupees per month. Now it's about 45, 50,000. After 9/11, Pakistanis living abroad are bringing their money back into the country and investing in property – land and housing. It's insecurity. Rather than investing abroad now, they feel they might as well invest money in Pakistan. A lot of it may be black money, for all you know.

'It has created a very superficial, artificial rise in costs. People have bought properties for eight lakhs [800,000 rupees], and in six to eight months it's worth 3.2 million. Six months ago, we were offered one kanal [about 500 square yards] for 450,000. Recently when I went to inquire about it, they said it was already worth 750,000. I feel the bubble's going to burst very soon.'

Zarina was opinionated and a good raconteur. I looked forward to returning to the guesthouse in the evenings, for her company. We usually ate dinner together and we watched a lot of television. She could often be found in the lounge with her feet up on a padded stool, smoking a cigarette and watching a movie or the news. Sometimes she read the Quran, especially after the fasting month of Ramzan began in late October, and when she did she covered her head with a scarf.

Her younger son, Zulqader, was usually around in the evenings. Zuly was tall and athletic, handsome and soft-spoken, with the particular kind of hook nose that I recognised as Kashmiri. (Kashmiris claim to be descended from Jews, and cite the Kashmiri nose as evidence.) He was 30 years old and a sales manager for a mobile phone company. He had a really cool mobile that did all sorts of nifty stuff. Once he used it to take my picture and email it to England. In the car on the way to see a local production of *Moulin Rouge*, he watched a Christina Aguilera music video on it.

'Does that thing make phone calls too?' I asked.

Moulin Rouge, directed by Shah Shahrahbeel, was performed and sung with great gusto, with actresses in daring sleeveless dresses and an outrageously camp drag queen who stole the show. The sell-out audience was spirited but, as I learned later, better behaved than was the norm in Lahore. There was a strong whiff of stern admonition in the tone of the woman who came on stage beforehand to recite a long list of acknowledgements and instructions. 'One more thing, ladies and gentlemen,' she said in conclusion. 'These kids have worked very hard for two months, so please remain in your seats for the curtain call.'

Moulin Rouge was the sort of thing one would not have seen in Lahore during the Zia years. I sat between Zarina and Zuly.

'The general perception of Pakistan is not this,' Zuly said to me. 'I wish that people in the West could see this side of Pakistan, where we're enjoying our lives.'

I said I wished so too.

'What's your perception of Pakistan?' he asked. 'Is it a fundamentalist state? Is it a progressive Islamic state?'

'I think it's a bit of both,' I said.

'General Musharraf says it's a moderate state.'

'Well, that's what he'd like it to be.'

Some musicians were on stage to entertain the audience before the play.

'Are these guys famous?' I asked.

'Nah,' said Zuly. 'This is just filler. Have you heard much Pakistani music?'

'No, I haven't.'

'You should listen to Nusrat Fateh Ali Khan.'

'I've never heard his music, but I've heard of him. He's well known in the West.'

'He's played with Peter Gabriel and Eddie Vedder.'

Zuly was knowledgeable about international tennis. One evening at the guesthouse, he asked who my favourite player was.

'Until he retires I have to say Agassi,' I said. 'He's so hardworking, and it's amazing how well he's doing at 33.'

'He is of Iranian descent,' noted Zarina. 'His father was from Iran. A-GAH-ssi' – she pronounced the name correctly. 'But everyone just says Agassi, because it's easier for Americans to pronounce.'

Zuly asked what kind of racket I used. I showed him my Wilson Profile passed down to me by my father, heavy and stiff, with a light head and a small sweet spot, old enough now to be a relic, the words 'West Germany' painted on the frame.

'My old strings were loose,' I said. 'Tariq said I should have tight strings.'

'Tight strings are better for a baseline game,' said Zuly. 'Actually, loose strings are good only if you serve and volley.'

'Tariq also says my racket is too heavy.'

'I think Tariq wants to sell you a new racket! I know him too well.'

I needed a haircut, so Zarina instructed Zuly to take me to get one. In his car on the way to Gulberg Main Market, he told me that his father's father had migrated from Kashmir in 1947, first to Amritsar in what became the Indian side of the Punjab, then to Pakistan.

'So you're a Malaysian Kashmiri,' I said.

'Yes.' He had a nice, ironic smile. 'Actually, my mother's mother was Irish.'

'I know. Your mother told me. So you're an Irish Malaysian Kashmiri.'

'And we think someone in our family was Portuguese.'

Waiting at the barbershop, he told me there would be Davis Cup tennis in Lahore again next weekend. 'South Africa,' he said.

'No, South Korea,' another guy sitting nearby corrected him.

'Are you still interested?' Zuly asked me.

'Oh, yes,' I said.

'But it's not at the Gymkhana,' said Zuly. 'It's at Defence, near where I live.'

I mentioned Tariq's brother. Azhar Noon had told me he had been very good, beating international players who came to Pakistan in the early 1990s. 'They spoke to the press and said they were surprised he wasn't playing internationally,' he had said. 'But his problem was that he didn't have any sponsorship.'

'Now we have one very good player,' said Zuly.

'The one who plays doubles with the Israeli?'

'Yes! Aisamul-Haq. He is doing well in doubles, but he has not yet made a mark in singles.'

'How old is he?'

'Twenty-two. There is actually a lot of discussion here about whether he should be playing with an Israeli.'

I had heard this. It reminded me of the letters I had read in the Pakistani papers in 1995, debating whether the cricket star Imran Khan should marry the Jewish heiress Jemima Goldsmith. Some said it was all right so long as she converted to Islam; others thought not.

'What do you think?' I asked Zuly.

He shrugged. 'I think there shouldn't be any problem.'

Some Beaconhouse teacher trainers came to the guesthouse for a few days. The general feeling was that they enjoyed working for Beaconhouse. 'There's a lot of job satisfaction,' said the senior woman in the group. We conversed over dinner. Both to pander to them and because it was true, I told them how dreadful I thought US media had become in the last couple of years.

'It's like Hitler,' said one of the younger ones. 'My father always said, "Don't believe everything they say about Hitler. It's all American propaganda."'

'He had his qualities,' added one of the other women.

A middle-aged woman, Mrs Kidwai, told a story about her flight from Karachi. There had been some sort of hassle to do with boarding or finding her seat. 'And then there appeared this enormous mountain of a man, with a huge beard like this,' she said, spreading her hands. He was one of those fundamentalists, she said, and she used the anecdote as a metaphor. 'They've taken up all our space in this country,' she complained.

Somehow the conversation turned to the O.J. Simpson murder trial. I said that in my opinion he did kill his wife, but there was more to it than that. Many black people in America were not unhappy to see him go free, I said, because they felt they were rarely given justice. 'It's like here, say you're a Christian in a village, and your Muslim neighbour wants your land,' I said. 'All he has to do is accuse you of blasphemy against the Quran or the Prophet.'

The women understood the analogy. 'Yes,' said one of the younger ones. 'Even the judges in such cases are afraid to rule in favour of a Christian.'

Late one evening Zarina and I watched a Bollywood movie on television. Shakoor and Nusrat were hanging around, Nusrat discreetly breastfeeding Hafsa. Shakoor had just got spectacles. He was delighted with them because his headaches had gone away and, I suspected, because they were a neat toy.

'One day only one movie,' he explained.

Zarina elaborated. 'There used to be a lot of these Indian movies on different channels,' she said. 'It got out of hand. It got so the kids were singing all the songs, and Urdu was getting mixed up with Hindi and what have you. So they banned them, the government.'

'So now they show only one Indian movie per day?'

'Well, the cable-wallahs got phone calls from people saying, "Why don't you show the Indian movies?" So they sneak them in.'

The girl in the movie was very pretty, and she was praying very piously in a Hindu temple while a roguishly handsome young man gazed soulfully at her from afar. I told Zarina that I thought the boy wanted to marry the girl but that she had decided to become a nun, or something, along the lines of *The Sound of Music*.

'Actually, I've seen this movie,' she said. 'He's a ne'er-do-well, a local hero. She's the daughter of a swami in the temple, and she's betrothed to a boy who's going to become a swami. The ne'er-do-well has never been particularly interested in girls, but she sparks something in him. But it ends horribly.' She paused, as if debating whether to ruin the ending for me. 'He gets sent to a place, very isolated, where people have all sorts of mental diseases. Her family says, "You might as well marry the other boy," but he breaks free and goes back. She realises too late that she loves him, and she commits suicide. He blows a fuse, and he probably ends up back in the loony bin.'

'Is it good or bad that they banned Indian movies?'

She considered the question. 'I don't know whether it's good or bad, but a lot of people miss them.'

The actor stripped to his waist.

'He loves taking off his clothes,' said Zarina. 'There isn't one movie they've made where he doesn't take off his shirt. He's a bodybuilder. He likes showing off his muscles.'

We watched some more. In a dream sequence, the boy and girl both were breaking into song.

'This is his first movie since he was in the clink for six months,' said Zarina. 'Drunken driving. Killed a pedestrian. I think this is her first movie.'

The next morning we watched *Fear Factor*, a show in which Miss USA contestants competed to hold their breath underwater, swim through rotten fish scales to find and drink a thermos full of 'fermented squid guts', and keep their balance atop a swerving tanker truck. Miss Louisiana edged out Miss Minnesota for the $50,000 prize, half of which went to a charity of her choice. The women all wore bikinis. I remarked to Zarina that it was rather undignified, but we both watched it through to the end.

'What do the government and the people in Pakistan think about shows with girls in bathing suits?' I asked.

'They're not Pakistani, so it's all right,' she said. 'Even the Pakistani models, they show a little leg, sleeveless, a bit of backless. The fundamentalists complain about the cable, that it's bad for the people. But they must watch it themselves, if they know what's on it!'

One day at tennis my doubles partner was Tariq Nasir Butt, owner of Variety Books, which he told me was better and more contemporary than Ferozsons near Regal Chowk in the city centre. The next day I went to Variety Books in a mood of anticipation. As I was leaving the office Omar Hassan Khan, the university's likeable young accountant, tall and slim with thick hair and enormous eyebrows that made him look like a Muppet, pulled up beside me in his car.

'Hello backpacker, do you want a ride?' he said cheerfully.

'Are you going anywhere near Liberty Market?'

But browsing at Variety Books was depressing, especially if it was true that this was the best bookstore in Lahore. Bookstores are oases, and a city without good ones is dreary. Variety sold cheap Indian editions of H.G. Wells and Conrad, pirated Penguins of *Animal Farm* and Khushwant Singh, pirated copies of the Harry Potter series, and imported hardcovers and recent paperbacks, mostly on Pakistan and Islam, at full price. These were potentially useful to me, but what did, for example, *Pakistan: In the Shadow of Jihad and Afghanistan* (a dreadful subtitle) by Mary Anne Weaver have to tell me that I couldn't as readily glean from *Pakistan: Eye of the Storm* (whose subtitle and cover photograph were equally hackneyed) by Owen Bennett Jones? Too many books about this part of the world kowtowed to the blinkered agenda and debased vocabulary of Western 'policymakers'. I later read Bennett Jones's book with great appreciation, which goes to show that you should never judge a book by its cover.

I bought a pirated copy of *Islam: A Short History* by Karen Armstrong for 160 rupees (just under $3) and a pad of lined paper. The till at Variety Books was a maddeningly convoluted assembly line: one man at one counter wrote up my purchase on a slip of paper; another at another counter took my money; a third gave me my book in a paper bag and my change. This system is common in the subcontinent and understandable as a measure to prevent employee graft, but it's still maddening.

As dusk fell I walked towards Gaddafi Stadium, named for the durable Libyan dictator because he had been great friends with Z.A. Bhutto. The streetscape was dusty, noisome and neon-lit, the kind of Asian city scene that made me feel at once vulnerable and nostalgic. It was rush hour, and traffic was picking up. Liberty Market, a horse-shoe-shaped row of shops around a park, seemed to be mostly jewellery stores. At the far corner was a bakery, Shezan Bakers & Confectioners.

Looking through the window, I resolved to buy a cream puff for old times' sake. In 1995 I had loved the cream puffs down the street from the YMCA on Fatima Jinnah Road. The bakery had the same assembly-line checkout process as the bookstore. The young man who handed me my cream puff was tickled to meet me.

'We see you first looking in glass,' he said cheerfully. 'Eat as soon as possible. Cream maybe melt.'

I walked on toward the stadium until I came to a large round-about. I didn't feel like walking across it, so I decided to save the Ferozsons outlet near the stadium for another day. Near the Grooms & Brides shop, a sorry-looking tomcat with a mangled ear eyed me sullenly. This was the Asia I had known and loved.

I struck a deal with the first taxi driver who offered me a ride back for 80 rupees instead of 100, but I paid him 100 anyway. His English was limited and his car was rickety, but he was cheerful and he told me the names of the roads, which helped me get my bearings. We went up Main Boulevard, past Pakistan's first McDonald's – there were now 20 in Lahore, he told me, and named their locations; there had been none in 1995 – turned left onto Jail Road, right onto Zafar Ali Road, and along the sewage canal to the Upper Mall, where a police barrier blocked the road for the first several months of my stay because of construction on a new underpass.

I told the driver I had been to Lahore before but didn't know this part of the city. The Lahore I knew was what I thought of as down-town, the stretch of the Mall between the Punjab Assembly and Regal Chowk, the zoo and Najam Sethi's Vanguard bookstore, plus Fatima Jinnah Road.

'Regal Chowk old city,' he said. 'Gulberg new city.'

On September 24, President Musharraf gave a speech to the United Nations General Assembly in New York. Zuly and I watched it on PTV.

'He looks good in a suit,' I remarked.

'Are you saying he shouldn't wear an army uniform?' asked Zuly, grinning.

'No. He looks good in that too.'

Later, just as Musharraf started speaking, I added: 'He takes good care of his hair too.' Musharraf, who had been a paratrooper, cut a dashing figure, and many Pakistanis appreciated the effort he made to present himself and the country as liberal and benign. He had famously allowed himself to be photographed holding his two pet Pekinese. Quite a few people I met knew him and spoke well of him. He enjoyed the social whirl, especially weddings. It was rumoured that his elderly mother made him dye his hair, except for a touch of grey at the temples to make him look distinguished.

The 'War on Terror', said Musharraf in his speech, 'must not be used by those who seek to use it to suppress other peoples.' The Huntingtonian thesis of a 'clash of civilizations' was 'a travesty'.

Islam was 'democracy in action' and 'must not be confused with a few extremists.' He specified Palestine and Kashmir as 'places where Muslim people are being suppressed' and insisted that 'Iraq cannot be allowed to remain an open wound. The Iraqi people must resume control of their resources and political destiny as soon as possible.' He urged 'peace with justice in the Middle East' and pointed out that 'the fate of the Palestinian people is the major factor in the public perception in the Islamic world.'

'India cites cross-border terrorism to refuse dialogue,' he said. 'It knows fully well that the Kashmir freedom movement is indigenous.' He called for a 'joint ceasefire along the Line of Control,' along with 'mutual nuclear restraint and a conventional arms balance'. He advocated increasing the number of non-permanent members on the UN Security Council, adding, in an obvious reference to India: 'Those states that violate UN resolutions have absolutely no credentials to aspire to permanent membership on the Security Council.'

In both what he said and how he said it, Musharraf was altogether more impressive than Prime Minister Jamali, a beefy man in a beard and shalwar kameez whom I later saw on PTV addressing the US Chamber of Commerce in Washington, DC, speaking haltingly and looking awkward, saying things like, 'Despite the image of my country that a casual observer may have, the socioeconomic indicators are encouraging.'

In early October, the South African national cricket team came to Pakistan for a competition called the Pepsi Cup. In September they had briefly backed out following a bomb blast in Karachi, but had been persuaded to go ahead with the tour after Karachi and Peshawar were dropped from the itinerary.

I watched part of the first match on television with Nusrat.

'South Africa and Australia best team,' she said. 'Pakistan up and down, up and down.'

'England is not very good,' I said.

'When England play in England, play good.'

'Who's winning?'

It wasn't that simple. 'Pakistan 277, eight overs. South Africa 95, no overs. No wicket.'

The batsman hit the ball and ran.

'Not out. Safe. He is home.'

I decided to try to get in to watch the second one-day match in the series, at Gaddafi Stadium. I had never watched a cricket match in person before. Two days later Shakoor drove me to the stadium on his motorbike, with Hafsa sitting in front of him grabbing the handlebars with her chubby little hands. She cried and threw tantrums if he left the house without taking her with him. 'No problem,' he assured me. It was true that, as one of the Beaconhouse women later put it to me, Pakistan is the freest country in the world because you can put a family of five on a motorbike and no one minds. But after the hair-raising ride to the stadium, I refused to let Shakoor take Hafsa any time he rode with me.

'Pakistan best security,' he said as we rode up to the police barriers outside the stadium. 'No terrorist.'

I handed him a 100-rupee note and guarded the motorbike until he returned, looking discouraged. 'No available.'

But then he had an idea. 'We try again. Counter no. Seventy-five ticket two hundred. Black.'

He persuaded the cops to let us through the barriers, and together we walked nearer the stadium and sidled up to some young men.

'Sir, three hundred,' said Shakoor.

'Two-fifty,' I countered.

The touts laughed.

In different circumstances I might have held my ground. But I wanted a ticket, it was the last minute, I was a foreigner, and a VIP ticket in the Imran Khan Enclosure would have set me back 1200 rupees.

A nervous moment followed, as policemen began crowding and bullying the cluster of men who had gathered around us. I thought we were being busted for ticket scalping, but Shakoor explained that they were more concerned about breaking up any gathering of half a dozen or more men. He suggested we step across the road. There I handed him a 500-rupee note which, in a comic pantomime, he passed behind his back to a tout.

Shakoor urged me to go inside early to be sure I got a seat, and warned me sternly: 'Sir, you no discuss anyone you America come. Some bad people. You any problem, go PCO call me.'

As I walked toward Gate 5, three young men latched onto me and asked where I was from. It was always the first question.

'America,' I said.

I walked on; they were becoming tiresome, and I started to wonder what their angle was. There's no privacy in Asia for a Westerner. But just then, they did something very kind that made me feel ashamed: they forced me into the long turnstile queue, near the front. The men in the queue (the queue was all men; women sat in a separate enclosure for families) were good-natured, even hospitable about the imposition. I thanked them, and I thanked the three young men, who grinned and waved as they walked away.

At the turnstile, five or six different men searched my bag redundantly. 'You are from South Africa?' one of them asked.

'No, from America,' I said.

I went inside to the general enclosure, the cheap seats. There were no seats, actually, only ranks of hard cement shelves. After a few hours, my lower back began to hurt and my butt got sore. Hawkers circulated selling dried lentils, chappatis and peanuts in greasy paper bags and disgusting artificially flavoured fruit drinks in little cardboard boxes. At the bottom, level with the pitch and separated from it by a high fence, were several faucets. The match began at midday. As the hot day wore on, many spectators went down to help themselves to water. I had neglected to bring bottled water, but I didn't dare go near the taps.

I was the only foreigner in the enclosure. As I climbed the steps, several groups of men vied good-naturedly for me to sit with them. One guy actually grabbed my knapsack off my shoulder and took it to his group, so I would have to sit with them. I did, but then for a reason I can't remember I moved and sat with a rival group.

'What do you think about Arnold?' a young guy asked me as we waited for the match to start. 'I like his movies very much.'

'I like his movies too, but I don't like him as a politician.'

'Yes. Now he is going to be governor of which state?'

'California.'

'Yes.'

'You know that California is the biggest state?' I said.

'Yes, I know.'

'I think that if Arnold wins in California, Bush will win California next year.'

'Yes.' He seemed to understand what I meant. 'He is too much supported by Jews. His father also was supported by Jews. But Muslim countries also supported his father. Now, George Bush is not gaining a good name.'

'No, he's not.'

The coin was being flipped to decide which team would bat first. A bearded man to my left said: 'Pakistani batsmen are not good chasers. It is a very tender matter what you decide to do. If you decide to bat first and you lose, they will say you were foolish.'

South Africa won the toss and opted to bowl first.

'But if Pakistan are not good chasers, South Africa should bat first,' I objected.

'But there is the dew problem,' he explained patiently. 'In day-and-night matches, there is too much dew, and it is difficult to hold the ball in your hand.'

The bearded man was Mohammed Faisal, a teacher of English and mathematics from a village near Gujranwalla, about 100 kilometres from Lahore. He was young, in his twenties. He had arrived that morning with 20 other young men in a Toyota pickup. This was his first visit to a proper stadium.

He wore a clean shalwar kameez and spoke English slowly but correctly. He might have been any of numerous severe-looking bearded men one passed daily in the street. Pakistan's citified elite, people like my tennis pals and my university colleagues, called such men 'beardies'.

He turned out to be a religious cricket fan.

'Pakistan!' shouted someone in the crowd.

'Zindabad!' shouted the entire enclosure as one. Long live Pakistan!

'Pakistan!'

'Zindabad!'

'Pakistan!'

'Zindabad!'

'Who's going to win?'

'Pakistan will win!'

'Allah-u-Akbar!'

God is great! Long live Pakistan!

'The behaviour of the spectators is the same in America?' Mohammed Faisal asked me. 'The raising of the slogans?'

'Oh, yes,' I said.

'Pakistan nation is very lazy,' he said. 'Therefore they can afford these day-long matches, five-day tests. Which cricket players have you heard of?'

'Imran Khan, and the South African captain who died in a plane crash.'

'Hansie Cronje.'

'Yes. He was corrupt.'

'He was corrupt,' he agreed. 'But he was a very good captain. And a very good player.'

'Imran Khan is very famous outside Pakistan,' I said.

'Because of Jemima?'

'Partly because of Jemima, but also because he was a great cricket player. Many people didn't want him to marry her,' I added, to see what he would say, 'because she was a Jew.'

'Yes.'

'But she converted to Islam.'

'Yes. Lady Diana was going to accept Islam too.'

The first batsman made out after 19 runs.

The man on the other side of Mohammed Faisal, who had a chubby face that was clean-shaven except for a small moustache, said a name and made what looked like the sign of the cross.

'Excuse me?' I said.

'Yusuf Youhana,' said Mohammed Faisal. 'He is the only Christian player. He is the backbone of the Pakistan team.'

Youhana hit a slow grounder that rolled only a few feet, but he and the other batsman ran for a run.

'He is a very good singles hitter, Yusuf Youhana,' said Mohammed Faisal.

A clean-shaven, jolly young guy sat on my other side. He was a Pathan named Naeem Khan. He came from the same district as Imran Khan, and he liked him. 'He speak about politicians, what they do wrong,' he said. 'Do you belong to intelligence?'

'No, I don't belong to intelligence.'

'Because you are writing down each and every thing we say.'

'It is a very childish question,' said Mohammed Faisal sternly.

A batsman made out by hitting a ball backwards that was caught by the wicketkeeper.

'It is a game of patience,' said Mohammed Faisal. 'If you want to make runs, you have to stay in. That ball was wide. He should have left it.'

The next batsman was Inzimam ul Haq, the Pakistan captain.

'Inzimam is a very lazy runner,' said Naeem Khan.

'South Africa is the best fielding team in the world,' said Mohammed Faisal. 'They are the second-best team in the world, after Australia.'

'But Pakistan won on Friday, so maybe Pakistan is better than South Africa,' I said.

They all chuckled.

'That is not to say that Pakistan is a weak team,' explained Mohammed Faisal. 'Pakistan is not a weak team. Pakistan is always in the top three in the world.'

'So Australia, South Africa, Pakistan ...'

'Yes.'

'India?'

They laughed nervously.

'Yes, then India and New Zealand.'

'What about Zimbabwe?'

'Zimbabwe is not so good.'

'It's a small country.'

'Zimbabwe is a small country,' he agreed. 'And they have not improved much over the last two decades.'

The scoreboard, to our left and across the pitch, was manually operated. Someone a couple of rows in front of us held up a handwritten sign saying, 'Where is Indian team? Rawalpindi Express is back on his track'. Inzimam retired hurt, replaced by Younis Khan. Around the time of Pakistan's 50th run, paper air-planes made out of cards with '4' on one side and '6' on the other, provided by the Slazenger company, began flying around in our section.

'These are very ill-mannered boys,' said Mohammed Faisal. 'Don't mind. Because such characters are everywhere in the world.'

'They are teasing you,' said Naeem Khan cheerfully.

'Should I ignore them?'

'Yes.'

'This stadium maximum 20,000,' said Naeem Khan. 'But in India – Bombay, Calcutta, Delhi – they have stadiums that hold one lakh. Eighty thousand, 90,000, one lakh people come to watch. You can imagine it is a tremendous atmosphere.'

When Yusuf Youhana reached 50 runs, everyone stood and cheered. When he hit a six, the crowd stood and chanted his name.

'Yusuf! Yusuf! Yusuf!'

'He is the first Christian to gain so much fame in Pakistan,' said Mohammed Faisal. 'He is our hero. We love him.'

Yusuf Youhana made out.

'Yusuf is out, after making 65 runs,' said Mohammed Faisal. 'I am very sad. He is my hero.' There was a twinkle in his eye, of pleasure and perhaps of benign, gentle cunning: he wanted me to think well of him because he considered a Christian his hero.

'Are you all from the same village?' I asked him.

'Yes, 15 or 20 boys.'

'Did you come here together?'

'Yes, in a Toyota.'

'Do you play cricket?'

'Very eagerly!' His eyes lit up. 'In our village, despite not having a good ground, our team is always a winner in internal tournaments, regional tournaments.'

Later he asked me: 'Do you enjoy fil-ims?'

'Yes, I enjoy some films. Do you? Hindi films?'

'I enjoy some Hindi fil-ims, but older fil-ims. I don't like new one. They have no morality. They are only dancing and fighting, no story. They only spread sex. I have not watched any fil-ims these last five–six years. But I enjoy some English fil-ims that are action fil-ims, of Arnold.'

The rowdies down the row put a paper visor on my head – it said 'Sufi Cooking Oils' – and hooted at me.

'Your presence has doubled their enjoyment,' said Mohammed Faisal.

An emissary from another group came up to me and asked, 'Where are you from?'

'I'm from America,' I said.

He acknowledged this answer with a nod and went away.

Mohammed Faisal laughed. 'He fears you. Everybody fears America.'

'What do you think of the Karachi bombing?' I asked. I meant the one that had happened the previous month, which had caused the South African team to consider backing out of this tour.

'Such unusual incidents could happen anywhere,' said Mohammed Faisal.

I asked what he thought of the New Zealand players who had decided not to come to Pakistan. New Zealand Cricket had given individual players the option of staying home without risking penalty. One could understand their point of view. I had never been to New Zealand, but I gathered it was not unlike Wisconsin ('America's Dairyland'), where I grew up. It must have shaken the players, and their families back home, when a suicide bomber had killed 14 people outside their hotel in Karachi the year before.

On the other hand, was it a proper cricket series between two national teams if fans in major cities were unable to attend matches, or if top players from one team didn't take part? And Pakistanis lived daily with the fact of bomb blasts. Why shouldn't New Zealanders, especially those who had chosen a public role as international cricketers, live with it as well?

'This kind of thing makes Pakistan seem like a dangerous country,' said Mohammed Faisal. 'Bangladesh toured recently, and it was entirely peaceful. They are hooman beings too. To say they will not come as white men is not a good gesture. They are raising it to the level of a political gesture.' He pronounced the word with a hard 'g'.

'Are there any black players on the South African team?' I asked.

'One or two.'

'In South Africa, football is for black people, cricket is for white people,' I said.

'It is because of this attitude that they were banned from international sport for more than 20 years,' he said. 'They came back in 1991. Till now, most of the players are white.'

Inzimam came back to bat, limping. He used a runner to run out his hits, which I hadn't known was allowed. In the last four balls of Pakistan's last over, Inzimam scored 14 runs. It was an exciting way to end Pakistan's batting turn, and the crowd was on its feet, cheering and chanting.

At halftime I took the opportunity to find a toilet under the stands. It was disgusting and crowded, with no discernible queue. It was every man for himself. I elbowed my way in and back out.

On my way back to my seat, another group beckoned and called to me, trying to lure me away from Mohammed Faisal and his friends. 'Are you African?' one of them asked.

'No, I'm American.'

'What are you doing?'

'I'm watching cricket.'

This met with general approval.

'Did you accomplish your mission?' asked Mohammed Faisal when I got back to my place next to him.

'Yes, I did.'

'It's like to go to the moon, to find a toilet in this place,' he said.

Someone in the row in front of us indicated my notebook and said, 'What is this?'

'Diary,' said Mohammed Faisal. 'Secret.' He had become my host and protector.

Pakistan was now fielding. Number 44 was in the outfield near us. Our enclosure cheered for him. He turned around and tipped his cap.

'This is Rawalpindi Express, Shoaib Akhtar,' said Mohammed Faisal. He was the fastest fast bowler on the Pakistan team. He bowled and looked like a wild man, with stringy hair flying all over the place as he ran. For now he was fielding and someone else was bowling.

'He should change his method of bowling,' commented Naeem Khan. 'Sometime batsman only tap ball and make four.'

South Africa's first over was a 'maiden over', with no runs scored; Mohammed Faisal explained the term to me. A white photographer with a ponytail, probably with South African media, walked around the pitch outside the boundary. When he passed our enclosure, the crowd cheered. He waved.

'India will not come to play cricket in Pakistan,' said Naeem Khan.

'Why not?' I asked.

'Because of the situation between India and Pakistan. Indian gummint will not let cricket team come. But I think they should come. That is other problem. Game is game.'

Near the end he said with satisfaction, 'Hundred seventy-seven runs, 41st over, eight wickets down. It is clear like a mirror that Pakistan will win.'

When the match was over, with Pakistan victorious 267 runs to 225, it was every man for himself again. Fans surged down toward the pitch, the water taps and the exit. The high fence between the stands and the pitch was there for a reason. I thought of English football fans.

'Pakistani people are so much naughty,' said Naeem Khan. His tone suggested that he was both embarrassed and a bit proud about this.

'Maybe I will come to your village sometime, if that's all right,' I said to Mohammed Faisal.

'Yes, of course,' he said. 'We would be honoured. You're not afraid of coming to a village where almost everyone is Muslim?'

'No, I'm not afraid,' I said. 'Should I be?'

They thought this was really funny.

'It was you who made our journey memorable,' said Mohammed Faisal. 'At first I didn't know what you would speak to us. I was a bit shy. But you speak to us very nicely. In my village I have no one I can speak English with.'

'Do you have email?' I asked.

'No. We don't have that facility. Only phone. We will meet again, *inshallah*.'

On my way out, a high-spirited young man shouted at me: 'You are South African?'

'No, American.'

He glared at me challengingly and demanded: 'Pakistani terrorists?'

'Excuse me?'

'Pakistani terrorists?'

'Pakistani good cricketers,' I replied.

'Your president say Pakistani terrorists.'

'He's not my president. I don't like him.'

'You don't like Bush?'

'No.'

'Very good!' he cried joyfully. 'I fuck for Bush!'

CHAPTER SEVEN

EDUCATING MYSELF
IN PUBLIC

The day after the cricket match, I stumbled downstairs to the lounge about eight in the evening after napping for two hours. Shakoor was in a panic.

'Sir, you no outside go,' he said. 'Terrorists!'

The Pakistani news was on the TV. A cleric-cum-politician named Maulana Azam Tariq had been killed outside Islamabad, gunned down in his car near a tollbooth on the motorway.

'You outside one man no,' Shakoor insisted. 'With me go. Sir, you never mind phone. I am safety. You no experience Pakistani people.'

I hadn't heard of Azam Tariq. Others told me later that he was a notorious extremist rabble-rouser who had got what was coming to him. Nusrat, who was watching the breaking news in Urdu with close attention, had a different view.

'He's milestone,' she said. 'Milestone.' I wasn't quite sure what she meant, but she said it with appreciation. 'He is a Sunni. He's killed, Shia. Shias terrorist. He is a regional Sunni leader.' He was one of four Sunni leaders in Jhang, she said, and a Member of the National Assembly. He and his driver, two security guards, and another MNA had all been gunned down in the attack on his car.

Zarina had been in Islamabad over the weekend.

'Mrs Zarina Sadik maybe this problem not come,' said Shakoor.

'But sir, this is not terrorism,' insisted Nusrat. 'This is two parties fighting. Shia–Sunni.' Two days earlier, 11 Shias had been killed in firing on a bus, on their way to a mosque. 'And Shias help Iran,' she added. 'I like Maulana Azam Tariq. I am very upset.'

'I am not very upset,' said Shakoor.

'He's a good man, sir. I like him,' said Nusrat. She supported Maulana Azam Tariq and his Islamist political party, Sipha-e-Sahaba. 'No terrorism, sir. This is the Pakistanis' problem. And this is the mind problem.'

We watched some more television. A Pakistani film came on, in which the groom's friends and relatives went to the bride's house to sing, but her father disapproved of him, or something, and there was lots of shooting and lots of men on horses.

'Very much bullet, but he's not die,' said Nusrat.

'Like Arnold movie,' I said.

'Yes.'

Next we watched Fox News. Bush gave a press conference along with Mwai Kibaki, the visiting President of Kenya. A reporter asked Bush about the Middle East.

'I expressed our nation's condolences for the murder of innocent people by the latest suicider,' he responded. 'The speech I gave on June 24, 2002, our policies have not changed.'

Another reporter asked about Iraq.

'We're makin' good progress in Iraq,' said Bush. 'Sometimes it's hard to tell, when you listen to the filter. The situation is improvin' on a daily basis.'

About aid to Kenya, Bush said: 'In many ways, we're the ones askin' for help. We asked, uh, the President of Kenya for help in the war on terror. And we appreciate that help.'

A reporter with no neck and comically perfect hair reported from Iraq.

'Fox News very bad,' I said to Nusrat.

'Wrong news?' she asked.

'Not always wrong, but very stupid.' I pointed at the reporter. 'Not like a reporter. Like a wrestler.'

The screen split between the reporter and a blonde anchor-woman with a square jaw. Nusrat laughed.

'She wrestler too!' she cried with glee.

It was only later in the week that Zarina made it back from Islamabad. I had missed her and even worried a little, though I knew she could take care of herself. Azam Tariq's supporters had rioted in Islamabad, burning down a cinema and trashing an outdoor food court in a shopping area.

'They're cashing in on the opportunity,' Zarina told me. 'You see, it's a banned party. They've been quiet for some time, and this is an opportunity for them to vent their feelings. In Jhang you've got both the Shias and the Sipha-e-Sahaba. So with two religious sects, they must be on red alert now.'

That Friday at the Beaconhouse head office, I met a friend of Zarina's who had a conspiracy theory that Azam Tariq had made a deal with Musharraf so that he could stand for election to the National Assembly, despite murder charges that were pending against him. Part of the deal, this guy posited, was that Azam Tariq would finger baddies among his own followers. Thus it was his own men, not the Shias, who had killed him.

There were always conspiracy theories, but the mysteries usually remained unsolved. Not that anyone went to too much trouble to solve them. Azam Tariq had lived and died by the sword and assassinations, like bomb blasts, were all too ordinary, and no one wanted to know too much about what was really going on anyway. I was catching history on the fly, and events always moved too quickly to allow for much leisure to ponder their significance. Soon there would be something new to panic or obsess about.

* * *

141

The semester had got underway at the university. It started with a ceremony at which Mrs Kasuri, the boss, introduced the visiting students from nearby countries. There were meant to be two from each member state of the South Asian Association for Regional Cooperation, plus Afghanistan. 'Unfortunately we could not have a girl from Afghanistan,' she said. 'Because as you know education for girls in Afghanistan was, um, off and on these last so many years. But we do have a young man from Afghanistan.'

I established a good working relationship with Taimur-ul-Hassan, my senior colleague in the incipient School of Media and Communications, who had edited several Pakistani dailies and worked with the courageous lawyer Asma Jehangir and others at the Human Rights Commission of Pakistan. Taimur was in his early forties, with a big bushy head of salt-and-pepper hair and a tidy moustache. He had an aristocratic Moghul background but had married for love, which had caused problems with his parents, and he had earned a good reputation but not much money as an unusually hardworking and honest journalist. 'He's a very good human being,' his wife, Zubera, told me with feeling. I found Taimur a kindred soul. He often spoke so fast I couldn't catch all his syllables.

'You are growing a beard?' he asked in surprise, a few days after we first met.

'Yes,' I admitted.

'Oh!' He affected startlement. 'Because you are coming here?'

'Partly.'

'We are having trouble with our own beardies, and you come here and grow a beard!'

I went to the office of Omar Hassan Khan, the accountant with Muppet eyebrows, to turn in my health insurance form. Omar's mobile phone rang; he looked at its screen, then turned and asked me:

'What is common between a man and a mouse?'

I was nonplussed and said so. He repeated the question.

'I don't know,' I said. 'Both have hair?'

'Come on, it's a joke! It has to do with what they do and want.'

'I give up.'

'Both are all the time trying to get into holes.'

'I'm shocked!' I said. 'That a good Muslim like yourself would say such a thing. And such a well dressed one, too.' He was wearing a suit because he had been out late the night before at a wedding, and he had no other pressed clothes.

'I didn't make it up,' he said. 'My friend who is very cynical about men sent it to me.'

'That's what your phone ringing was about?'

'Actually,' he said, his eyebrows dancing playfully, 'as good Muslims we are very strict about our practices. But no harm is done to anyone by making a joke.'

I settled into a routine of walking in the morning from the guest-house to the university – the three-story building next to the Shell station – then in the afternoon across Zafar Ali Road to the Gym-khana for an hour or two of doubles on the grass courts, then in the evening back to the guesthouse. Landmarks and people along the sides of this triangle became familiar: the cats that lived in the dumpster outside the Montessori school; the man who sold news-papers on the corner; the burly policeman with the long black beard, who manned the traffic barrier on the Upper Mall; the beggar who sat with his artificial leg across the footpath, the leg a silent rebuke each time I stepped aside to avoid it; the youths in their Shell uniforms, who never failed to wave and grin; the cops on the bridge over the sewage canal who insisted I drink tea with them.

The neighbourhood yielded its nuances to me as time passed. One evening as I walked back from the Gymkhana, a skinny teenager fell into step with me. When I saw a palm tree in silhouette in front of a house wall – all the houses in this elite neighbourhood were surrounded by high walls – I said it was beautiful, just for something to say.

'This is a fucking house,' he said, and I saw it in a different way.

Another day, as I cut through a makeshift tea stall near the Upper Mall intersection, a policeman asked, 'Where is your residence?'

'Scotch Corner,' I said and gestured vaguely.

'You only one man?'

'No.' I gestured and stammered to suggest that I was staying with others, which I sort of was.

'Where is your wife?'

'In England.'

This was his cue to leer and make gestures with his hands, shaping his fingers to make an oblong hole and a round one, offering me either a woman or a boy, whichever I liked. In fact, I could have this boy right here. The boy smiled at me encouragingly. Feeling queasy, I declined politely and escaped.

I had never taught before, and I didn't know what to expect of my students in terms of English fluency or general knowledge. Taimur asked me to write a course outline, but no one gave me any guidance in how to do so. I took this to mean I had carte blanche. I took as my premise that teaching is like reporting, in that you can transmit only what you yourself know. I decided to try to convey things I had learned from experience as a working reporter and editor: the importance of acquiring and deploying authority – that is, of knowing what you're talking about – and never writing beyond your authority; the importance of honesty, and of initiative. I taught my students the phrases 'shoe leather' and 'elbow grease' and 'the first draft of history'. I assigned them a piece called 'Travel Writing: The Point of It', in which Paul Theroux advocates writing that's 'prescient without making predictions' and argues: 'I have always felt that the truth is prophetic, and that if you describe what you see and give it life with your imagination, then what you write ought to have lasting value, no matter what the mood of your prose.'

I cited James Fallows, who says he likes being a journalist because it's a way to get paid to educate oneself in public. I told the students that, in his book *Breaking the News*, Fallows claims journalism is 'not a profession' in the sense that, unlike dentistry or the law, it has no formal credentials or codified set of standards to which all practitioners must adhere. This leaves the door open to phonies and charlatans, but it also means that any ambitious and talented young guy or gal can show up in Bangkok, as I did, claim to be a journalist, and make his or her way. Gavin Young had fallen into journalism as a drunken man falls into a pond. It was a hard road, and not likely to be a lucrative one, so I told the students that if they were in it for the money, they shouldn't go into journalism.

I had been inspired by the tradition established by David Astor, the great editor of the *Observer* who had cultivated George Orwell, Arthur Koestler, Sebastian Haffner, and other fine writers in the middle of the 20th century, and who had almost single-handedly championed Nelson Mandela and the African National Congress in Britain through the darkest years of apartheid. Through my slight personal connection with Gavin Young, who had been a later and very fine practitioner of the paper's foreign reporting, I felt myself to be carrying forward that tradition. And I admired Astor's personal mission statement: 'I edit the *Observer* for myself and my friends.'

I made my students read Anthony Sampson's long obituary of Astor and several pieces from Young's collection *Worlds Apart*, including his prize-winning coverage of the Bangladesh War and his report on the hanging of Z.A. Bhutto. I also gave them excerpts from the Library of America collection *Reporting Vietnam*. I had in mind that having them read exemplary pieces of reporting on historically significant events – the first draft of history – might also fill gaps in their historical knowledge. This turned out to be atrocious, as I learned from their blank looks when I made allusions in lectures. When I got the blank looks I would back up and devote the next half hour to a thumbnail sketch of the Berlin Wall, Tiananmen Square, the Khmer Rouge, or the Holocaust. 'In Beijing, the capital of China, there's a huge square ...' I was no expert on any of these subjects, but I knew a lot more about them than my students did, and by the end of the semester they knew more than they had.

To their credit, almost all my students were eager to learn. They also were good-natured, charming and respectful. They called me 'Sir' or even 'Sir Ethan' and never sat down if I was standing. There were ten of them in their early twenties, enrolled for a two-year master's degree, plus Amit Kumar Shrivastava, an earnest and demanding 18-year-old Indian who was at BNU and in Pakistan on a special basis. Most of the students were from the upper reaches of the Lahori elite, and most were female.

What was more, the women were much livelier and more obviously intelligent than the men, and more hardworking. The three Pakistani guys blossomed later on, but at first they seemed dull and intimidated by the girls. I found this strange, but was told the tables would turn when they married. 'You have to be very courageous to make something of yourself in this part of the world,' my boss, Navid Shahzad, told me. 'There's so much that gets sucked out of your soul if you're a woman.' Mrs Shahzad was an impressive person in her own right: a teacher, intellectual and actress who had made a celebrated 'love marriage'; I could only guess at the depths of personal experience from which she spoke.

As a new institution, BNU couldn't yet be academically selective, but it charged high fees and could do so because of the Beaconhouse School System's 28-year track record. When I entered the classroom for the first lecture I had trouble pronouncing names and couldn't tell one student from another; five months later I not only knew each one as an individual but could articulate how he or she had grown.

A tall, effervescent young woman named Sadaf Daha was one of the brightest and a member of the clique I dubbed the Gang of Three. Sadaf was a US citizen, born in 1980 in Connecticut, where her father was doing his medical residency. Because the US didn't allow dual citizenship she was not also a Pakistani citizen, even though she had grown up in Pakistan. In February 2003, she had been deported from Pakistan.

'For me it was like the end of the world, like I wouldn't get to see anybody ever again,' she told me.

She had flown on Emirates Airlines from Boston to Lahore via London and Dubai. She had expected to get a visa on arrival in Lahore, as used to be possible for Americans. 'They gave it in the newspaper that if you're an American living in Pakistan, you don't need a visa,' she explained. 'The guy at Heathrow Airport, he said, "You can go. You're not going to have any problem."'

The immigration officials at Lahore, all men, had grabbed her arm and would not allow her even to touch her mother, who had had to remain on the other side of a glass wall. They had forced her to board a plane back to Dubai. 'It was the Eid holidays, so nothing could be done,' she said. On the plane back to Dubai she had asked: 'What are you going to do to me? I don't even have money to call my mother.'

'We'll let you know when we get there,' they had told her.

In Dubai, she was not allowed to leave the premises of the airport. 'They didn't give me a hotel room or anything,' she said. 'They're supposed to, but they didn't. There was this lady who took care of me. She was a total stranger. She arranged money for me, which my father sent.'

She was still indignant. 'Okay, even if I was deported because I didn't have a visa, they didn't have the right to harass me. Especially in Pakistan, where they're not even supposed to touch women. It messed me up for quite some time. It made me feel insecure, just the thought that I couldn't do anything about it.'

I asked if she was now legally resident in Pakistan.

'I will be,' she said. 'I'll get a Pakistan Origin Card. It's like a permanent visa.'

But why had they treated her so harshly?

'He said, "If one of us had gone to the US, this is what the *goras* [whites] would have done to us. So this is revenge." I said, "So do it to them, not to one of your own!"'

If they went on to become journalists, most of my students would be Pakistani journalists reporting to a Pakistani audience. The concept of 'the gentleman living abroad', defined by Western imperialism and exemplified by *Observer* men such as Young and Neal Ascherson, or Hemingway, or Alistair Cooke, or Fowler in *The Quiet American*, was irrelevant to their context. It also was outmoded in the age of the internet. The conditions of global communication had changed drastically, even since I had been their age. They were chatting online daily with young people in England and Spain and wherever else. International journalism – reporting local events across national borders – had to mean something new and different to them.

'I know that for myself as author, the internet has never seemed more miraculously human than in the two weeks following the attacks,' Jay Rosen, Chair of the Department of Journalism at New York University and my collaborator on a collection of writings published as a book less than three weeks after 11 September 2001, had written. 'Being connected is such a mysterious good, I don't think we understand a tenth of it.' Much of the material in the book had been published first in the online publication I had launched, BlueEar.com, which subscriber Dorothy Mills praised on 16 September as providing 'a breadth of information that we could not have found in any university because of its amazingly wide member-ship among intelligent people around the world.'

I saw my semester in Lahore as a chance to build on this, by connecting my Pakistani students directly to mostly Western readers and interlocutors, and vice versa, via the web. I felt what we were doing on BlueEar.com represented legitimate innovation in commu-nication and journalism. The heady days of the internet boom were past, but the new medium was still there, its potential still not fully realised. 'Now the distance between author and reader is shrinking,' the novelist Jonathan Franzen had written. 'Instead of Olympian figures speaking to the masses below, we have matching diasporas.' Or, as Jay Rosen put it: 'The most basic act of journalism, by no means limited to journalists, is when someone says to us, "I was there, you weren't, let me tell you about it".'

I required each student to choose a topic to follow locally in Lahore, to write one article per week on it for BlueEar.com and to read and take part in the daily debate there. I learned quite a bit from their pieces about Pakistan, on topics ranging from fashion to heroin addicts to pop music.

I was fairly lenient with the students. Taimur was sterner, espe-cially when it came to *The Beacon*, the student paper we were trying to launch. One day in the computer lab, I found myself button-holed by Sadaf and Zunera Khalid, a charming and sensitive girl who could seem ditzy but who impressed me greatly later in the semester.

'Sir,' Zunera pouted, 'Sir Taimur wants us to write about *serious* things, like Quaid-e-Azam and all that.'

'Quaid-e-Azam is so *boring*,' sighed Sadaf.

Zunera complained that others were giving copy for *The Beacon* to Neelum Zia, a prim and pious girl who was in charge of page layout, rather than to her as editor. I advised her to confront Neelum directly and assert her authority.

'Yes,' she said. 'But I am a Scorpion, and Neelum is a Scorpion, and Scorpions have the tendency to be hyper.'

Sadaf came to my desk one day, feeling discouraged. Her BlueEar.com topic was women's issues. 'Sir, I don't know what to write about!' she cried. She was starting to find writing stories about oppressed women's misery repetitive and boring.

I said that her restlessness was salutary and that, if the tales of woe were boring her, the writer, imagine how readers might come to feel. I said this was a real and chronic problem for writers who want to depict the world truly and to tell people things they ought to know. I suggested she consider writing about other aspects of women's experience in Pakistan: issues of women's dress and the Islamic principle of feminine modesty, or the positive side of being a woman – how men often are very polite to women, for example.

This cheered her up. 'Sir, you *are* a genius!' she gushed.

One of my male students, Ahmed Usman Chaudhry, came to my desk and asked, 'Do you know of this play *The Importance of Being Earnest?*'

'Yes,' I said. 'Why do you ask?'

I had seen posters at Kinnaird College, where I had been on the panel of judges for a spirited if rather stilted and old-fashioned debate between the Kinnaird girls and the Government College boys, sponsored by the Kinnaird economics department, on the proposition 'Men Save More Than Women'. The play was being put on at Kinnaird, by senior students from a Beaconhouse school.

'Because my father and I were planning to attend it,' said Usman. 'Of course it interests him as a professor of literature. But he has had to go to our ancestral village because of a family marriage. So I have two passes, and perhaps you would like to accompany me?'

He picked me up that evening on his motorbike.

'How is traffic in Lahore?' he asked over his shoulder.

'I used to live in Bangkok,' I said. 'Compared to Bangkok, traffic in Lahore is fine.'

'Lahoris don't obey traffic laws,' he said. 'They never stop at lights unless there is a policeman – and he has a car or a motorbike. If he is on foot, they don't stop. One time I was in traffic, and I came to a light. I obeyed the light, but my professor also was there, and he didn't stop.'

'He wasn't setting a good example, was he?'

'No, he wasn't! And he was a professor of Islamic Studies. What a contrast!'

'Was your father disappointed that he couldn't come tonight?'

'Yes, he was disappointed. But this marriage also is important in our family. And I couldn't replace my father in that marriage, because all the relatives want to see him. They don't want to see me.'

We made our way into the auditorium and sat down. 'I wanted to read this play before watching it, but I was not able to do so due to lack of time,' said Usman as we waited for the curtain to rise.

When a tall, husky boy dressed as a butler walked on stage and said, 'Mr Ernest Worthing has driven in from town. He has brought his luggage with him,' Usman turned to me and whispered: 'This one is my friend.'

There was shouting and whistling when the curtain opened and closed. 'It's something normal in the culture of Lahore,' said Usman. The play was thoroughly entertaining and well done, with impeccable British accents all round. Afterwards the director, Omair Rana, congratulated the audience: 'It's very rare to find an audience of your sort, that actually understands and reacts at the right moments.'

One of my female students, Zainab Bashir, had gone twice to see *Moulin Rouge*. Zainab had an incisive mind, excellent clothes sense, and very dignified bearing. I had my own impressions of *Moulin Rouge*, but I wanted to know what a fashionable young Pakistani thought. Zainab was the one writing for BlueEar.com about pop music.

'I think it was very bold of Shah Shahrahbeel to bring out such a play, knowing that our public is very closed-minded,' she told me. 'One of my friends saw it on Monday, and all they could talk about was, "You've got to check out the dresses. They were sleeveless spaghetti straps, low backs, low fronts." On Friday the crowd was really rowdy and passing their own comments during the play. Naturally people were laughing at their jokes, but the actors tried to ignore them.' There was 'a lot of gate-crashing,' she added. 'On Tuesday they were more of an uncle-aunty thing. But on Friday it was mostly youngsters.'

Did the rowdiness ruin her enjoyment of the play?

'Yeah, it did,' she said. Zainab didn't suffer fools.

Malaysian Prime Minister Mahathir Mohamad, who was retiring at the end of October after 22 years in office, gave a speech to a summit of the Organisation of the Islamic Conference on 16 October that ignited one of the periodic firestorms of controversy for which he is well known. About three-quarters of the way through a 4200-word speech, what Mahathir actually said was:

We are actually very strong. One point three billion people cannot be simply wiped out. The Europeans killed 6 million Jews out of 12 million. But today the Jews rule this world by proxy. They get others to fight and die for them.

We may not be able to do that. We may not be able to unite all the 1.3 billion Muslims. We may not be able to get all the Muslim governments to act in concert. But even if we can get a third of the ummah [worldwide body of Muslim believers] and a third of the Muslim states to act together, we can already do something. Remember that the Prophet did not have many followers when he went to Madinah. But he united the Ansars and the Muhajirins and eventually he became strong enough to defend Islam.

Mahathir was characteristically unrepentant in the face of the predictable avalanche of outrage his remarks sparked. Most Western writers condemned him outright, but Paul Krugman of the *New York Times* wrote:

> ...That tells you, more accurately than any poll, just how strong the rising tide of anti-Americanism and anti-Semitism among Muslims in Southeast Asia has become. Thanks to its war in Iraq and its unconditional support for Ariel Sharon, Washington has squandered post-9/11 sympathy and brought relations with the Muslim world to a new low.
>
> And bear in mind that Mr Mahathir's remarks were written before the world learned about the views of Lt Gen William 'My God Is Bigger Than Yours' Boykin. By making it clear that he sees nothing wrong with giving an important post in the war on terror to someone who believes, and says openly, that Allah is a false idol – General Boykin denies that's what he meant, but his denial was implausible even by current standards – Donald Rumsfeld has gone a long way toward confirming the Muslim world's worst fears.

Frequent BlueEar.com contributor Michael Brenner asserted: 'Krugman is wrong ... Mahathir's speech and his attempt to justify it as anti-Zionism is the best evidence yet that there is no qualitative difference between anti-Zionism and anti-Semitism.' Michael also had a letter published in the *New York Times*. I took the speech as an occasion to see if anything fruitful could emerge from honest debate between seemingly irreconcilable Muslim and Western views.

I required my students to read the speech in full.

'It was very moving,' said Zainab. 'I was close to tears.'

'For the first time, somebody is trying to bridge the gap between

Muslims and the West,' said Ayela Deen, a plump girl who was both bossy and well liked enough to be the class leader.

'I think he's a star for being so bold,' said a girl named Warda Khalid.

'It's like a wake-up call for the Muslims,' said Sadaf.

'Jews consider themselves a big part of the speech,' said Zunera. 'I would say that they feel guilty.'

'They have taken one sentence out of Mahathir's speech and put all the emphasis on that,' said Sadaf.

'I think they are not getting the point that he is just addressing the Muslim community,' said Neelum.

'It's like the Pope addressing the Christian community,' suggested Zainab. 'A lot of the American vote comes from the Jews also. And that is why America is biased.'

'People just need a reason to condemn Islam,' said Ayela. 'And it's our own doing as well. I mean, why don't we get visas? I think 50 per cent we should blame ourselves for it.'

Ayla Hassan was from Karachi and kept herself a little apart from the rest of the class. 'America has been an illusion: that if you live there you have a good life,' she said. 'On that particular day, when there was an attack on the Twin Towers, there were Jew sweepers working there. But they did not come to work that particular day. I read in the Quran that there is a prediction that these two very beautiful buildings will be destroyed.'

I also made them read Krugman's column, his follow-up and one by Richard Cohen of the *Washington Post*.

'Most of these people, I think they should come here before they start commenting,' said Zainab. 'They act as if they know everything!' Other Muslim leaders, she said, appreciated Mahathir's speech. 'But no one is going to do anything about it. Because they all have so many internal problems, and no one wants to get on the wrong side of America.'

I explained the Jewish Diaspora in broad outline and did my best, as a Western Gentile, to convey the perspectives and sensibilities that arose in large part from Jews' more recent experience of the Holocaust. I told them about my own visit to Auschwitz in 1990.

'You speak as if you're all for the Jews,' complained Zainab.

I kept up the tennis almost daily, usually bringing my kit to the office in the morning and dashing out at three o'clock, when the gents started arriving. Most of them had similar priorities. 'All my daily activities are geared so that I can be free by 3.30,' Omar Qayyum told me. 'This is the best part of my day,' said a businessman named Mian Mohammed Amjad. 'I have friends whom I can joke to.' I liked Mian-sahib a lot. He had the strangest service motion I've ever seen, arms and legs flailing for several seconds before he hit the ball. It was hard to believe, what with all the flailing, that he could actually hit the ball over the net into the court. Other than that, he wasn't a bad tennis player for a man in his seventies.

The ball boys liked me, and I came to know several of them individually. My favourite was a teenaged Pathan named Suleiman Khan, who was his widowed mother's sole support. A couple of them could play competently. The best player among them, a lanky, dark-skinned Christian named Jamil, was also the senior ball boy. Jamil had little English but was pleasant company, and whenever I played him I thought of Paul Theroux's short story 'The Tennis Court', in which Western expats in Malaysia use a ball boy as a stealth weapon to humiliate a Japanese businessman. When they were free, the ball boys played a modified version of doubles, using their bare hands and playing within the service boxes on a spare court. The most thoughtful of the gents, Butt-sahib, told me he had urged the club to provide a few secondhand rackets for their use, but his proposal had gone nowhere. Most of the ball boys were dark-skinned and, as they told me eagerly, Christian. They asked if I was Christian too. I told them yes, because I knew it would please them.

Not all the gents had as much time for the ball boys as I did, and it was true that some were lazy and had bad attitudes. One day I overheard Rashid Rehman and another member discussing how the ball boys really should have uniforms. 'When I was secretary, this is what I did,' said Rashid. 'But they don't wear them.'

'It's a disgrace,' said the other man. This man no longer played since heart surgery, but he walked briskly around the courts for exercise, and he always complimented some aspect of my game when he passed behind me. 'And second objection I have is that they're always sitting around over there.'

'These ball boys get yelled at a lot, but they don't seem to work very hard,' I observed to Sajjad Gul, the filmmaker.

'Oh, you have to,' he said. 'I buy them a Coke every day, but I expect them to work.'

I put in training sessions with Tariq as often as I could. I knew how expensive this much coaching would be in England or the US. 'Lovely shot, yaar,' Tariq would say, to encourage me. As my technique improved under his tutelage, I started feeling my oats. 'No good,' he said sternly, when I tried something fancy.

'But lots of topspin!' I objected.

'No, no! I'm no like. Hit proper.'

Rashid Rehman was lean and self-contained and had an intense, forbidding look about him that was underscored by his headband and white beard. One time in doubles he served to me, on the ad side. I called his serve out. 'A liner isn't a fault,' he growled.

'Excuse me?'

'A liner isn't a fault,' he repeated. 'My serve was in.'

As intimidated as I felt, I decided I had to stand my ground. It helped that I knew I was right. 'With respect, Rashid-sahib, the serve was out.'

After the set I went up to him and stammered that I didn't want any bad feelings and had honestly believed his serve was out. 'Ethan,' he said jovially, 'you take these things far too seriously!'

I wrote an article about tennis at the Gymkhana for *The Friday Times*, Najam Sethi's weekly paper. I didn't have time to check with Rashid Rehman whether it was all right to mention his name, so I wrote: 'I knew somebody who knew somebody who was kind enough to sponsor me as a guest member.' The first time I saw him after the article was published, he said, 'I want to talk to you.' He took his session with Tariq, then called me over. 'First of all,' he said, 'when you practice your backhand, hit all the way through. Never mind if it goes long. Otherwise, you'll never learn to hit it properly with topspin.'

'Thanks,' I said.

'Now, about your article. I noticed that you wrote that you "knew somebody who knew somebody." Names are forbidden?'

I explained that I had been cautious because I hadn't had time to check with him. He told me he had been imagining a policy against mentioning him in *The Friday Times*. This was the first hint I had of the longstanding and complex relationships among Rashid Rehman, his younger brother Asad, Najam Sethi and the journalist Ahmed Rashid. Later I learned more about the history the four men shared, which was intertwined with a significant episode in the country's history. The world of the Pakistani elite, especially in Lahore, was a social hothouse where everybody knew everybody else. It could be stifling, and it could be a minefield. After a few gaffes I learned to take care whom I mentioned, to whom, and how. You never knew who would turn out be whose cousin or son-in-law.

In October, Omar Qayyum and an army colonel from the Defence Club organised an inter-club tournament, in which Omar invited me to take part. I lost my first-round doubles match 7–5 6–3. The partner I got stuck with accused me of not volleying well, which was rather rich considering how weak his serve was. Afterwards I sat on the grass, leaning against a chain link fence, and chatted with Omar's son Saad.

Saad was 18 years old, thin and fit, with a quiet manner. The first time I spoke to him he had seemed standoffish, even arrogant. He definitely was proud. 'They think we live in caves, or we live on the trees, or something,' he said about Westerners, with obvious disdain. But he had begun warming to me, and his manners were well polished.

As dusk fell and we waited for the last match to finish so we could all have tea and cakes, Saad and I discussed his college plans. He would be going to Indiana University, in the US, in late December or early January. It would be the first time he would see snow. He had been to America before, though – he was in fact a US citizen, thanks to his father's long stint working there. So, unlike many young Pakistanis, he would have no trouble entering the US. He carried a US passport and a Pakistan Origin Card and could come and go between the two countries as it suited him.

'I think I'll study and get my degree in USA, then come back and live in Pakistan,' he said. 'Living here is much nicer, I think. What do you think?'

'I agree,' I said.

'You can't have servants there,' he pointed out. 'Here, you can relax and enjoy life.'

I grew fond of Saad and later, when he left for Indiana, I missed him. 'I'm going to avoid three things while I'm there,' he said earnestly. 'I'm going to avoid getting into any fights, I'm going to avoid drinking, and I'm going to avoid girls.' He laughed. 'Actually, I won't avoid talking to girls. But I will avoid them in a sexual manner.'

A few days later Defence Club swept the finals of the tournament, and a frail old man sitting in a chair – a former Davis Cup player for Pakistan, I was told – ceremonially gave out the trophies. Tariq Rahim, the big man, gave a short speech. 'On behalf of the Gymkhana Tennis Club, I extend you a hearty welcome,' he said. 'And before I invite you for cup of tea, let me just say that Defence Club will have to invite us over as soon as Ramzan is finished.' There were hearty chuckles all round.

'How did your match go?' I asked Shaqil-sahib, a jovial, pear-shaped man.

'I lost,' he said.

That was all he seemed inclined to say, so I left it at that. But later, near the hors d'oeuvre table, I asked, 'So did you play well, even though you lost?'

'I had four bloody Marys this afternoon,' he said, more cheerfully. 'So I wasn't seeing the court very straight!'

I exchanged hellos with Saad.

'Everybody is going to be sad for a week or so because we lost the tournament,' he said with a smile.

Saad and I moved over to the hard courts, which were floodlit, and played singles. I was up 4–1, but he evened it at 4–4. I broke to make it 5–4 and served for the set, but he broke back to make it 5–5. At 6–6 we played a tiebreak, which Saad won 7–2. I was angry with myself for squandering the lead and found myself shouting when I made errors, mostly on overheads. Shaking hands at the net I said, 'It was a good set.'

'You should have won it, though,' said Saad.

'I'm going to win the next one.'

'We'll see.'

Tariq, who had watched from a chair on my side of the net, admonished me about losing my temper.

'Is part of the game, yaar,' he said. 'I play, I get hangry, I speak to myself, "Come on, come on, next point."' But he had kind words too. 'Your game one month ago and now, very different.'

'Better?'

'*Much* better.'

As I changed my shoes and packed up my kit, Asif, aged eight, arrived for his lesson. Asif was big for eight and pretty good.

'Asif, *hit* the ball!' Tariq yelled.

I chatted with Asif's father, Dr Salman Shah, director of the Lahore College of Business Administration and Economics. 'He knows all the rankings, the Swedish Open, the Australian Open, the French Open,' he said. 'He doesn't understand why I don't know all that stuff!'

We talked about the situation of Muslims in India, which he compared to the situation of blacks in the US. This caught my interest, because I had noted the same parallel when I was in India in the mid-1990s. Both groups were disadvantaged socially, economically and politically. Neither had a political party it could naturally call home, and were taken for granted by the ostensibly more liberal party. Both were concentrated in urban areas. Coincidentally but strikingly, each made up about 12 per cent of its country's population. What C.L.R. James said about black Americans could also be said of Indian Muslims: 'There never was a minority which was so much flesh of the flesh and blood of the blood of the majority.' V.S. Naipaul, a pukka Brahmin and a some-time protégé of James, wrote in *An Area of Darkness* that, in Trinidad, 'at an early age I understood that Muslims were some-what more different than others. They were not to be trusted; they would always do you down; and point was given to this by the presence close to my grandmother's house of a Muslim, in whose cap and grey beard, avowals of his especial difference, lay every sort of threat.'

'Imagine what America would be like if they hadn't given the blacks their rights over the last 20–30 years,' said Salman Shah to me. 'It would be a holy mess. Muslims in India have not resorted to violence in 50 years. But now they're starting to.'

'Now they're going to build that Ram temple,' I said. I had heard of plans to build a Hindu temple to the god Ram on the site of the mosque fanatical Hindus had torn down in Ayodhya in 1992.

'Yes. That Ram temple might be important to their religion or whatever, but if they build it, they will permanently alienate a major portion of their population.'

I remarked that he was the first person I had met who had made the comparison between black Americans and Indian Muslims, but that it had occurred to me too.

'Well, I lived in America for a long time,' he said.

Friends in the West got the not unfounded impression that I was living the life of a pukka sahib. 'In the next email I want to hear that you are at least doing a few hours work a week and that there is the odd occasion when you are not playing tennis,' my regular opponent Dave Penny wrote. Andy Badenoch, my editor at the *Observer* News Service, imagined 'tiffin and sipping gin beneath the ceiling fan – steadily worked by the punka wallah – among the manicured lawns and starched white jackets of the club staff.'

I didn't mind. The world of the Gymkhana would be what it was with or without me, and for a time I was happy to be part of it. I told myself tennis was a way of penetrating the networks of the Pakistani elite, and to an extent this was true. It also got me in shape – I lost 20 pounds during five months in Pakistan – and drained the tension from my back and shoulders after a day at the office.

And it was the perfect diversion for a writer. I found tennis soothing because, although a line call could be ambiguous or wrong, at least in theory every ball was either in or out. This is not the case in the worlds of literature and journalism. 'I am so sick of this trade of authorship, that I have a much greater ambition to be the best racket-player, than the best prose-writer of the age,' wrote William Hazlitt in 1820. 'The critics look askance at one's best-meant efforts, but the face of a racket-player is the face of a friend. There is no juggling here. If the stroke is a good one, the hit tells. They do not keep two scores to mark the game, with Whig and Tory notches.'

CHAPTER EIGHT

RHYTHMS OF RAMZAN

The 27th of October was the first day of Ramzan, the Muslim holy month, in Iraq and Malaysia but not in Pakistan. 'It depends on this moon sighting,' Zarina explained as we watched the news. The news was that there had been several suicide bombings in Baghdad, including on Red Cross headquarters, with at least 34 people killed and 200 injured. Zarina's personal news was that she had sealed the deal for her new house.

I asked her what it was like to adjust to the rhythms of Ramzan, when Muslims are meant to fast every day between sunrise and sunset. 'The first few days are pretty rough,' she said. 'After that, your body gets used to the new routine.' Her son Zuly told me he always took a half-hour nap after breaking his fast in the evening. Zarina also said that in Pakistan, 2.5 per cent was taken out of all bank accounts on the first day of Ramzan, for a fund meant to aid the poor. I wondered if this applied to my account at Askari Bank, where my salary was deposited.

'You're a non-Muslim,' she assured me.

But I noticed later, when I looked at my statement, that 2.5 per cent *zakat* tax had been taken out.

After the news there was an interview show on Geo, Pakistan's new private channel. The show's format was that interviewers and cameramen spent a day following around a celebrity or public figure. Today's episode was on Benazir Bhutto. They showed her in her London flat and riding in a Mercedes. It was mostly in Urdu. Zarina explained that it was a 'day in the life' type thing, not very political. Benazir claimed she would have done unspecified things differently to do with Iraq if she were prime minister today, and that her email was bugged, but otherwise she talked mostly of domestic matters and did things like lay cutlery on a dining table. She wore a white headscarf and a blue dress over white trousers.

'She's the worst-dressed woman I've ever seen,' said Zarina.

'She is awfully frumpy,' I agreed.

'She's *very* frumpy.'

In one scene she sat on a couch with her children, one of whom sat beside her on the arm of the couch.

'That kid needs a haircut!' I said.

'That's a girl,' said Zarina.

The girl said she wanted to join the army when she grew up. Was this the one with whom Benazir had been famously pregnant during the 1988 election? 'Why do you want to join the military?' Benazir asked her in English.

'I think they're really cool, and we need them,' said the daughter in a sloppy British accent.

'And we might stop military coups by good people joining them,' Benazir prompted her.

'Yeah, that too.'

Zarina translated the parts that were in Urdu. 'She says the general is anti her because she was born and bred in luxury, and he has nothing to show, so "He doesn't like the way I live, my lifestyle." Isn't that stupid? The kids can't even reply in Urdu. Isn't that a shame? "I like the military. I think they're cool." What a stupid interview.'

The next morning everyone in the guesthouse – Shakoor and Nusrat, Zarina and her elder son Ahmed – was up at 4 am to eat before dawn. I joined them. I intended to join them every day, but that didn't end up happening. I got into the habit of eating breakfast discreetly on my own most mornings at my usual time, then trying to make it until *iftar*, the breaking of the fast, in the evening. Iftar was a pleasant custom, with a convivial vibe and tasty foods, such as spicy fruit salad and pakoras with special yoghurt sauce.

At the university, I ran into Omar Hassan Khan in the corridor. 'How's the first day of Ramzan treating you?' I asked.

'I haven't felt anything yet,' he said. 'But I feel more pious.'

'The beginning of the month of Ramzan is always contentious,' Taimur told me in our office. 'This has led to some chaos and quibbling among clerics, and to some extent has been used as a political issue. Routinely there have been disputes about beginning of Ramzan between NWFP [North-West Frontier Province] and Punjab, because of the geographical situation. This has been a perennial problem in Pakistan. If so much technological equipment and satellites are available, why can't they just come up with a uniform moon sighting?'

It was a rhetorical question. 'There have been attempts at the gummint level to streamline things,' he added. 'They have formed a committee.'

Ramzan, he said, was 'a mix of a month of restraint and getting ready for the festival' – Eid, the great feast that marks the end of fasting, when families gather and children are given money and presents. 'Generally, during this month, economic productivity is quite low. Open taking of food was banned during Zia's days. According to the Shia sect, they end their fasting half an hour earlier than Sunnis.'

'Why?'

'Ask them.'

I said I had watched the Benazir Bhutto interview. This prompted a non-stop rant from Taimur that went on for at least 20 minutes. I just kept my head down and took notes.

'Emotions were high because we had been through hell in Zia's days, and we thought Benazir Bhutto might be able to change things,' he said. 'She is so arrogant. She doesn't take any counsel. She thinks she is a wisdom unto herself.' There had been a hung parliament after the 1988 election. 'She could have opted to sit in opposition and wait her time, but she chose to compromise with the establishment. So where do we stand? Where do people like us stand, who thought she would take on the establishment? She cannot say anything to people of Pakistan. People of Pakistan brought that woman twice to power. People of Pakistan owe nothing to Benazir Bhutto. She turned out to be a weak woman, in fact. A weak, emotional woman. At least she could have organised the Pakistan People's Party at the grassroots level. There was not a party office in Lahore, when she was in power. Zardari' – Benazir's infamous husband, Asif Ali Zardari – 'is in fact Baloch. Zardaris are people who used to do business with these camels.'

Taimur remembered the euphoria at Benazir's return from exile in 1986. He was a representative specimen of a liberal Pakistani who had been stirred by the populism of her father, Z.A. Bhutto, and who had invested in her his hopes that a better era would follow Zia's death. 'Bhutto's picture is still in my wallet,' Taimur said. 'But this woman is dishonest, corrupt, revengeful, reactionary and incompetent. She may be a good opposition leader, but she cannot run a good government. If you talk about merit, I think Musharraf has served the interests of secular classes more than she did. She really disappointed us. She took that dream away from us.'

Ramzan took a toll on tennis. 'You're tired?' I said in surprise to Tariq at the end of a Sunday morning lesson. 'I'm fresh!'

'You drinking water,' he said. 'I'm *rosa*.' *Rosa* meant the daily Ramzan fast.

'I'm tired today,' I told Butt-sahib another day. This was not the bookstore owner Tariq Nasir Butt, but a different, laconic man with an Islamic-style beard-without-moustache.

'Did you eat lunch?' he asked.

'No.'

'But you are not fasting.'

'I'm not fasting, but I don't like to eat when others are fasting.'

'Actually,' he said – Butt-sahib had a penchant for impromptu sermonettes – 'fasting allows us the opportunity to feel what poverty is like. Resources blong to Creator. People blong to Creator. And he who is in command must distribute resources fairly, to all. This is divine law. It's very clear. If there is rule of law – divine law – then there will be peace in the world.'

As I was lacing up my tennis shoes one afternoon Shaqil-sahib said to me, 'Do you know Mullah Omar?'

'From Afghanistan?'

'Yes. You're looking like him.' He meant my beard. 'You'd better watch out. FBI might get you!'

Omar Qayyum and I beat Shaqil-sahib and Saad 6–4 in doubles that day, then I played singles against Butt-sahib. We stopped at 6–6 because the ball boys were more restless than usual to take down the nets. Dusk was falling earlier now, around 5.20, and people hurried home for iftar. I often felt lonesome if I was outdoors at iftar time, seeing groups of people sitting or standing together, sharing food on the street or in a shop or office. Seeing Tariq and the ball boys huddled together, convivially breaking the fast in the deepening shadow near the red brick clubhouse that was under construction, I hurried home. I didn't wait for them to invite me to join them, though they would have if it had occurred to them or if I had asked.

I found Zarina in the lounge, wearing a headscarf and reading the Quran. While we took iftar, the BBC reported Pakistan's response to the latest peace overture from India. India was proposing opening a bus service between Srinagar and Muzaffarabad, the capitals of the two sides of Kashmir. On CNN, Pakistani foreign secretary Riaz Khokar said Pakistan welcomed the proposal in principle but, since the road went through disputed territory, it must be manned by UN personnel and travellers must carry UN documents.

'Imagine that,' I said. 'A bus service from Srinagar to Muzaffarabad!'

'They're quite close to each other,' said Zarina.

'I know, but what a wild concept. I'd love to be on the first bus.'

'It would probably get blown up!'

My student Adnan Latif invited me to visit Lahore's Moghul-era old city with him one afternoon early in Ramzan. 'Have you had your lunch?' he asked politely when he picked me up in his car at the university.

'No, I haven't eaten lunch,' I said.

'We can get your lunch.'

'No, thank you. I won't eat lunch today.'

'Are you fasting?'

'No, but I don't want to eat when other people are fasting.'

I didn't know what to make of Adnan at first, but I grew to like him. He joined the class several weeks late and was physically and socially awkward, tall and gaunt and darker-skinned than most of the others. His English was not good. He had a reckless streak, but I found him gentle and thoughtful. The girls complained that he made rude remarks to them. His father was a wealthy fruit merchant. 'My brother is also businessman,' he told me. 'He imports coconuts from Sri Lanka.'

We drove down the Mall, past landmarks I had known nearly a decade earlier: the Governor's House, Jinnah Gardens, the zoo, the Avari Hotel where I used to go for the air conditioning and to buy newspapers, Wapda House, the Punjab Assembly and Regal Chowk where I had witnessed a riot on my first day in Pakistan, the GPO, the telecom office where I had gone to send faxes, the Catholic cathedral, the Lahore Museum. This downtown area was the Lahore I had known, back then.

'My mother said, "Mr Adnan, please at least get your master's" ,' Adnan told me. 'Money is not a problem. She also has master's degree.'

'What is her master's in?'

'She has master's degree in Islamyat, from Punjab University.'

I winced when Adnan nearly collided with another car.

'Don't worry,' he said. 'Because traffic is the major problem in Lahore. I also don't have side mirror.' He had once had an accident with a bus. 'When he went to police station, my father angry. He say, "Why you break the bus mirror?" But otherwise he not angry. He always love me. He say, "Anyone hit your car, just let them go away. Forget them."'

We arrived at a bazaar near a big and splendid stone mosque, the Data Darbar mosque. 'Lots of Afghani beggars everywhere in Lahore,' said Adnan. 'People buy rice there and distribute to poor people, like Afghanis.'

'For Ramzan?'

'No, throughout the year. Thursday night every time I come here and give some money to the poor people. My dad also.'

We turned onto a crowded side street and parked. A wide outdoor staircase led up to the vast courtyard of the mosque.

'Sir, problem is, we going upstairs barefooted.'

'Of course,' I said and took off my sneakers and socks.

Upstairs Adnan said, 'This is our religious man's grave.' It was the shrine of a saint named Hazrat Data Ganj Baksh Ali Hajveri, a covered room at one end of the marble courtyard.

'When did he live?' I asked.

'Twelfth century, I think. This door is made of gold.' He showed me a plaque in Urdu on the wall. 'Prime minister of Pakistan,

Zulfikar Ali Bhutto, opened it, 24 December 1974. You see that green box? People come here and throw down some money in these box. When he open these box he collect lots of money.' On each side of the courtyard, just outside the entrances to the mosque proper, were five large fans that were turned on in hot weather. 'And this marble is also hot,' said Adnan. On the first day of November, at four in the afternoon, the marble was cool to my bare feet.

A man approached us and said, in English, 'Hello, Mr Adnan.'

'Hello, Mr Usman,' said Adnan.

'You are from where?' the man asked me.

'From America,' I said.

'He is my teacher,' said Adnan.

'Are you Muslim?' asked the man.

'No.'

The man left.

'Is he your friend?' I asked Adnan.

'My grandfather was very famous,' he said. 'He was councillor. He stand for elections. That is why lots of people know me.'

A large crowd of men were inside the mosque, praying in unison. 'It is time for *namaz*,' said Adnan.

'Would you like to pray? I can wait for you.'

'No. As you like. I pray later.'

We went down the stairs, then back up so Adnan could take a few snaps with his digital camera. As we re-entered the courtyard, prayers ended and the crowd streamed out of the mosque toward the saint's grave.

The streets were congested as usual with bicycles, three-wheeled motor rickshaws, horse-driven tongas and motorbikes. I saw a fully veiled woman carrying fruit. At one of the gates in the Moghal wall, fruit was for sale – bananas, pomegranates, apples. Mangoes were out of season; I had eaten some of the last of them when I arrived in mid-September. Citrus was coming in. Vendors were also selling samosas, pakoras, nan and bowls of fruit salad covered in bright red sauce from carts.

'Iftari foods,' said Adnan. 'People come here and purchase and take home. There is very hustle and bustle. Sir, that's the Lahori Gate.' Over the arch I read:

LAHOREE GATE
Rebuilt 1864
Sir ROBERT MONTGOMERY, K.C.E.
Being Lieutenant Governor
T.R. FORSYTH, C.B.
Commissioner
CAPTAIN HALL, Deputy Commissioner

I bumped into a small man. 'Good morning,' he said.

'Good morning,' I said back.

'He doesn't understand English, but he knows about "Good morning",' said Adnan happily. 'I also don't speak English very well. But Sir Taimur, he says I should speak English, never mind grammatical mistakes. Firstly I must speak English.'

'These are very old houses,' I said. Some parts of the houses looked old, in carved wood. Other parts were concrete. At a shop we saw chickens in cages and a blind man shouting. I asked Adnan what he was saying.

'He is saying everybody is dying, that is why you pray God as much as possible.'

'Is he a beggar?'

'Just like.'

Open sewage flowed down the gutters of the narrow alley where we walked past meat hanging on hooks. 'You see, without even covering the meat, lots of germs,' said Adnan. 'In front of sewerage.' We walked past a man using an old black, pedal-driven sewing machine and a barbershop, and stopped to greet a tooth-less old-timer hunched over a burning hookah.

'This is my grandfather's friend,' Adnan told me. 'He is very rich man. He has lots of agricultural land. His son lives in Defence. But he doesn't want to go Defence. He say, "This where I spent my young age, I like here, I death here."'

One of the famous things about Lahore is Basant, the folk festival in February that seems to be all about flying kites. I quizzed quite a few people about it but could never discern any deeper purpose or meaning. In November it was still several months away, but already on people's minds. You saw colourful paper kites for sale in the markets. There was currently a ban on kite-flying. This was controversial because kite-flying was considered great fun, but there were legitimate safety concerns: children sometimes fell off rooftops and ran into traffic. And the more competitive young men doctored their strings to make them sharp so they could sever rivals' strings in aerial battles.

'But nowadays gummint has great objection over flying kites,' said Adnan.

'Why?' I asked.

'Because sometimes people cut their necks. I think gummint return his objection in Basant. Only Basant. Because lots of foreigners come here and enjoy, and gummint collect lots of foreign currency. Also, bureaucrats also like the Basant activities because meet each other and eat food and congrats.'

We had been walking around inside the old city walls and were now back at the Lahori Gate, where a man tended a large cart piled with dates.

'That's the dates,' said Adnan. 'People purchase because Prophet says, "You open your rosa with dates".'

'Do you open your rosa with dates?'

'Yes.'

'Every day during Ramzan?'

'Yes. But not dates like that. Better quality dates. Fifty or sixty rupees per kg. And that is I think so 35 rupees per kg. Sir, I think it's iftari. I will open my fast. Firstly I will take some water and something, then we will go outside and eat.' He bought some dates. 'These are expensive than other dates. I will eat only one.'

'Why?'

'There is lot of dust. But dates are good – good for health.'

A siren sounded.

'It is the indication to open your fast,' said Adnan.

'But we ate before the siren.'

'But there was already one announcement from the mosque. It's not a problem.'

A man trudged past us pulling a cart that was meant to be drawn by a horse.

'This is old tradition,' Adnan told me. 'But nowadays people prefer rickshaws, like this. Front is bike.' I looked more closely at the rickshaw and, sure enough, the front of the vehicle was a Suzuki motorcycle. The rear wheel had been cut off and a passenger contraption welded onto the frame, with two benches, one facing forward, the other backward.

'Sir,' said Adnan, 'one of my uncle is living in Chicago, and one of my uncle is living in UK, in Birming-gum. And which uncle is living in Birming-gum, he say, "Mr Adnan, you want to visit in London, please you come here." But my mother say, "Firstly you complete your master's. If you get visa before you complete master's, I will not allow you to go." My father was very angry on me. He say, "Why are you going UK? What are doing there? Here you have lots of servants." He is great angry on me. In this way he is very strict man. He won't allow me to go abroad. He say, "You stay here, take care of your business." But I would like to go abroad.'

We were back in his car, driving along a crowded boulevard. On a median island stood some sheep and goats. 'Because Eid is coming and people sacrifice,' said Adnan.

'When we met the old man, was that goat for sacrifice?' I asked.

'No! Because it is black. That is our religious thing, that you get black goat and give it to poor person.'

We passed the train station. A huge new sign over the entrance said LAHORE RAILWAY STATION and, at both ends, 'Coca-Cola'. Near the station were a number of hotels. Most cost four or five hundred rupees per night, said Adnan. The Lahore Hotel was better and cost 1,000 or 1,200. Near the hotels was another big sign saying BIKE MARKET. New and used motorbikes were for sale. In Pakistan the word 'bike' means motorbike; a bicycle is a cycle.

It didn't occur to me this time or on several other visits to reflect on the blood-soaked historical significance of Lahore Station – this very station, built to last and in dignified style by the British, now sponsored by Coca-Cola, was where trains had arrived in 1947 filled with corpses. 'The summer of 1947 was not like other Indian summers,' is the unforgettable first line of Khushwant Singh's classic novel *Train to Pakistan*. It was only near the end of my stay, when I walked past it with an Englishwoman, a Sanskrit scholar named Isabelle Onians, that she reminded me of it.

Oh yes, I thought then. But it was hard to summon the appropriate feelings, and even the twinge of guilt I felt made me annoyed with myself. When the great baseball stadium Comiskey Park was needlessly torn down in Chicago, I told a friend I was sorry I had never seen a game there. 'You should be pissed off,' he corrected me, 'that you can't see a game there *now*.' Of course I rued the death and destruction of the Partition, but its only importance now lay in how the events and choices of that time informed or pre-empted the choices we, the living, made now. That importance was immense and in itself was ample reason to study history. But an earned and applied understanding of history, complete with a tragic sense and a chastened view of human nature, was crucially different from nostalgia and cheap liberal hope.

Adnan had other things on his mind. 'Our railway system is very bad,' he said. 'Only one time I travelled by railway.'

'Where did you go?'

'From Lahore to Rawalpindi.'

'I also took the train from Lahore to Rawalpindi, in 1995,' I said.

'What was your experience of railway?'

'It was slow. Six hours.'

'Yes! It is slow. When I take my car to Islamabad by motorway, it take only three hours and 30 minutes. Police stop me and give me penalty ticket 600 rupees, because he say I'm driving too fastly. I was drive hundred-seventy kilometres per hour, in this car. That was my first experience of motorway.'

It was dark now. We went to Food Street, an impressive strip of restaurants serving kebabs, rice dishes, different kinds of nan, and other delicacies.

'Are you hungry?' I asked Adnan.

'Not much.'

'But you ate only two dates.'

'Yes, I am hungry, but not much. No problem.'

'You ate this morning?'

'I ate two parathas, and some piece of chicken and one egg, and some bananas, and one cup of coffee.'

'At four o'clock?'

'At 4.30. My elder sister or mother prepares, then they intercom me at 4.30. Because my bedroom is upstairs.'

We sat down and ordered some kebabs.

'My younger brother keep fast,' said Adnan. 'He is just nine years old. At three o'clock he say, "Mum, when will rosa open? Because I am hungry." She say, "Be patient for one hour and a half. Then you can eat anything you want." Everybody loves him. He is a lovely child, and a naughty child. He studies at English medium school. I studied at good school, very famous school, but not English medium.'

'Do you wish your parents had sent you to an English medium school?'

'No, because our family is a business-oriented family. Whenever anyone completes his graduation, my father gives him money and says, "Go, start your business."'

One of Adnan's sisters was in her first year of medical studies. The other was in the second year of a master's course in psychology at Punjab University.

'What will she do after she gets her master's?' I asked.

'I think it will be time for her to get married.'

'Will she also work?'

'Yes, she can work if she wants. There is no objection from my family.'

'But maybe her husband won't want her to work?'

'That is up to him. But my father is very strong, and that man won't go against my father.'

We stopped at a McDonald's for ice cream. It was one of only two times in my five months in Lahore that I set foot inside a Western fast food place, and the other time was only to use the toilet. The McDonald's franchise in Lahore was held by Shahbaz Sharif, the more intelligent younger brother of Nawaz Sharif. Both brothers were now in exile. I remarked to Adnan that McDonald's must have been very popular when it first came to Lahore in 1998. There were ads on television commemorating the five-year anniversary.

'Yes, it was very popular,' he said. 'But our religious person, like maulanas, say it's not good foreigner company open their branch in Pakistan. 'You don't go McDonald, blah, blah, blah.' But people don't care about maulanas. People has own life, as like me. I do what I want. I answering in front of God, not maulanas. That is why I don't care maulanas. Otherwise I belong to religious family. My father went in 1997 to Saudi Arabia, to Mecca. My father did his Haj, along with my mum. My father is religious man, but he also don't care about maulanas.'

We went in, ordered sundaes and sat down.

'Strawberry is the best flavour,' said Adnan. 'I like it.'

On another day I found myself at Liberty Market at iftar. A sign on the door of Variety Books said EID CARDS AVAILABLE NOW. The call to prayer came abruptly from the mosque across the street, behind the colourful and aromatic row of flower stalls, and the store staff started drinking water and eating samosas. In the horseshoe-shaped park, small private clusters of people broke the fast together, sitting on the grass. At a stand selling pakoras and samosas the young man insisted I take both; I took two pakoras and one samosa, and he refused payment.

Back at the guesthouse, a young boy was shown singing 'Allah-u-akbar' on the television. 'Karachi iftar,' Shakoor explained.

'Different?'

'Half hour later.'

'Why?'

'Sun problem.'

Just before Shakoor and Nusrat gave me dinner, Hafsa threw a tantrum. She was delightful most of the time, curious and alert, but wilful and in danger of being spoiled. Whenever she cried Shakoor would pick her up, so she learned to cry in order to be picked up and to get her way. This time she refused to give Nusrat some sharp kitchen utensils. When I took them out of her hand, she fell on the floor and screamed. Shakoor picked her up and took her with him to the shop to buy fruit.

This sort of thing was starting to cramp my style, and I decided to discuss it with Nusrat. Feeling foolish, I gave a long speech about how if Hafsa behaved badly, in my opinion she didn't deserve to be picked up and should be left alone. I said that a lot of it was Shakoor's fault because he spoiled her.

'Sir, he's like baby,' said Nusrat. 'Sometimes very much.'

'Yes,' I agreed.

'He say, "I'm right, you wrong."'

'But he's wrong,' I said.

'In Pakistan, all men always right.'

'But that's not true.'

'Yes.'

Shakoor either suffered or feigned chronic headaches; it was hard to tell, because he really was bone lazy. He was a sad sack, with the grudges of the enlisted man. 'Hi. How are you?' I said to him once.

'Head problem, work problem, baby problem,' was his reply. 'Problem, problem, problem. I no fresh man.'

You could cut the tension with a knife that day around the guest-house. 'You and Shakoor are fighting?' I said to Nusrat.

'Not fighting, but not speaking,' she said. 'All day rosa. I tell him go to market, buy fruit. He sleeping all day.'

Shakoor had a long and animated conversation in Urdu with Zarina.

'He'll always be what he is,' Zarina said to me. 'He's complaining about her. I told him, 'You're *nothing* without her."

I asked Zarina what ethnic groups Shakoor and Nusrat belonged to.

'She is a Pathan,' she said.

'Is he a Pathan too?'

'I don't know what he is. Whatever he is, he's incorrigible.'

This was true, but he was also delightful company. A few days into Ramzan I was up at 3 am, awakened by mosquitoes dive-bombing into my ears and by ceaseless prayer amplified over the loudspeaker at the mosque down the street. Later I learned that this was what you might call a Quran-a-thon: a recitation of the entire Quran during the holy month. When I gave up trying to sleep and went downstairs to get coffee, I found Nusrat in the kitchen. She and Shakoor were both awake and eating breakfast by four o'clock. Coffee in Pakistan, incidentally, always means Nescafe instant. You get used to it.

At 5.30, I went down again to send 38 emails I had just written. On the television was an American talk show about unusually fat babies. Shakoor was sitting on the couch under a blanket, with a kitchen towel on his head, reading the Quran. He was a *hafiz* – he had memorised the Quran – and very devout. When he finished reading, he kissed the Quran several times before putting it back on its stand.

'Sir, *bachchi*, two hundred pound!' he said, thrilled at the sheer weirdness of it.

On a Saturday morning during Ramzan, Usman came to the guest-house on his motorbike to take me to the office. It was my day off, but my presence was required by popular demand. The classroom and other rooms allotted to our School of Media and Communications were bare; I had urged the students to put their stamp on it. An alcove of the office Taimur and I shared would work as a student lounge. The students ran with the idea, and Zainab composed a memo to Mrs Shahzad that featured a wish list of furniture and other things they wanted. Mrs Shahzad was supportive and supplied a table and chairs and a couple of couches. I bought maps of Pakistan, Asia and the world for the classroom walls.

So this Saturday morning the students were painting, and they wanted me there. I sat behind Usman on his motorbike. Because both the Upper Mall and Zafar Ali Road were boulevards – Zafar Ali Road's median was the sewage canal – we had to do a U-turn in front of the Gymkhana, then go all the way down Zafar Ali Road to Jail Road and back almost to the Upper Mall again. As we rode, I told Usman that I had been to a party the night before at the house of Ahmed Rashid, the journalist and author of the well-timed bestseller *Taliban*, and that Imran Khan had been there. Usman was impressed.

'Imran Khan is very popular among many people here, including me,' he said. 'I think the next most popular cricketer in Pakistan is Wasim Akram.'

'Is Wasim Akram also retired, or is he still playing?'

'He retired last year, after the World Cup.'

'Are the current stars also popular, like Inzimam and Yusuf Youhana?' I was pleased with myself for being able to drop a couple of names, as if I knew anything about Pakistani cricket.

'Yes, they are popular. But I think Imran Khan and Wasim Akram are superstars because not only are they great cricketers, but they are also handsome.'

I ended up spending a lot of time with Usman. He would become perhaps my most important friend in Pakistan. He had an incisive sensibility that I appreciated and a striver's ambition that I recognised and found congenial.

At the office, the students were painting the alcove in a jazzy pattern of orange and purple stripes. A copy of the 'Books & Authors' supplement from the Karachi-based daily *Dawn* was among the newspapers covering the floor.

'I think you're using some of my newspapers,' I said.

'My father reads 'Books & Authors' regularly,' said Usman. 'But books are so much expensive in Pakistan, especially foreign books, like that book *Homeland*' – my friend Nick Ryan's book about far-right movements in Europe and the US, which I had edited, and parts of which I had assigned the students to read. 'How much would that book cost?'

'About £20, 2,000 rupees,' I said.

'Yes! You see? Recently I looked up online a book about Wasim Akram. I was very much interested to get this book. But then I saw the price – $22! I thought when a pirated copy is sold in Pakistan, I will buy that. Pirated books and CDs are a blessing for us, truly. You can buy a CD for 35 or 40 rupees, containing many softwares. In West, you pay much more and get only one software. So truly it is a blessing for us, even though there is a hue and cry from America that Pakistan should protect intellectual copyrights and things like that.'

This gave me an idea. A few days later I asked Usman to take me to Hafeez Centre, the shopping centre on Main Boulevard that specialised in computers and electronics. We went on his motorbike in mid-afternoon after classes finished. Because it was Ramzan and banks closed early, I had been unable to get cash from my account via the helpful university accountant, Omar Hassan Khan.

'I don't like the early timings in Ramzan,' Usman complained. 'Even in time of Prophet, peace be upon him, people used to fight wars during Ramzan.'

'You think that if they could fight wars, you could keep the banks open?'

'Yes. I think they should have normal timings during Ramzan.'

'You think it's cheating to close early?'

'Yes.'

Usman had a populist sensibility and ideas of economic and social justice that he had learned from his father. His family was not wealthy like most of the other students', and he was keenly aware of the expense of his university fees. His plan in life was to make something of himself, but by the same token he was alert to how the deck was stacked.

'Beef is very expensive,' he said. 'Six months back, it was 80 rupees per kg. Now it's hundred rupees per kg. Because Pakistani beef is exported to UAE for 400 rupees per kg. Same with citrus fruit, and mangoes. Local people are left with B and C class oranges.'

At Hafeez Centre he explained that you could buy non-branded computer systems and get good deals if you were prepared to mix 'n' match. 'First you select the casing,' he said. 'Then you select the hard drive. Then you select the processor. Then you select the motherboard, then they assemble for you. Because branded systems are very expensive.'

I saw branded, used keyboards for 100 rupees, about £1.

'Branded new ones are available for 900 or 1,000 rupees,' said Usman.

I saw a non-branded system advertised on a flyer in a shop window for 4,999 rupees – about £50 or $85. 'Good price,' I said.

'Yeah, but normally good system is available for 10,000 rupees,' he said. £100. 'Branded system – branded used system.' He gestured around at all the shops. 'You see, full of used systems. We can call it technology transfer.'

Usman was in a hurry to get home in time for iftar.

'When people throw iftar parties during Ramzan, is that good or bad?' I asked. Some rich people took Ramzan as an occasion to throw lavish evening parties at the five-star hotels.

'It is a tradition – religious tradition,' said Usman. 'Even if I don't fast – I do fast, but even if I don't fast – if I give iftar party, I get same reward as he who keeps the fast.'

'But aren't you supposed to give food to the poor? Do people give food to the poor?'

'Usually people give iftar parties for same class.'

'Isn't that cheating?'

He misheard me. 'Yes, lot of eating.'

'No,' I said. 'Isn't that *cheating*?'

As he dropped me off in front of the Odeon Hair Salon ('Serving Lahore's Elite since 1956'), Usman said: 'People waste lot of money on useless pursuits. Not in Pakistan, but everywhere in the world.'

One Friday morning, instead of the usual computer lab time, I gathered the students in their newly decorated lounge to watch *The Quiet American*, the adaptation of Graham Greene's novel starring Michael Caine and Brendan Fraser. The novel had long been a touchstone for me; I had read it at least four times and had bought a pirated copy on the street in Hanoi. It was prescient about the Vietnam War and, intriguingly, Greene wrote in his autobiography *Ways of Escape* that it includes more direct reportage than any of his other novels. It also is one of three novels that are required reading for any Westerner living in Southeast Asia. (The other two are *Burmese Days* by George Orwell and *A Woman of Bangkok* by Jack Reynolds.)

The dangerously innocent title character, Pyle, can be taken as a personification, almost a caricature, of his country. The narrator's famous line is: 'I never knew a man who had better motives for all the trouble he caused.' The narrator, Fowler, is a grizzled foreign correspondent for *The Times* of London. 'I am a reporter; God exists only for leader-writers,' he says in the novel. The two men are rivals for the love of a Vietnamese woman, Phuong. I thought the movie would expose the students to a bit of history as well as give us an occasion to discuss the practice and history of international journalism.

Ayela Deen rented it and brought it in. The pirated DVD started skipping and freezing during the climactic scene, so she had to get another copy over the weekend so we could finish watching it on Monday. The girls had a lot to say about it.

'I don't think he should have been killed,' complained Zunera. 'That's sad.'

'She's such a loser,' said Ayela.

'Yeah, she's like a porcelain doll,' said Sadaf. 'She is so ugly. They should have selected a more beautiful girl. It would have been believable that he would leave his wife.'

I thought Do Hai Yen was gorgeous, and that the reserve and tact with which she played Phuong were exquisite.

'This is the first nice dress she's worn in the entire film,' said Zainab during the last scene.

'She should have gone for the younger one,' said Sadaf.

'Uh, excuse me, but he just died,' said Zainab.

'He shouldn't have died,' said Sadaf.

'I feel sorry for the hero,' said Zunera.

'Who's the hero?' I asked. I thought the hero was Fowler.

'Pyle,' she said.

On 15 November, while I was watching the *World Sport* show on CNN covering the tennis Masters semi-finals (Roddick v Federer, Agassi v Schuettler), a 'Breaking News' item scrolled across the screen: 16 people – 17, 20, 23: it was hard to keep pace, as the number kept rising – had been killed by two car bomb attacks on synagogues in Istanbul. I watched the unfolding story with Nusrat and Shakoor. They didn't understand the word 'synagogue'.

'Like mosques for Jewish people,' I told them.

'Everywhere world problem,' said Nusrat, ruefully.

After a while I changed the channel to the sitcom *Friends*.

'This much better,' she said. 'No problems. Always happy, happy, happy!'

Nusrat and I watched quite a few reruns of *Friends* together. Sometimes we took turns controlling the remote: she would watch an Indian soap opera, then I would switch to *Friends*. She didn't understand much of the dialogue, but she enjoyed the zaniness of some of the episodes, like the one where Joey and Chandler leave Ross' baby on the bus, or the one where Ross is rushing everyone to get ready for a fancy-dress function at his museum. She thought it was funny that they all sat around together all the time in the same coffee shop, and she was curious about the things she learned from the show about life in America. She liked trying to keep track of who was associated with whom and in what way. I cringed whenever I watched anything sexually suggestive with her, or when I had to interpret certain differences between Pakistani and American customs. 'Women and women marriage?' she asked me, puzzled, when there was a scene showing Ross talking with his ex-wife and her lesbian lover.

Like many Pakistanis, including some educated ones, Nusrat thought that no Jews had died in the World Trade Center and that US intelligence had known about and declined to prevent the 11 September attacks. But she was intelligent and curious about the world outside Pakistan, while at the same time maintaining a strong sense of who she was: she had integrity, in a context that had meaning and purpose for her. She always dressed and behaved with great decorum. She knew that I was from a different, non-Muslim world, and that was all right with her. She had enough human sympathy and imagination to consider how strange Pakistani mores might seem to me. 'Sir, see my burkah!' she said, and showed it to me, one time when she was preparing to visit her home village in the North-West Frontier Province. I smiled, imagining her in the village or on the bus, to the eye just another faceless Ninja Turtle, and thinking how privileged I was to have come to know her as an individual.

Friends was shown on an all-sitcom cable channel that used a voting system to determine which show to air next. Whenever an episode finished, for the next five minutes the screen would show a chart listing the options and a phone number, with a numbered code for voting. We watched *Friends* on this channel most often because it was the show people voted for the most. At the university, I often caught my students watching *Friends* when they should have been watching the news on Geo or CNN or the BBC. But *Mr Bean* was popular too, partly because its humour was visual rather than verbal. Nusrat liked it because Mr Bean reminded her of her husband. She also liked *Full House* because the kids were cute, and a 1970s-era British show about an English class for immigrants called *Mind Your Language*, which is funny but no longer shown in Britain because it's considered racist. ('What is the population of England?' the stern headmistress asks the class. 'English,' answers one of the students. 'Not anymore,' rejoins the headmistress.)

A steady stream of bad news was coming out of Iraq. The day after the synagogue bombings in Istanbul, 17 US soldiers were killed when two Black Hawk helicopters collided and crashed under fire, and we watched a BBC talk show on which a *Wall Street Journal* reporter, a German radio journalist, and an Arab reporter discussed how the situation in Iraq might affect the presidential election in the US.

'About American election,' I explained to Nusrat.

'And Bush is win election?'

'Bush *wants* to win election.'

'But Pakistani news say Bush popularity very down.'

'Yes.' I thought about how to express some complex things. 'Bush didn't win the last election,' I said.

The Nepali word *nakkali* had come to mind the previous day, when I had discussed with Shakoor an internet access card he had bought for me that had turned out to be nakkali. The shopkeeper had refused to give a refund. I had felt especially disgusted that the guy's policy was no refund if the card had been scratched to reveal the username – the only way to tell if it worked was to scratch it. It was a bait and switch trick, but what the hell, this was Asia. 'Shop man cheating man,' Shakoor had said to me in commiseration.

'Nakkali election,' I explained to Nusrat. I wondered if the word meant the same in Urdu as in Nepali; some words, including numbers, are the same or very similar in the two languages.

Nusrat's face brightened and she laughed.

'Every year in Pakistan is nakkali election,' she said. 'Musharraf is nakkali referendum. Jamali is nakkali prime minister. All politicians nakkali.'

I learned a lot from watching TV with Nusrat. On 24 November the 'Breaking News' on CNN was that John Mohammed, the sniper who had terrorised the Washington, DC area in the autumn of 2002, had been sentenced to death. I explained the story and the verdict to Nusrat. The news gave me the same chill I had felt when Timothy McVeigh was executed. She thought the sentence was just fine. Then she said:

'Sir, before 30 years my father killed a man. Big man!' She gestured to indicate a fat man. 'Another man killed my father's cousin. And he attempt my father. My father attempt another man's brother and kill him. He is in jail seven years. Then he relief …'

'Released?'

'Yes, release. And then he married. He supposed to in jail 14 years, but thanks to Allah he release. Then he married. Pathans.'

Zarina Sadik returned, after a week or more packing up her household in Islamabad to move to her new house in the Defence area of Lahore. She had found supervising and negotiating with the movers trying. 'He told me 8 to 4.30 they would work,' she told me. 'I said, 'Look, I'll give your men iftar and dinner. There's a mosque down the street.' So they worked until 8.30.'

I had been lonely in the guesthouse without her, but her absence also spurred me to take more initiative on my own behalf and coincided with what I felt as a turning point. I was now nearly halfway through my time in Lahore, and I felt both greater urgency and a preemptive nostalgia. The passage of time is a sad thing.

By way of greeting, Zarina shook my hand. Hugs weren't the done thing here between women and men. On the other hand, men hugged each other all the time.

'It's getting cold in Islamabad,' Zarina said.

It was already chilly in the mornings and evenings even here in Lahore. I had started to feel the change of season riding behind Shakoor on his motorbike without a jacket.

We sat together in the lounge, one last time. 'Would you like more grandchildren?' I asked.

'Yes, I'd like a couple more,' she said. 'I'd like a couple of little girls running around.'

'You should nag your sons, then.'

'I've been nagging them for years. My sister said to me, "Tell your sons to stop firing blanks!"'

The next morning, well after sunrise, I found her in the lounge drinking tea and smoking a cigarette.

'You're not keeping the fast,' I said.

'It's too much for me, with all the packing and moving,' she admitted.

'It's permissible to break the fast when you're travelling, right?'

'No, there's no excuse for me. It's just beyond me this year.'

CHAPTER NINE

WHAT I DID DURING EID

In October I had gone to Islamabad to visit a fascinating German woman, Helga Ahmed. She was a friend of Isa Daudpota's, and I had included her piece on Western media, Afghan refugees and historical memory in the collection of writings I edited after 11 September 2001. Helga and her Pakistani husband Jamil had met in 1955, when Helga was 18 years old, at the British Council in London. Jamil was now retired from a long career in the civil service. In their early married life he had been posted in remote areas without electricity or running water, and they had no car; they had used a horse-drawn tonga or walked. Jamil had a reputation for unbending integrity. 'All the other boys used to go in their fathers' official cars, and I rode on a cycle until the cycle was stolen,' their son Temur told me.

In the 1970s, Jamil had been posted to Kabul as the Minister for Economic Affairs at the Pakistani embassy. The family had lived through the 1978 coup that preceded the Russian invasion of Afghanistan. 'The whole thing was like a comic opera,' remembered Jamil. 'This fellow in Ariana Airlines, he was having an affair with a girl in the royal family, Daoud's family. The royal family decided to kill him. He looked like a Communist newspaper editor, who was killed instead. I'm glad I was able to be there, seeing things happen before my eyes. Because reading it in a book is different from actually seeing it.'

In the early 1980s Jamil had been posted to Quetta, capital of Pakistan's remote Balochistan province, where they had seen Afghan mujahedin tell girls shopping in the market: 'If we see you again with your bare hands, we will chop them off.'

'When the Westerners say female education was stopped because of the Taliban, it was stopped because of the mujahideen much earlier,' said Helga. 'The Kalashnikov took over. There were more of these freedom fighters moving around than our own people.'

Helga had found her calling as a one-woman jihad against societal evils. She was what Americans call a buttinski — someone who butts into other people's business. 'In Pakistan we have too many NGOs,' she complained. 'And the NGOs are absolutely useless. They're only interested in perpetuating themselves.' When I asked if she had converted to Islam, she told me, 'I did. But it didn't make any difference, because my parents had already left the Church. We were neither Catholics nor Protestants. But I use it when I have arguments. I quote the Quran and say I am a very good Mussulman.'

One of Helga's hobbyhorses was biogas plants, vats that produce gas for cooking from fermented animal dung. I went one day to see them in a village outside Rawalpindi, with Helga and her daughter-in-law, Fawzya Minallah.

'What about the human thing?' asked Fawzya. 'Can't they use that?'

'Ja, but that is much more complicated in our Muslim society,' said Helga. 'We tried that, but they rejected it.'

Fawzya was frankly admiring. 'Other women of Auntie Helga's — how shall I say? — age and class, they are busy in coffee malls, having chitchat,' she told me. 'She spends her time here.'

Fawzya was an artist and took pleasure in beautiful, well-crafted things. She pointed out the design on the outer wall of the village mosque. 'Do you see what they've made that out of? Broken plates and dishes!' Admiring a carved doorway she said, 'All this must be very old. So beautiful. I love these.' She made visits to French Colony, the Christian slum in Islamabad, where she taught the children to draw and make Christmas cards. She didn't go through any NGO or intermediary; she just showed up. When they saw her, the children cried, '*Drawing-wallah bhaji!* – Drawing auntie!'

'I've never seen myself doing big, ambitious things,' she told me. 'I see myself doing small, intimate things.'

Fawzya also had been a political cartoonist for the newspaper *The Muslim* during the Zia regime. She showed me some of her cartoons. One depicted Uncle Sam tossing wind-up dolls, labelled with names like Marcos, Samoza and Duvalier, into the trash. One doll had no name and was shown from the back, holding a whip. 'I got a call from this guy,' said Fawzya, 'and he said, "Can you tell me who is this one?" I said, "The best art keeps you guessing." He said, "It looks like Zia ul Haq." I said, "Well, you're right!"'

Helga had left her mark on the village. 'See that plant?' said Fawzya. 'That's basil. That's Auntie Helga. You will see it at my mother's house, and at my house too. Auntie Helga is always telling us to grow it. So you can see the influence of one person.'

'When I go back to Germany, my friends are going into the woods and the meadows to pick plants to make their herbal tea,' said Helga. 'Even today. So you see it is around us, at least for my generation.'

As we drove back to Islamabad she said to me: 'You noticed in the village there was no reaction to you.'

'I wasn't sure whether I should greet the women or not,' I said.

'No, in the village it's a very open society. They don't keep purdah. That happens when you are moving towards the city.'

'Why?'

'You see, in the villages, in one way or another everybody is related to one another.'

She pointed out some rock formations. 'If you ever come this way again, these rocks will be nonexistent,' she said in a tone that expressed severe disapproval in its very matter-of-factness. 'Already they have made white marks, what has to be cut.'

'There's a lot of this kind of formation in Colorado,' I said.

'Ah cha,' she said. 'But they don't cut it down. Look at these trees.'

The dead trees were Indian rosewood. 'They've been dying out all over the Punjab,' said Helga. 'Their roots aren't finding enough moisture.' New housing and eucalyptus were using up all the ground water. Helga stopped the pickup and spoke to two men sitting by the roadside.

'They have no idea,' she said. 'I ask him why the trees have died, he doesn't know. I ask him what kind of trees he's planting, he says eucalyptus. I ask if he knows that it causes a lot of problems, he says yes, he knows. I ask him if he knows why, he doesn't know.' She spoke again to the man in Urdu. I caught the word 'Australia.' The British- and American-owned Pakistan Tobacco Company used 100,000 eucalyptus trees only for the curing of tobacco leaves, and one eucalyptus tree consumed 70 litres of water per day and grew for seven years before being cut. 'So where does your water table go to? And we are blaming the common man for deforestation. My other problem with tobacco is the pesticides.'

I saw her in action again when she dropped me off at the shuttle from Islamabad to the Daewoo bus station in Rawalpindi. 'Hello,' she said to several young men standing around smoking.

'Hello, Auntie,' they said.

'You fellows seem to be enjoying your smokes.'

'Yeah,' said one of them sheepishly.

'Do you know what tobacco does to you?'

At the end of November I returned, because Fawzya had invited me to spend Eid, the festival that marks the end of Ramzan, with her family. I took the opportunity of a long holiday from classes to get out of Lahore. I stayed overnight with Helga and Jamil, then rode with Fawzya, her husband Temur and their two young sons to her family's house in Sirikot, a large village in the hills in the North-West Frontier Province.

'Islamabad is going to extend to here,' said Fawzya, at least 20 minutes outside the city. 'It's going to have a severe water problem.'

Temur was driving. The boys and I were in the back seat. We passed an obelisk on a hill, which Temur said was called the Nicholson Monument. 'This man was named Nicholson, and he was a sort of a political agent in this area in the British time,' he said. 'And he was pretty terrible. He raised a regiment of Pathans. Pathans, as you know, will fight for anyone who pays them. So in 1857 he raised a regiment of Pathans and went to fight against this Mutiny in Delhi. And in Delhi he was wounded, and he died of his wounds. Some of these Pathans, they worshipped him like he was a god.'

'Even though they were Muslims?'

'Even though they were Muslims.'

I thought of the Matopos, the rock formation I had visited in southern Zimbabwe where Cecil Rhodes had asked to be buried, and of the strangely anachronistic reverence in which many Zimbabweans, black and white, held him still.

We went through a town called Hassan Abdal.

'This is a Sikh centre,' said Temur.

'Are there still Sikhs living here?'

'Yeah, very few, but pilgrims come from India every year for a festival.'

Outside the town, nomads lived in tents along the roadside. These were 'criminal tribes', said Temur. Certain tribes had to register with the police whenever they went to a new town. The term dated from the British time.

'Lots of eucalyptus,' I remarked.

'Fawzya's father is responsible for some of it,' said Temur.

'Yah,' Fawzya acknowledged. 'At that time I think there was not an awareness. It was just this amazing tree that grew so fast.'

The boys were eating chocolate chip cookies. 'You know in Ramzan, even if you're not fasting, you have to be very careful about not eating in public,' said Fawzya. 'So when it's over, it feels strange.'

I told her that in 1995 two men had approached me on the street in Lahore and politely asked me to put away the Coke I was drinking.

'It's so stupid,' she said. 'In other Muslim countries, in liberal countries like Thailand and Malaysia, they don't make you feel that way. Here they're so touchy. I have very low blood pressure, so when I fast I get terrible headaches. Even though I don't keep rosa, I go to my mother's house, where she has a very elaborate iftar every day. I really like the atmosphere. But nowadays the trend is for even young kids to keep rosa. The Quran says you should keep rosa from age twelve, but nowadays kids as young as six are keeping rosa.'

The boys started saying, 'Are we there yet?'

'Yes, we're here,' said Temur. 'Would you like to get out?'

'No! Tell the truth!' They smacked him on the face from behind his headrest.

'We are here. You can get out if you want.'

'No! Are we there yet!? How much longer?'

The younger boy had round glasses like Harry Potter.

'Hey, Harry Potter, are you bored yet?' I said.

'Harry Potter. I'm not Harry Potter.' He pointed at his brother. '*You're* Harry Potter!'

'You know what you are?' said the older brother, and whispered in his ear.

'I know you are, but what am I?' said Harry Potter.

'I know you are, but what am I?' said his brother.

We turned left onto a smaller road and headed towards the mountains. The road was lined by eucalyptus, with open fields behind.

'These are the eucalyptus Fawzya's father planted,' said Temur.

'There used to be a *really* big Afghan refugee camp right here, but now it's finished,' Fawzya told me.

'Did they go back?'

'Yes. They've been here for 15 years.'

The road twisted through the mountains. In the far distance were snow-capped peaks.

'That is the Hindu Kush,' Temur told me.

'Is that in Afghanistan?'

'No. Afghanistan is very far from here. That is towards Gilgit area.'

'Do you see that blue thing down there?' said Fawzya. 'That is the lake of the Tarbela dam. And it is so much lower than it used to be.'

'It's a bit better this year,' said Temur. 'But it will be lower soon, because they'll have to release some water for the crop season.'

Fawzya's family home in Sirikot was a spacious two-story house on a hilltop, overlooking the village. On the walls were snapshots of family members with Z.A. Bhutto, Gaddafi ('my best wishes/ Col. M.G.'), Princess Diana and the boxer Mohammed Ali. There were also posed group pictures with captions: 'Farewell to Hon. Mr. Justice Qaisar Khan on retirement on 30-7-1978', 'Cambridge University Faculty of Law 1996', 'University of Peshawar Economic Society 1952–53'. We had an informal but ample meal of different kinds of rice and meat, then whiled away the afternoon.

Fawzya's mother had been a Member of the National Assembly in the Zia time. 'Did you worry about Fawzya, when she was drawing the cartoons?' I asked her as I helped myself to a second helping.

She laughed. 'She even made a cartoon of me!' she said. It had depicted Zia giving plots of land to MNAs, who followed him like the Pied Piper.

From the balcony, I watched the boys lighting firecrackers in a plastic Coke bottle and a metal can. Fawzya and one of her brothers stood below me, also watching. Fawzya admonished them in Urdu or Pushtu; I caught the English phrase 'dangerous fumes'.

'These are firecrackers?' I asked her brother.

'Yes,' he replied. 'Eid special.'

'And Fawzya doesn't approve.'

'Yes. I went and bought toys for all the kids. And they all got guns, except for Fawzya's son. He said, 'No, I'll have a car.''

In the lounge, the conversation turned to politics. 'If there's one thing that Bhutto deserved to be hanged for, it's for rebuilding the army after 1971,' said Temur.

'I'm not sure he deserved to hang for that,' said Fawzya's sister-in-law, Ghazala.

'If there's one thing he deserved it for, it was that,' Temur insisted. 'He should have kept it down when he had the chance. Instead he gave it a free hand in Balochistan, and he created a monster.'

Talk about politics and history in Pakistan always seemed to revolve around what-ifs and regrets. 'It would have been so easy to rebuild Afghanistan,' said Temur, who had worked there in UN anti-narcotics programmes. 'All you needed was to choose one credible man to be in charge – Karzai is a nonentity – and a bit of money. Use it to employ a lot of people in big projects, so they're busy doing something useful, instead of lying around smoking cannabis and thinking about whom to kill.'

Night fell, and I found myself outside looking out over the village with the quieter of Fawzya's two brothers, Akmal. The village was fully lit by electricity, but stars were visible in the clear night sky.

WHAT I DID DURING EID

The only sound was the chirp of crickets.

'Your book that you're writing,' said Akmal politely. 'Is it fiction or non-fiction?'

It always irritated me when Pakistanis asked about my book, because next they usually told me what sort of book to write. 'You can't write a book about Pakistan unless you learn Urdu fluently/travel everywhere in the country/spend a lot of time in Peshawar' was a refrain I heard often.

'Non-fiction,' I said. 'I want it to be a book of journalism and contemporary history, a portrayal of this country in this historical moment, but one that people will still want to read ten or 20 years from now. I think a lot of books of journalism suffer by becoming dated too quickly.'

'There have been some books about Pakistan that have proven very popular, such as the one called *Waiting for Allah*,' he said. 'And the other one.'

'*Breaking the Curfew*.'

'Yes.'

'Which one is better?'

He paused for thought. 'Frankly,' he said, 'I can't remember which is which. Which is the one that was written by Christina Lamb?'

'*Waiting for Allah*.'

'Yes. I remember that I liked her descriptions of things, like houses in Islamabad. But other than that, I can't remember much. It's been too long.'

I pointed out that *Waiting for Allah* was published in 1991 and *Breaking the Curfew* by Emma Duncan was published in 1989. 'Part of my purpose with my book,' I said, 'is to update the story. Those books were published 15 years ago. A lot has happened since then.'

'A lot has happened since then,' he agreed.

I told him I had first visited Pakistan in the mid-1990s.

'That was when people took an interest in politics and debated things,' he said. 'Now, nobody talks about politics.'

'Why not?'

'I think they realise that the army is in power for the foreseeable future, and that the only force that can offer any resistance to the army is the mullahs.'

'What if the mullahs were to come in?'

'The top mullahs have always supported the army. But the lower-ranking ones, and those who support them, have their own priorities. And they have jihadis and guns of their own.'

'So Musharraf has to be careful with the mullahs,' I suggested as we walked back inside to dinner.

'Yes. Or he will be destroyed by this Frankenstein's monster he has created.'

'Just like Bhutto was destroyed by the Frankenstein's monster he created?'

'Yes.'

I stayed up late talking with Ghazala and her husband, Fawzya's other brother Athar. Like many Pakistani married couples, Ghazala and Athar were first cousins. Both were lawyers.

'I was actually very depressed on the 12th of October 1999' – the day of the coup – 'though I had no love lost for Nawaz Sharif,' said Athar. 'Because one thing I believe in very strongly is the supremacy of the constitution. For democracy to work, it needs at least 25–30 years uninterrupted. Supremacy of the constitution is closely linked to rule of law, because if the supreme law is not respected, who will respect other laws?'

In February 2000, Musharraf had required Supreme Court justices to take a fresh oath.

'The first thing I do when I get out of bed is, I pick up the newspaper and scan the headlines,' Athar said. 'I saw this headline that said the Supreme Court justices were to take a fresh oath that day. It was not announced a day earlier; it was announced the same day. There at home I wrote a handwritten petition, and I went to the Supreme Court. Because my father-in-law used to be a justice of the Supreme Court, the steno typist had become like part of our family. He was then the deputy registrar of the Court. He said, "What are you doing here?" I said that I have a petition.

'I saw the justices coming out from the corridor, and they were being led by the senior-most justice, Justice Irshad Hassan Khan. He was the senior-most because reportedly the Chief Justice then, Justice Saeed-uz-Zaman Siddiqui, was detained that day and not allowed to go out of his house, because they didn't want that he should be administered the new oath. The effect of that was that Justice Irshad Hassan Khan was then to become the Chief Justice of the Supreme Court of Pakistan.

'I approached him, and I said, "Your lordship, I have a grievance." He said, "What is it about?" I said it was about the oath that they had to take. And the moment they heard that, they all rushed to their parked cars, and he asked me to submit it to the office of the registrar. I had not expected that. I thought that they would at least hear me and summarily dismiss my grievance. Because there is a plethora of case law that says a technicality should not interfere with justice. So they should at least hear my petition. They didn't expect that I would come alone, just like that. Because here in Pakistan, people think that anything that happens is part of some conspiracy, or part of some big plan.'

Athar had then gone into the chambers of Justice Nasir Aslam Zahed, where he found the five justices who had decided not to take the new oath.

'You see, in Pakistan there's an elite class, a very strong elite class,' he explained. 'Democracy doesn't suit that elite class, because it diminishes their role. If you are exposed to life in Lahore, you will become aware of who is that elite class. The elite class, they are one, and all these stories relate to elite class. Here, you see, because there are no institutions, personalities are what matter. If I am a very resourceful person, everyone will want to get close to me.'

Justice Nasir Aslam Zahed, who was retiring in two weeks, said: 'Young man, we appreciate what you state in your petition. But we have already decided not to take the oath.'

'I give Nasir Aslam Zahed the benefit of doubt, because as Chief Justice of the Sindh High Court he had a good reputation for public interest litigation,' Athar told me. 'Even if someone sent him a telegram or a handwritten letter, he would convert it into a petition. So I give him benefit of the doubt. But at that time it was his action that was causing my petition not to be entertained. He was arguing on behalf of all the justices. He was asking me not to embarrass them. Because everyone is afraid of the army. I can understand their dilemma. They might have thought I was from some agency. Because as I told you, in Pakistan anything that you do, the first impression is that there has to be something behind this.

'There's one question you haven't asked me, and that I think you should ask me,' he added. 'If I took this petition to the Supreme Court, why did I take a position as a minister in the same government?'

Athar had been Minister of Law and Local Government in the NWFP provincial government before the elections of 10 October 2002.

'Everyone had accepted that timeframe of three years,' he said. Musharraf had promised elections within three years of the coup. 'There was no protest. I was probably genuinely convinced that what General Pervez Musharraf was doing, he was doing to improve the situation.'

'At the time, it seemed to be the right decision,' said Ghazala. 'But as time has passed, all this accountability stuff has turned out to be a farce.'

'I have actually to come across a person who would actually leave power,' said Athar. 'Because it's a beautiful feeling when you are there. I've taken a few drives in official limousines, and it's a beautiful feeling. Musharraf is not evil, you see. But the compromises he has made …'

At another point, Ghazala said: 'People in America are totally brainwashed by this Fox News.'

I explained to her what I thought about America: that anyone there can know the truth if he or she wants, but most don't want to make the effort; that 11 September had been such a shock because it brutally demonstrated to Americans what the world is really like; that Americans prefer to locate evil outside themselves.

'But it's good not to know the truth,' said Athar. 'Ignorance is bliss.'

The Minallahs were Pathans, and most of their connections were in the Frontier. I asked them what it had been like here during the war in Afghanistan.

'In Peshawar, everyone was depressed,' said Athar. 'In Islamabad there was a bit less of a feeling of depression or resentment. In Lahore, it was practically nonexistent. All the restaurants were open. They were too far from the actual scene, you see.' People in the Frontier 'voted for the mullahs, without being fanatics. They voted for the mullahs out of reaction against the present government or against the United States. And then there was also another fear, of Pakistan being one of the targets. Because until 9/11, Pakistan was on the verge of being declared a terrorist state.'

Near midnight, Athar concluded: 'This is a very fertile country, in every way. And there are so many intelligent people here. They need good leadership.'

'All the flaws of the system and of the man notwithstanding, can Musharraf provide that leadership?' I asked.

'The system does not favour him. I think he has missed that opportunity.'

* * *

Ghazala's father, Syed G. Safdar Shah, had been Chief Justice of the Peshawar High Court. 'From my childhood, I always remember him being depressed about Pakistan,' Ghazala told me the next day, sitting on a charpoy behind the house. 'He was always upset about what was going on.'

Ghazala's father and Z.A. Bhutto had been adversaries. 'They knew each other from their student days,' she said. 'You could say there was a personality clash. He didn't dislike Bhutto as such, but when he disliked anything that Bhutto did, he openly criticised him. Bhutto had a major problem with that.' Bhutto, she said, had changed the retirement age for judges in order to force her father off the bench. When Bhutto went on trial for murder, 'Zia was trying to shape the Supreme Court, to get the judges who would give a verdict against Bhutto. And he thought my father would be an ideal candidate, because of his grudge against Bhutto.'

But her father had refused to join the slim majority that condemned Bhutto to hang. 'It was a split decision, four to three. But you don't hang a person on such a split decision. My father was absolutely, 100 per cent convinced that it was a conspiracy, that no way could someone be convicted of murder based on such evidence.'

The family had been forced into exile in Britain. 'You can't imagine the state of our family at the time. We were so upset because we were *personally* involved in it. He was very guilty about the fact that because of what he did, the whole family was uprooted, even though we kept drumming it into him that we were proud of what he did. Anybody who knew my father, any of the lawyers in the Frontier, knew that he would never do anything against his conscience.'

Her father died in Britain in December 1986. Earlier that year, Benazir Bhutto had returned to Pakistan. 'The day before, she called up my father and had a long conversation with him,' Ghazala said.

'And he was advising her, because maybe he thought she would do better than her father. They used to visit us quite often in London, her and her mother. You could say that she and her mother had a special thing for my father, because they knew he had reasons to go with Zia, but he didn't. They had a lot of respect for him for that reason. I remember him telling her that "Don't surround yourself with sycophants." I remember that word. And he told her to listen to criticism and not to make the same mistakes which her father did. The vote bank for the PPP is still there, because of her father, despite the fact that she blew it twice.'

I asked Ghazala if she thought Benazir could ever come back, or if she wanted to.

'For somebody who has had the taste of power, for her to live in a flat in central London must be suffocating,' she said. 'She's far too ambitious ever to give up politics. The problem is that every time they come into power, the whole of their time is spent obliging their sycophants and taking revenge on their enemies. And I can't imagine it would be any different next time.'

Within 24 hours, I felt comfortable and familiar with this effortlessly hospitable family. I told Ghazala that I felt it as a great privilege and gift, a fringe benefit – rather a central benefit – of my work, to have met so many kind and interesting people and seen so many places around the world. 'I see that as a tribute to Pakistani hospitality,' I said.

'Well, you're not exactly the most difficult person to welcome,' she said, graciously.

Akmal took me on a short walk, to a hilltop where we could see neighbouring valleys and part of the lake created by the Tarbela dam, to a madrassa or religious school where we had tea, and to a cemetery. Back at the house he asked if I wanted to see the dam and lake from the other end of the village before it got dark. I said sure, so we got in his car.

'The valley where the dam is now used to be very fertile,' he said.

'So is the dam a good thing?'

'For the people of this area, yes, because it provides them with employment. But the people who used to live in that valley lost their land.'

'Were they given compensation?'

'Litigations are still going on.'

On the way down to the village, we passed four men we had met at the madrassa. Akmal offered them a ride to the top of a nearby hill, so all four crammed into the back seat, and we went there instead. Half a dozen times, we passed pairs or small groups of men on the road. Each time we stopped to greet them with handshakes and ritual hugs.

'*Assalam-u-aleikum.*'

'*Wa aleikum assalam.*'

I felt at once bereft and liberated by the sensation of being out of email contact. Temur and Fawzya had gone back to Islamabad, and I had sent my laptop back with them.

'I'm glad to be unreachable,' I said.

'Actually, you can access internet even here,' Akmal informed me. 'I checked my email yesterday.'

'That destroys my illusion,' I said, and he laughed.

There was a melancholy about this family. Perhaps they had experienced too much history. Ghazala and Athar and their teenagers and Athar's mother returned to Islamabad, leaving me alone with Akmal. At dinner the next evening, he told me about his plan to emigrate to Canada. He was an accountant, with a master's degree in accountancy and a bachelor's in medicine.

'I have two reasons,' he said. 'One is that one should have an international passport other than one's own, so that one can travel freely. Second is that I feel obligation to my son. At least I feel secure that my daughter has a choice.' His daughter was three, and his son was six. His daughter had been born in the United States.

'I think these borders will become more and more impermeable,' said Akmal. 'I see it as a natural phenomenon, the way population in developing countries is increasing and population in developed countries is static. It's like in science, where all these molecules from unsaturated try to enter saturated.'

After 11 September, Canada had raised the eligibility score needed to qualify for 'skilled worker immigration'. Points were awarded for age, language proficiency, work experience, academic qualifications. 'You have to get so many points out of a hundred,' Akmal explained. 'Before September 11 it was 70, then they raised it to 75. Now they lowered it to 67. I have 72. My greatest fear while applying for a visa is standing in the queue. It's a nightmare. It makes you feel small. Now it's good they've started doing it through the mail. Before that, people used to get up at five o'clock in the morning to stand in the queues. But it's again extremely inconvenient, because you have to plan at least one month ahead.'

I kept Akmal and the cook waiting the next morning, while I wrote up notes in my notebook. We planned to climb a small mountain nearby.

'Even close to noon we're in shadow,' I observed at the bottom.

'Yes, it's strange,' he said. 'At this time of year, sometimes you're too hot in the sun, and then you're cold.'

'You're never completely comfortable,' I agreed. 'Does it get hot here in the summer?'

'Yes. For few weeks it is hot. Few years back, you didn't need an air conditioner. But now climate has changed, and one really needs an air conditioner in the summer.'

The terraced fields on the hillside were dry, stony and empty. Akmal said some would be planted to wheat. Flat stones – slate – lay scattered everywhere, and retaining walls for the fields had been made from them, without cement.

'This slate is everywhere, even in the fields,' I said.

'This is a real problem with this Tarbela dam,' he said. 'Because the catchment area is filling up. Every time it rains, these slates go down and fill up the catchment area. Musharraf is always talking about how we need new dams, like this Kalabagh dam. And he's right, because these other dams are filling up.'

'But won't the Kalabagh dam have the same problem?'

'At least in the short term, at least for next 20–25 years, it will solve the problems we have because the other dams are filling up.'

'Then what?'

'I don't know!'

Halfway up the mountain, Akmal said he needed a rest. He was my age, in his late thirties, but plump and unfit. We saw a couple of small clusters of people in the distance below, walking along the road. The madrassa we had visited the day before was on the hilltop opposite.

'This is new road to Islamabad,' said Akmal.

'Not the one we came on?'

'No. This one is under construction. That one is 19 kilometres of mountainous terrain. This one is ten kilometres. And plus, this one is not so tortuous as the other one, I think.'

The cook and another servant had driven up in the family's Suzuki van and were waiting for us here. We drove the rest of the way up along a narrow, hair-raising road, through several small villages. When the van got stuck we walked the rest of the way, along a ridge.

'This mountain is called Mountain of Martyrs,' said Akmal. 'Because when the Sikhs invaded Sirikot, the local people sent their women and children up to hide. But then the children were discovered, and about 150 children were killed by the Sikhs.'

'Is this the top?' I asked.

'Yes. This is where they say the children were killed.'

Two local men laid out a rug for us with water, tea and biscuits.

'You sit here, sit there,' said one. 'No sofa.'

'No chair,' said the cook. 'This is chair!' He pointed at a rock.

In Asia, you can never just hike somewhere and then sit down and relax; you have to be served and told what to notice. I felt irritable, wanting the solitude I knew I couldn't have. I sat on a rock writing notes, including the previous sentence. An old man squatted on the slate and read what I had written, without asking permission. A younger man with an especially well-groomed beard greeted me.

'He is our holy pir,' he said. 'Imam. We are his followers.'

The old man read my words haltingly aloud, to show that he could read English. It turned out he was a teacher in a local high school.

There was a small shrine on this hilltop, festooned with bits of coloured cloth. 'Have you been to Tata Durbar in Lahore?' Akmal asked me. 'That is the most famous shrine in Pakistan.'

'Is that the one with the famous drummer?'

'Yes. Papu Sai or something like that.'

'Yes, I've been there,' I said. I had spent several hours at the Shah Jamal shrine one Thursday night listening to Navid Shahzad's son, Farhad, jam on the drums with Papu Sai. It had been quite an experience, with frenzied dancing and hypnotic, endless drumming well into the wee hours, and a pervasive aroma of ganja.

'Actually, such big shrines can be very lucrative,' said Akmal. 'People give millions of rupees in donations. So caretakers of such shrines inevitably become involved in underworld.'

'What sorts of things do they get involved in?'

'Drug trafficking. About five years back there was a battle over who would control Tata Durbar, and eight or nine people were killed. The man who was responsible for the murders fled and took asylum in England. They sent two assassins there.'

'And the assassins killed him in England?'

'No! He killed the two assassins.'

The next day, Akmal and I went to a fish picnic on the other side of the dam. The guest of honour was Pir Saber Shah, the leader of the madrassa we had visited, which was in the Sufi tradition and for historical reasons had many followers in Bangladesh. The pir was a large, jovial, middle-aged man with a fair beard and flat Afghan hat. I had returned the night before to the madrassa to interview him because he was working with Beaconhouse in a project called The Educators, to provide education at lower cost to local communities and to children outside the elite class. He described his madrassa as a liberal one. 'There are so many madrassas which teach Islam, but they don't know about the modern developments and require-ments,' he said. 'The world is becoming a global village, and we are living in that village. Among all religions there must be under-standing.' After our interview he had given us dinner and invited us to the fish picnic in his honour the next day. He supported Nawaz Sharif's faction of the Pakistan Muslim League, and the picnic was a political function.

We went in his car, and he drove. When we passed pedestrians on the road, he waved and smiled.

'Everybody knows you,' I said.

'Yes, of course,' he said, beaming.

We talked about Bush. 'He is the second Hitler,' he said.

The plan had been that Athar would return on Sunday and he and I would drive to Peshawar. When Akmal and I returned from the picnic on Saturday, Athar was at the house. He had to return to Islamabad, so I went with him.

'So what's been happening in the world the last three days?' I asked.

'Not much, except two more US soldiers were killed yesterday in Baghdad,' said Athar. And Bush had made a surprise visit to US troops celebrating Thanksgiving.

'Would you like to hear some Pathan music?' he asked when we were on the road. He put on a CD. Pathan folk music was played on a guitar-like instrument called a *chebab*, accompanied by a *tabla* drum, and had a lonesome, rustic sound. To me it sounded like lonesome, rustic music from my own country. The female singer was 'a very well-known Pushtu singer,' Athar said.

He translated some of the lyrics for me. 'She is saying that she has returned from a very faraway place, and she cannot find her beloved.' The next song, he said, 'should be sung by a man, even though the singer is a woman. He is saying to his wife that "I have been granted a visa for Dubai" – He's going there to work, you know – "and now I must send you back to your father's house."'

In Islamabad I met Awais Ahmed Chaudhry, a former travel agent. The word 'former' is operative. Boyish and quietly sad, he wore a plaid lumberjack shirt and spoke with an American accent. Islamabad, a planned city built in the 1960s, is famously sedate and dull amid the hurly-burly of Pakistan. Walking from the Super Market shopping area to Jinnah Super, we crossed a bridge over a stream. 'My father told me when he was growing up he used to bathe and swim in this stream,' Awais said. 'But now it's a sewer. An open sewer.' Sitting by the fountain in the Jinnah Super shopping area, eating chicken tikka with paratha and drinking fruit shakes, he told me about his business.

'Before, I used to have at least ten groups a year,' he said. 'Some years I used to have 20 groups. They used to come from Germany, from Italy. In 1999 I had a group from Russia, and one from Georgia.' His customers had been 'mostly from Europe, not America. I had just one American – just one person. His name is Mr Jay Sieger, from Alaska. He used to come every year, but this year he didn't come, because he's afraid. He told me, especially after Daniel Pearl, that he's afraid. He tells me he can come if I come to the airport to pick him up and stay with him all the time. But I told him that I can come to the airport to pick him up, but I cannot stay with him all the time. So instead of Pakistan, he went to Nepal.'

'Is he Jewish?' I asked, thinking of Daniel Pearl.

'I don't know. I never asked him. He's a very friendly, open person, just like you. I once told him that he has to do some home-work before he comes here. Number one, he has to dye his hair black. Number two, he has to learn some Urdu. I told him he has to wear a shalwar kameez and one of those Afghan hats.'

'No wonder he's not coming. You scared him away!'

He laughed. 'No, I told him in a joking way. But he's definitely coming next year, because it's K2's fiftieth anniversary. He wouldn't miss that.'

A man with green eyes and wearing a skullcap, green shalwar kameez and knit vest approached us and offered to repair Awais's shoes. I had an annoying hole in the sole of my right boot, so I took the opportunity to ask him to fix it.

'Country America?' the man asked.

'Yes.'

'Afghani,' he said.

'I didn't get many mountaineers,' said Awais. 'I used to get more trekkers. Just to trek to the base of the mountain and spend maybe one day there and then go back. Just to be there and have K2 beside you is a dream come true.'

The shoe guy finished repairing my boot and asked for 500 rupees, nearly $10. It was a shocking amount. Awais haggled with him, and we settled on 195 rupees for my boot plus the repair and polishing he had done on Awais's shoes.

'Even that is too much, I think,' said Awais.

'That's all right,' I said, unhappy but resigned. 'I'm white.'

'Sorry.' He went on: 'It was okay before 9/11. Just after 9/11, the flights were messed up. It was very difficult to find an airplane!

The flights were grounded in the US, but also in the Middle East. Gulf Air and Emirates, their schedules got messed up. I had a group that was visiting the Chitral area during 9/11. It's near the Afghan border – not very near, but close. They have a mountain there called Tirich Mir. I got a call from that group from a PCO. They didn't call, but they asked the guide to call me. I think they saw it on television, because on the PTV English news they showed it. They still had five–six days left there. They had to see the Kailash people there – it's a special tribe there; they're not Muslim. They follow more like the Greek religion. Their women wear headgear out of shells.

'But they got kind of frantic. They told me to get them on the first flight out of Pakistan. So I did, but still they had to spend five or six more days in Islamabad. And during five or six days they didn't even leave their hotel. I think if they were Italians or Germans, it might have been okay. But they were British. But it wasn't really 9/11 that affected things. It was the aftermath, some things that resulted from 9/11, the fallout. The Afghan war, the Indian and Pakistani border tensions that lasted for about a year, the 11 French people that got massacred in the Sheraton Hotel bomb. We got emails from seven French groups. They just said, "We're not coming, man."'

Awais was 34 years old, born in Pakistan but raised in Saudi Arabia. His father was a chemical engineer who worked for SAFCO, Saudi Arabia Fertilizer Company. When he was 16, his family had moved to the US. His father sent him to the University of North Texas in Denton to get a bachelor's degree in computer science. 'He gave me $10,000. To my dad it was a lot of money, but I knew it wouldn't last that long, so that I had to get a job.' His first job was cleaning toilets.

'I don't think you should write this,' he said. 'Oh, why not, you can write it. It was not just cleaning toilets, it was mopping floors, cleaning carpets. Part of the job was cleaning toilets. But it's something that – when I think back about it, it irritates me.'

He had good memories of Texas, though. 'I was near Denton, driving towards Oklahoma,' he remembered. 'I had a flat tyre, and there was no town nearby. And this really nice gentleman stopped, and he took my tyre about 30 miles north towards Oklahoma, and he brought it back, and he even helped me put it back on the car. And when he left he just said, "Jesus loves you." I said, "What do I owe you? I want to pay you something." And he just said, "Jesus loves you." That touched me so much. He was a true Christian.'

Awais had returned to Pakistan in 1996. He had been given a Green Card to work in the US, but it had lapsed because he had stayed out of the US for more than six months.

'After 9/11, the people that were inside Pakistan began to leave,' he said. 'The American Center was shut down.'

'The USIS library was shut down, wasn't it?' I said.

'Yes it was. It's still shut down.'

'I used to go to the USIS library.' On my previous visits to Pakistan, especially before the internet came along, the USIS library in Islamabad had been a haven.

'Me too. I used to have membership there. They had really good books, and really nice tapes: documentaries, scientific, concerning all subjects. They used to have magazines. My favourite was *The Economist*, and I used to go there and read it.'

'They had *The Economist*?'

'I can't remember. It was either at USIS or at the British Council.'

I explained that USIS stocked American publications, and the British Council carried British ones.

'It doesn't matter,' said Awais. 'Both are closed.'

'Do you feel at home in Pakistan?' I asked.

'Well, no.'

I asked why he had come back.

'I asked my parents to come to America, and they didn't want to stay. So finally I had to choose between America and my parents, and I had to choose my parents. They said their relatives and all their friends are in Pakistan, and they were born here and they're gonna die here. But I personally think the US would have been better. Because to me, the US offers everything a person can dream for.' But he had returned to Pakistan and made the best of it, until the autumn of 2001.

'The number one thing that made the tourists not come to Pakistan,' he said, 'was this: the US government gave the Afghan government about 45 days to think it over and turn over Osama bin Laden. The Taliban turned them down, and had the whole country bombed to hell. All the Americans asked the Taliban to do was to hand over Osama bin Laden. They didn't ask them to shave off their beards or let girls go to school.

'During those 45 days, and during the bombing, every day at the Afghan embassy here in Islamabad, the Taliban was giving daily briefings to the press of the world. From where? From the Taliban embassy here in Islamabad. It made my blood boil. Every day on BBC or CNN it would say, 'Taliban briefing from Islamabad.' I had some journalists from KBS – Korean Broadcasting System. I was taking them to their daily press briefing at the Afghan embassy. I was really amazed, that here we are at war with these people, and they're on international television.

'That was so stupid of the Pakistani government. That's the single thing that ruined the tourism industry in Pakistan. Even to a layman it showed that the Pakistani government is collaborating with the Taliban, or even that the two were the same. I don't know what else is damaged, but it ruined my business.'

'So Islamabad was pretty crazy during that time,' I suggested.

'The place was swarming with camera people and reporters. They used to go all around the city and to Peshawar. And then for the final two–three minutes they would go to the roof of the Marriott, where they could get the government building in the background. The Marriott was full to the brim with journalists. And you could not find a room in the Pearl Continental in Peshawar. You couldn't get a guesthouse in Peshawar that had a room. Journalists were forced to rent houses for six–seven months. I even met Amy Kellogg from Fox News in the elevator at the Marriott. She was going somewhere, and we went from the fifth floor to the lobby. It was amazing, somebody you've been seeing on TV for so long, and suddenly you meet them face to face. I think she's a very beautiful lady. I missed Geraldo, though.'

A lot of water had gone under the bridge since 1995, when the Taliban's rise had been a leitmotif in the Pakistani papers. The general feeling then had been that this mysterious new group may have been fanatical, but at least they were bringing a measure of stability to large areas of Afghanistan, and surely that couldn't be worse than the factional chaos that had prevailed since the Russians left. Tony Davis had been in Kabul in September 1996 when the Taliban captured the capital, and had had to battle his own editors at *Asiaweek* to get the story in the magazine. People in Hong Kong, he had told me ruefully, weren't interested in 'a bunch of nig-nogs and ragheads' fighting among themselves in remote Afghanistan.

Awais invited me back to his house. His wife brought us hot chocolate and graham crackers in the room he used as an office, and he introduced me to his parents. He had three children: Gohar, age three; Omar, two; and ten-month-old Mariam. This surprised me; he hadn't seemed like a family man. The two boys were alert and charming. They drew with crayons while Awais and I talked. 'You know the younger one, Omar, he beats up the older one,' said Awais. 'And the older one cries and runs away.'

Omar babbled happily.

'Does he speak any proper words yet?' I asked.

'In Urdu he speaks some words. He calls me Baba, and he calls his mother Mama.'

In Awais's office were three computers. 'This one is on all the time, connected to the internet,' he said. 'This one you can watch TV on. And this is the fax machine where –'

'Where you got the faxes saying 'We're not coming'?'

'Yeah.'

He turned on the middle computer, tuned to Fox News. Seven or eight Spanish intelligence agents had been killed; two more US soldiers had been killed in Baghdad; two Japanese diplomats had been killed near Tikrit. On the third computer, Awais opened bbc.co.uk, cnn.com and msnbc.com.

'I have this habit of opening these chats, just in case I get a customer from it,' he said.

'Have you ever?'

'Yes, when I had my website, VisitPakistan.com.'

'Now you have another website?'

'Yes, but that's just for K2 – k2chronicles.com. It's empty right now. It's already too late for it, though. A website needs about six months to get itself recognised by the search engines. I should have built my website during the summer, so it would be in the search engines now, by December. I've basically given up, though.'

Fox News was reporting something about Michael Jackson.

'He used to be a handsome man, back when his *Thriller* album came out,' said Awais. 'I like Fox News. It brings back memories.'

'Memories of what?'

'Memories of America, actually. It's like a fairy tale place, where everything is in order.'

From Islamabad I went to Peshawar. The last time I had made this journey, in January 1999, had been in a white minivan with a dozen or more young men. In the conversation between a bearded guy in the seat behind me and another next to me by the window, I had caught an English word.

'Journalist.'

'Journalist?'

'Journalist.'

I turned around to introduce myself. I figured if they were going to talk about me, they might as well talk to me. 'Hi,' I said over my shoulder to the guy behind me.

'You are journalist?'

'Yes.'

'From America?'

'Yes.'

He said nothing.

I felt I should say something, so I said: 'America bombed Afghanistan. I'm sorry.'

He smiled then and said, 'It's all right. That is politics. We have a saying in our language: "Sometimes the mother is up and the father is down. Sometimes the father is up and the mother is down." You understand?'

'Sure.'

'But America should be careful,' he added. 'Politics is a dangerous field. There must be a response. Newton's third law.'

I scribbled in my notebook.

'If you want to write my name also, you can write it,' he said. 'Noor Alam, from tribal areas of Pakistan.'

I looked out the window. 'The sunset is very beautiful,' I said.

'Yes it is,' agreed Noor Alam. 'There must be some Creator of all this: the sun, the sky, the land, the mountains. Don't you think?'

At his house in Lahore before the Eid holiday, I had asked Ahmed Rashid if he would rethink a year-old article in *The New York Review of Books*, in which he had made some strong assertions: 'A crisis is clearly impending: it may occur just before the [10 October 2002] elections, when Musharraf will have to allow limited campaigning and party rallies in order to give at least the appearance of normal political life ... Few Westerners seem to realize how grave Pakistan's situation has become.'

No, he told me, he stood by what he had written: 'There's a very swift deterioration, if you look at all indicators. Has fundamentalism been checked since 9/11? No, it hasn't.' As for Afghanistan, which he had been covering for more than two decades, 'It's very bad. The whole of this year there's been enormous neglect. The money hasn't come. The international peacekeepers haven't come. And then of course Iraq, which has preoccupied the world for the last year. The Taliban are resurgent. The economic resurgence hasn't begun. The warlords are still rampant. I think Iraq has had a hugely negative effect on Afghanistan. And the effect on Pakistan has been that it's led to a huge upsurge in anti-Westernism. It's had more of an impact than even the war in Afghanistan, which was next door.'

I had learned to look critically at claims of impending doom for Pakistan, if only because doom was always impending here. Predicting it was a parlour game for journalists. For example: 'Some ugly spectres are haunting Pakistan these days: the spectre of an ugly end to the [current] government; violence and civil chaos; even, perhaps, an Islamic revolution. [Recent events] have led many to wonder if a major upheaval is brewing in Pakistan. Well, yes, surely something along those lines is indeed on the cards.' I had written that, in an unsigned leader published in the *Bangkok Post* the day Benazir Bhutto fell from power for the second time. I had said some rude things in that piece, prompting the Pakistani ambassador to Thailand to storm into the paper's office and the editor to print a humiliating apology, after which I was *persona non grata* at the *Bangkok Post*. I had struck a nerve, but it was also true that seven years later the oft-predicted major upheaval hadn't quite happened yet, although doom was clearly still impending.

Now, as I returned to Peshawar on the Daewoo bus, I thought of something else Ahmed Rashid had said to me: 'Peshawar at the moment is like another country, it really is. You really get a sense that it has little to do with this part of Pakistan.'

Athar Minallah had given me the name of a young lawyer, Atif Ali Khan. We met in the coffee shop of the Pearl Continental hotel. He was 28 years old, a graduate of the International Islamic University in Islamabad, which taught shariah and law as practiced in Pakistan, and had earned a master's degree in international law from American University in Washington, DC. That clearly had been a formative experience, and he had been elected to speak for his LLM class at AU. He had appreciated the diversity of the student population. 'At AU this was another chance I had, to interact with Jewish students,' he said. 'Being there, interacting with other human beings, you see that it's a whole different ball game.'

Atif Ali Khan was slightly built, with a long black beard and hair that was just starting to grow back. 'I've just come back from Mecca,' he explained. 'That's why I have the shaved head.'

'But I think not on Haj, right?' I said. He seemed too young.

'No,' he confirmed. 'It was the *umra*, the smaller pilgrimage.'

He was well dressed, in a dark Western-style suit. He exuded the self-confidence of an intelligent, ambitious young man, a guy who's going places. I liked him immediately.

He told me frankly that his views were very close to those of the Taliban. Whenever I meet someone whose background and opinions differ sharply from my own, my practice is to suspend judgement and listen patiently. You never know what you might learn. In the no man's land between where you're at and where I'm at is where we find our common humanity.

In May 1999 Atif Ali Khan moved to New York, where he worked several months for the Organisation of the Islamic Conference at the UN. 'It was a good experience,' he said. 'I left on the 31st of December 1999 and flew through the millennium. They actually stopped the plane in Ireland at midnight, because of this Y2K.' In January 2000, he started working for the firm of Afridi Shah Minallah. Athar, he told me, 'is a very senior lawyer. He's like a big brother to us.' He left in June 2001 to open his own firm.

The US Consulate in Peshawar contacted him to assist on some property matters. Then, in August 2001, he learned that some French NGO workers had been captured by the Taliban. 'I had my experience in shariah and international law,' he told me, 'and I said, "By the way, if I could be of any help, I'd be happy to."' On 4 September, a woman from the US Consulate called to ask if his offer still stood. Eight foreign-aid workers with the Christian NGO Shelter Now International were being held by the Taliban in Kabul, and the Consulate needed help securing their release.

On 11 September, 'afternoon our time, but before the planes hit the towers, they told me I had been appointed counsel and that I should drop the property work and concentrate on this, and they were looking at transportation to get me into Kabul,' he said. 'In the evening we learned that the planes had hit the towers.' For two weeks he tried to get flights into Kabul. 'On the 26th we entered into a contract with the parents of the aid workers and came to terms, and it was decided that I would go to Kabul on the 28th.' He travelled overland via Jalalabad. 'The ride from Jalalabad to Kabul was one hell of a ride,' he said.

The aid workers were four Germans – one of whom, Georg Taubmann, I later realised I had interviewed in Peshawar in 1999 – two Australians and two Americans, Dayna Curry and Heather Mercer. The case received a lot of coverage in the US and elsewhere. After they were released, the two women secured a book deal, made speeches around the United States and met George Bush at the White House. Many media reports claimed the missionaries faced the death penalty for spreading Christianity.

'I don't understand this kind of journalism,' said Atif. 'Even when my case was going on, these networks like CNN and BBC were saying that these people were going to be hanged for what they had done. And legally that wasn't the position at all. It really infuriates me. I think good journalists tend to earn respect over time. One of them that I admire is Robert Fisk of *The Independent*. Now, when I go to the site, you have to pay for his articles. I feel that he's a lone voice among this whole horde of other Western journalists, who tries to show a balanced picture. The role that Fox News played was really pathetic. I got interviewed by someone live on Fox in Islamabad, and I didn't like my interview. I found CNN to be more professional than Fox.'

The case had been lucrative for him and had helped establish him professionally. 'But it was not a very good experience for me, in the sense of how the parents and the international people interacted with me. As long as the case was going on, they were all sweet and honey. But the day the case was over, they shut their doors to me. That was hurting to me. I did not expect that at all. I had the worst experience with Heather's father. And I did not receive the balance of my fee. I sued Shelter Now International over here, and there was a consensual decree in which they agreed that they were responsible and I was paid the balance.'

While the case was still pending, Atif had shuttled back and forth, delivering letters and clothing for the prisoners and once spending two hours running around Kabul looking for a doctor for Heather. 'She had some problems,' he said. 'She was mentally unstabilised a bit. At one point I thought she was really losing it.'

He believed the US Consulate had asked him to take the case 'because my political views were similar to the regime at the time. But even in terms of their interaction with my clients, the Taliban went out of their way to be helpful. Even these girls, when they came out and they were being interviewed in Islamabad, they praised the Taliban.'

If they weren't at risk of being hanged, what punishment did the missionaries face, if they hadn't been freed?

'They were arrested for preaching Christianity,' he said. 'That was against the laws of Afghanistan. There was a decree from Mullah Omar that anyone caught doing this, that they should be incarcerated for seven to ten days and then banished from the country.' Apostasy – converting from Islam to another religion – was another matter. 'That is punishable by death. That is like when someone commits treason in a country.' Preaching Christianity 'could lead to the changing of faith. So the person doing the preaching would not be given the death sentence, but he would be given a lighter sentence to stop him from doing so.'

We finished coffee and drove to his office in the Saddar area of Peshawar so he could give me some articles about the case and introduce me to Mr Afridi of Afridi Shah Minallah. Mr Afridi wasn't around, but Atif and I talked some more. His enthusiasm for his work led me to ask if he had read John Grisham's legal thrillers.

'Yes, I like them a lot,' he said. 'I used to read them all. In *The Chamber*, I think, he goes on and on and on about some legal details, and the dramatism suffers, but I really like *The Runaway Jury*. *The Chamber* was good, though, the way it told about the death penalty and gave both sides.'

I asked him about Dayna and Heather themselves.

'Yes. Very nice. I have their book with me. Oh, it's not here. I think it's at home. They've written a book.'

'They sent you a copy?'

He laughed. 'No, I had to buy a copy. I thought they would send me a copy, but they didn't. They say nice things. They've said nice things about me, and fair.'

'Would you like to get into politics?' I asked.

'Absolutely. I love politics. I would like to contribute at the national level. And I would like to make a new kind of politics, a more honest kind of politics. In AU we were having a seminar on the Lewinsky issue. My turn came at the end of the session. I rose and I said, "People you elect are a reflection of what you are. If you elect him and then you criticise him for what he does, you yourselves do the same." So people in Pakistan will get good leaders only when they correct their own mistakes. If I go into an office and I pay bribes, how can I criticise a leader for being corrupt? Allah says in the Quran that Allah does not change the destiny of nations who do not want to change themselves. And speaking out only will not make a difference.

'I'm aligned with the Jamaat-i-Islami, and I can appreciate their kind of politics. But one thing I've realised is that the army has a role to play, and one can make contacts with them as well. At least the army is sincere and wants to serve the country. Grand reality at this time is that everyone knows that there is no government. It's Musharraf who's running things. It's a puppet show. Real power is with the president.'

I asked if he thought the 1999 coup had been justified.

'I think at that particular time it was justified. And it is justified every time it happens, because there are certain conditions. At the time that Nawaz Sharif was overthrown, people wanted him to go. Because he was taking on every other pillar, every segment. I don't know about Kargil, because it's very hazy. But what he did was unpopular with the people as well. I was in America at the time, in DC, and Pakistanis there were saying this is no way for a self-respecting leader to act, to come and plead to get out of the mess he had made for himself.'

'Do you think Musharraf is in for the long term?'

'Yes. There are only two threats to him. One is if there's a coup within the army, and the other is if he's assassinated.'

'I've been told by others that there's not much chance of any coup within the army – that the army is very disciplined.'

'That appears to be the case. And that's one reason he's been pressurised to take off his uniform. Once he takes off his uniform, his power is lost.'

'So it's a real conundrum for him.'

'Yes it is. You have to play democracy, and you have to play the army as well.'

'These are all Afghani people,' Ehson Ullah told me as we wended our way past storefronts, produce stalls and women in blue burkahs to the Afghan English Language and Computer Center off University Road. I had browsed in bookshops along University Road the night before, when it had exuded the post-apocalyptic vibe of Asian cities after dark: traffic dust mixing with pollution; ghostly figures shrouded in earth-coloured blankets against the chill. The sinister aspect of the streets of Peshawar lifted with the morning fog and exposed to unsparing daylight the ramshackle scruffiness of it all.

Ehson Ullah, a young Afghan refugee, was the servant of the family of Anwar Zeb Khan, proprietor of Zeb Traders, which held the Peshawar and NWFP franchise for the metal and plastic pipes, traffic cones and street lamps manufactured by Polycon Pakistan (Pvt) Ltd of Lahore. Polycon was run by the family of Fazal Qadir Khan, a polite 23-year-old with whom I played tennis a few times in the evenings on the hard courts at the Lahore Gymkhana. Ehson Ullah happened to be sitting in the office when, out of courtesy and curiosity, I called on his employer.

'I study one book,' he told me. 'I have to study six books. All Afghani people are wanting to learn the English and speak the English. *Because* is *need* the English.'

At the Afghan Center, boys were milling about in the small court-yard. On the courtyard wall were Quranic sayings in English: 'Seeking knowledge is obligatory for every muslim (man and woman)' and 'O Lord! Increase me in my knowledge.' I greeted the boys and shook each one's hand in turn. 'How are you?' I asked them.

'Fine thanks, and you?' they answered.

The young man who introduced himself as the principal was small, with a delicate mustache. His name was Abdul Ghani Azimi, and he was 20 years old.

'Have you ever been to Afghanistan?' I asked in his small office off the courtyard.

'I have been there twice,' he said.

The school had 300 students, girls as well as boys. 'We have old persons as well, the age of 40 or 45. We made the Center only to learn something. Not for making deal or business. Just for making people to learn something and finishing ignorancy. Not just from our country, but from the world. We are not taking from them money, the students who are orphans. How can we? They have no money.'

'So the students who are not orphans, do you take money from them?'

'Yeah, why not? We have to rent and salaries for teachers.' For students who were not orphans, the fee was 300 rupees per 75-day semester.

Out of the corner of my eye, I saw that a man had laid a prayer rug and was praying.

'Do you also have religious education here?' I asked.

'In here no,' said the principal. 'Only English and computers.' They had Pentium II computers and taught programs such as DOS, Word, Excel and PowerPoint. I asked what kinds of jobs the students aspired to.

'Especially they want to work in NGOs. But mostly they want to work to rebuild their country.'

'Are they all hoping to go back to Afghanistan?'

'Yeah, yeah, why not? Absolutely.'

Ghani himself had been born in a refugee camp.

'What was it like?' I asked.

'It was good.'

'Do you live in a camp now?'

'Yeah, why not?'

I noticed that I had only two blank pages left in my notebook. 'Do you know where I can get another notebook like this?' I asked.

'No, brother. You are our guest. I will send a man to buy a notebook and I will give it to you as a gift. You know, Afghani people, if someone comes to our home, we really appreciate the person. Afghani people love hospitality. Is that right?'

'Yes, it's right.'

'Sir, these are all Afghani people,' interjected Ehson Ullah. 'All want to learn English.'

Ghani had met US soldiers in Afghanistan, though he wasn't sure exactly when.

'What was it like meeting American troops?'

'Interesting.'

'Tell me more.'

'I met them in Jalalabad. We discussed the point a lot about revolution in Afghanistan.'

'Would you like to –?' I meant would he like to return.

'Why not?'

'When?'

'When the peace come in Afghanistan. We are just waiting. Our country.'

'What was it like in Jalalabad?'

'The first time it was not good. The people had guns and ignorancy was a lot there. But the second time when I was there, people were attract to learn something.'

He showed me around the classrooms. In the first were seven

or eight boys of various ages. I asked them where they were born, and where they had celebrated the recent Eid festival. Several had celebrated Eid in Afghanistan, with relatives in Jalalabad or Kabul. I spoke the longest with an 11-year-old named Bacha Khan. He said he had four brothers 'above' him and that they were all younger than he was. I explained that if they were younger, then he was 'above' them and they were 'below' him. I asked if he had any sisters. Yes, he had six sisters. Were they older or younger? They were all older. The eldest was 18 and already married and living in Jalalabad. His father had stayed with her there, but she had not been home – that is, to Peshawar – for Eid. She might visit, *inshallah*, and then the family would get to meet her husband. Their house in the refugee camp was too small. No wonder, I thought.

All the boys were Pathans. Did they speak Urdu? Only a little, said Bacha Khan.

'Do you speak more Urdu, or more English?' I asked.

'Same.'

'I'm sorry,' I said. 'I don't speak Pushtu, and only a little Urdu. But I speak good English.'

He grinned. 'Because you are Englishman!'

In another classroom, nearly two dozen boys were crowded around the sides of a small room. These were beginners in English. 'What is your name?' I asked one of them.

'Sir, my name is Abdullah,' he said.

'How old are you?'

'Fine thanks, and you?'

The teacher corrected him, and all the boys laughed.

I met Ghani Azimi again the next morning because he had offered to show me around his refugee camp, 40 minutes' walk from the school. It was sprawling but not overcrowded and was called Ghundi Camp. The houses were made of khaki-coloured, sun-baked earth and the fields were planted to spinach and radishes. We visited two schools in the camp. In one, a one-story cement building sponsored or supported by an NGO called Ockendon International, unveiled women teachers taught in indoor class-rooms. The other was a collection of tents. At both schools, the boys left their shoes outside and sat crossed-legged on the floor. Some classes were reciting the Quran; others were learning English. The blackboard in front of one tent had a picture of a rifle drawn in chalk. The boys took turns approaching the board and reciting, 'G-U-N, gun'. Girls went to school separately starting at one in the afternoon, the head teacher said. In his office, a poster showed three children and two balloons:

Reading of (use of (has)(have))
Eid Day

It is Eid Day. The children are very happy. They have a lots of fun. The children count their Eidi. Aslam has thirty rupees. Salman has twenty rupees and Saira has thirty five.

When we left the second school, half a dozen boys followed us, making wisecracks and generally being high-spirited. I asked Ghani if the water buffalo tethered by the roadside belonged to Afghans. No, he said, they belonged to Pakistanis. Afghans could never afford to own buffaloes. We sat for a few minutes in a barbershop that also had shower stalls. While we were there, a man came out of one of the stalls half naked and looking startled by my presence.

We stopped again at the stall of a young tailor who had three old-fashioned black sewing machines and a computer that was busy defragmenting its hard drive. The tailor was named Sherin Agha and was Ghani's cousin. He said someone had recommended he defrag his computer because it had been running slow. While we sat there, the defragging process went from 40 to 41 per cent complete. He asked me how much longer it would take.

'At least a few hours,' I said.

Further along I noticed that some of the houses were in ruins, with roofs missing and walls broken and partly or entirely gone. Some lots with house walls still around them were being planted to crops. It seemed a gentle, organic kind of ruination, since the houses had been made of earth in the first place: dust to dust. But I wondered why they were ruined.

'Because the owners went back to Afghanistan,' said Ghani.

But why had they destroyed their houses? Why not leave them for other people to live in?

He laughed. 'They are not thinking of other people.'

We had walked in a circle around the camp and were back near the entrance. Here a shop sold vegetables: potatoes, carrots, radishes, onions. It also sold sugarcane, which Ghani acknowledged didn't grow around here, but was sold in the market. Little inch-long chunks of chewed-up sugarcane littered the ground, such as I had seen in Haiti and all around Asia. Boys used sticks to propel tyre rims along the ground, as in Nepal.

We briefly visited a small mosque and looked at some gravestones, then Ghani insisted on giving me tea in his own house. Tea became lunch. It started with almonds and delicious, sweet raisins, then rice with tiny raisins, yoghurt, nan, onions and tomatoes, and chicken.

Ghani and his mother lived with his uncle and aunt, who had taken them in when his father died eight years ago, when he was 12. His uncle, Haji Mukhtar, looked wizened and rustic, and it was star- tling to learn that he was 35, three years younger than I was. He spoke no English. He had worked in Pakistan and in Saudi Arabia as a labourer and had left home to fight the Russians at age 12. His mother had not been happy about that, so he had had to sneak away.

'He said they were not allowing us, but that was our duty to free our country from Russia,' Ghani translated. 'He said Pakistan destroyed our country. Pakistan made us opposite each one. "I was opposite to Taliban from the beginning. All of Taliban were agent of Pakistan, therefore I was opposite of them." He says 85 per cent of people are thinking that Pakistan ISI [Inter-Services Intelligence] is protecting Osama and Mullah Mohammed Omar.'

Haji Mukhtar had lived a while in Lahore, where he was a 'honey businessman', but he had been shot in the leg by *goondas* or robbers, so had returned from Lahore to Peshawar.

'He says the American, London, French and Germany troops in Afghanistan, if they work for our country, we will never forget their kindness,' said Ghani.

'Are they working for the country?' I asked.

'Right now we understand that they are protecting themselves, because there are some terrorists in Afghanistan. After one–two years, if they are not working for our country, then we will be a little angry.'

Haji Mukhtar's two small daughters came in and cuddled on each side of him. He enfolded them gently with his arms. His eight-year-old son presented himself to us.

'What sport do you think is best?' Ghani asked me, still translating for his uncle.

'I think tennis is best,' I said.

'His son is learning tae kwon do. He said if child is little busy, he won't be naughty.'

The boy demonstrated his skills, kicking the air.

'So if he is robbed by goondas, he can protect himself,' I said.

Both men laughed. 'He said that is our problem, therefore he is learning tae kwon do.'

Near the end of the long, languorous lunch, I summoned the nerve to ask Ghani, 'How did your father die?'

'Taliban killed him,' he said.

The Taliban had tried to force his father to join them to fight against the warlord Ahmed Shah Massoud, but he had refused. Using the excuse that his beard was not long enough, they had killed him. 'First they attached his hands with a rope, then they beat him, then they shot him.' They refused to give his body to the family until they paid a bribe. He was buried in Jalalabad.

I watched the gentle youth's face as he told me these things. He kept his composure, but with effort, and his eyes were moist.

'If I could find them,' he said, 'and I have power, I would not leave them alive.'

CHAPTER TEN

'LADIES AND GENTLEMEN, WE'VE GOT HIM!'

'Please down your newspaper so the camera man can take our picture,' said the chubby-cheeked, smiling young man in the bus seat beside me. A security man was coming down the aisle, recording the faces of all passengers.

After Peshawar I had spent a few more days in Islamabad, and now I was returning to Lahore. I didn't want company or conversation; I wanted to shut down and recharge my batteries. The paper I was reading was *Daily Times*, the new companion to *The Friday Times*, launched in 2002. I had begun writing a weekly column on its op-ed page for Ejaz Haider, the journalist who made headlines when, in January 2003 as a visiting scholar at the Brookings Institute, he was picked up on the streets of Washington by the US Immigration and Naturalization Service on suspicion of being Pakistani. I was rereading my latest column, the way a baseball player admires his own home run.

I lowered the paper grudgingly, without acknowledging his request. During the entire first half of the journey I gave him only one perfunctory smile. At the rest stop, I felt a tap on my shoulder.

'Excuse me, you are from which country?'

'America,' I said.

'I am also Christian.'

He asked what I wanted to eat. I said I didn't really feel like eating, but needed to use the toilet. So he escorted me to the gents. What I really wanted was to be alone in my fatigue, at the end of a long trip and a long day. But solitude was the one thing his solicitous hospitality couldn't provide, so I gave up and sat down with him at a table outside, and we ordered barbecued chicken and roti.

His name was Asim Peter. He was 24 years old and worked as a secretary for Dongfang Electric Corporation, a Chinese company working on a hydroelectric project on a canal near Attock, several hours the other side of Islamabad. 'This is a big project, to supply 1440 megawatts per year,' he said. There were about 75 Chinese people at the site. 'But before this, when the project was at the peak, maybe 100–120 people.' His job entailed preparing transport, telephone, electricity and other bills. He had been there 11 months. It had been a good experience. 'You know, we can buy each and every thing in our life: house, car. But we can't buy the experience.'

He had a B.Comm. degree and intended to go for a master's. Pakistanis I met seemed very concerned with academic degrees. 'I think I will do something for computer science,' said Asim. 'I just want chance to go abroad.' His fiancée was his cousin and also 24. He had loved her since he was nine. 'She will don't want me to go,' he said. 'But she is giving me courage. You know, if you want to make something in life, you must to do something.'

This was the third time in the last month that he had made the long, two-leg bus journey to Lahore. Before that, it had been two months since he had been home. He had come for his birthday on 14 November, then again during the Eid holiday, and now to make his application to the London School of Science and Technology. He had learned about the school by chatting on MSN Messenger, where he had met Azeem Khan, the school's International Liaison Manager. He had to send some documents to England to support his application. 'I think I spend like 1800 rupees on the DHL,' he said.

Back on the bus, Asim told me he was Catholic. 'But my father has five brothers, and we all live together in one house. And some are Catholic, some are Protestant.'

He had noticed the picture accompanying my *Daily Times* column, and had guessed it was me. He asked where I stayed in Lahore. I told him; it was very near his family's house. I suggested we share a ride. At the bus station he found a motor rickshaw and settled with the driver, and off we went.

The pollution and bustle on Lahore's streets, even close to midnight, were jarring after the serenity of Islamabad. I remarked on this to Asim in the rickshaw.

'Lahore is the heart of Pakistan,' he said with feeling. 'Here you can do each and every thing. You can see girls, and cinema, and fun fair. In Peshawar, nothing.'

After a few minutes the rickshaw broke down. The driver was a briskly cheerful small, dark guy with a moustache. He removed a metal part that might have been a spark plug, blew on it thoughtfully, and put it back on. That seemed to work, and we were on our way again.

'He is a Christian,' said Asim. I caught the driver's eye in the rear-view mirror. He smiled through his moustache. 'Whenever I see my religion people I am very happy.'

Asim and the driver chatted some more.

'You know, he got deported from Denmark,' Asim told me.

'Oh really?' I said politely. I caught the driver's eye again in the side mirror.

'Bad luck!' he said cheerfully.

The driver's name was Javed Masih. 'Masih mean Jesus,' said Asim. 'Masih' is a very common surname among Pakistani Christians and actually means 'Messiah'.

The next morning, Asim came to the guesthouse. It was a Sunday, and he had invited me to attend church with him. One of my intentions was to catch people in Pakistan going through their humdrum regular activities. This is, it seems to me, the advantage travel writing has over crisis-driven journalism. 'It's been very difficult to get other stories in that don't have to do with al-Qaeda,' Ahmed Rashid told me, speaking of his gigs with *The Daily Telegraph* and the *Far Eastern Economic Review*. But there's always a lot more going on than what people notice most readily, and much of what is true is subtle and requires patience to glean.

So I went to church with Asim. On the way, we stopped at the John Medical Store run by his uncle. 'See, John Medical Store,' he said, pointing at a sign in the flowing Arabic script. We sat and chatted with Asim's affable uncle, John Daniel, who gave us bottles of Pepsi. 'Welcome, brother,' he said. 'This is your store, if you need any medicine or anything. We are brothers in the Lord Jesus Christ.'

I told him my name and spelled it for him. He wrote it down. 'No,' I said. 'Not K.C. C-a-s-e-y.'

'Oh, I thought it was K.C.,' he said. 'I am also J.D.,' he added with a laugh. 'J.D. can also mean "Jesus disciple". My son also is studying abroad. MBBS, medical doctor.'

'That's great,' I said.

'In Latvia.'

'Really?'

'Yes. In Riga.'

'Very cold there, I think.'

'Yes! Minus 30 degrees!'

Today was 7 December, warm and sunny in Lahore.

'He tried to study in Seattle in USA,' said John Daniel. 'But he could not get a visa. USA visas are becoming more and more difficult. They say, "You are too young, you will stay."'

Asim and I walked on to the Christ for Pakistan Church, on a side street near the railroad tracks. The cross on the door was red. 'For some reason, in Pakistan they always paint the crosses red,' Fawzya

Minallah had told me. 'Even in the Christian colony in Islamabad. I want to ask them why, but they don't know.' Inside was a small dais with six wooden chairs and a lectern with plastic flowers on it. We came in at the tail end of the early service and sat along a side wall. The congregation was singing rousing songs, accompanied by an older man with grey hair dyed orange with henna, who played the harmonium and tabla drum. 'He is the choir incharge,' Asim whispered to me. I took out my notebook. 'These are holy songs,' said Asim. I couldn't tell if he was rebuking me or only explaining. I put my notebook away.

One song had the word *shukriya*, thank you, repeated over and over. 'We are saying thank you to God for all the achievements he give us,' Asim explained. About another song he said: 'We are saying our Jesus' words are sweet and pure more than gold.' There was a reading – Luke 12:17–21. 'There is a rich man, and he has a very great harvest,' the man sitting to my left translated. 'And he says, "I am a great man, and now is my time to rest and enjoy." But he doesn't know when will come the time for death.'

The first service ended, and the room filled up for the second service. Before it started, Asim introduced me to Pastor Yaqub Bhatti. The pastor wore a light brown polyester suit and welcomed me jovially, in a manner reminiscent of Protestant preachers in Florida, Atlanta and Nashville – all places he made a point of telling me he had visited. 'Journalists are the true representatives of the people,' he remarked. 'Because they get down to the grassroots.' He asked where in America I was from.

'Wisconsin,' I said. 'It's near Chicago.'

'Chicago is in Indiana, I think,' he said.

'Actually, it's in Illinois, but right next to Indiana.'

During the part of the service set aside for announcements, he singled me out as a first-time visitor, calling me 'Brother Ethan Casey,' and asked me to stand up. In English he said: 'In future this is your church, whenever you have the time to come. Welcome.'

Then he gave his sermon in Urdu. Asim translated: 'Pastor is saying that he had a conversation with a donkey. Donkey say, "I am lucky because God ride on me." People say him donkey, but he is the lucky one.'

I met Asim several more times, and even went to church with him again on Christmas Day. 'Yeah, mostly friends are Muslim,' he told me when I asked. 'No problem. We eat together, drink together, same like the family members.'

'Do they tell you you should become Muslim?' I asked.

'Sometimes. I tell them we should not talk about the faith. Firstly we are the human beings. Then we are something else.'

'Do you ever feel it's difficult to be a Christian in Pakistan?'

'No,' he said. 'They have the majority here. They can do. But here is a minority of Christians. If somebody say something against our religion, what we can do? You know, Christmas come on the Quaid-e-Azam day. So they just celebrate the Quaid-e-Azam day. Our Christian community leader, Peter Gill, made it so there will be two holidays, 25th and 26th. He told the gummint, 'Muslims have so many holidays. We are part of this country too."

I asked him what would happen if a Christian and a Muslim fell in love.

'Sometime if a Christian boy loves a Muslim girl, and the parents don't agree, so they run away.' In such a case, the girl might convert to Christianity. 'But if they found, maybe they will be killed. Specially they will kill the girl. Maybe they kill the boy also.'

His fiancée, whose name was Noreen Fernandes, was a Christian. But even so he had worries. 'From my childhood I am loving to her,' he said. 'We play together in the childhood. But you know, when I was in matric, I told my other cousin that I love her. So she gave the message that "He loves you." So she came in my house and she ask me, "Do you love me?" "Y-y-yes," I say, like that. She say, "If you love me, why don't you say?" I say, "I have no courage."'

'But then for a while she refuse to marry me. Because their society and our society are a little different.' I didn't understand this; both Asim and Noreen were Christians. 'They are the Anglo-Indians,' he explained. 'And we are the simple Punjabis. There is some difference between their culture and our culture. They are modern people. Actually, there was a problem. That problem was this: she want to live alone. We live all together, all the family. My parents said, "If she want to marriage you, she should to live here." For last three–four–five years, I am in this situation. So you tell me one thing: what do you suggest?'

A journalist is accustomed to asking questions, not answering them. His question threw me.

'She's just waiting for me,' he said. 'If she agree to living with my family, we would get married next month. So you tell me, what should I do? Because one side I don't want to leave my family. And other side I don't want to leave my love.'

The conversation had crossed a line. It was no longer an interview; this was a serious personal matter for Asim and he needed someone to give him something: comfort, or reassurance, or sage advice. All I knew to do was to listen.

'I think you have a smaller problem than if you loved a Muslim girl,' I said.

'But I think it's a big problem,' he said.

'But not as big as if you loved a Muslim girl.'

'She said, "I don't want you to leave your parents, but this house is very small,"' he told me. 'Our house is inside the street. My father is bigger than all the brothers; he is the eldest. So they are all living together. My father say we are living together last so many years, and my brothers are also married, and they also live in same house. You know, when a girl gets married she brings a dowry. We don't have space for more things. And you know, when people get married there are some secret things, private things, between the husband and the wife. Some happiness, some badness. Without these things, life is not complete.'

On Monday morning, I went into the office clean-shaven.

'Sir, you look 19,' said my student Sadaf.

Shakoor didn't like it. To him, being beardless was unmanly and un-Islamic. 'Sir, you are no Ethan Casey!' he said in half-feigned, half-genuine shock.

On Thursday at tennis, Shaqil-sahib stroked his own chin and said, 'Hey! What's this?'

'I decided not to join the Taliban after all,' I said.

'They're not letting people with beards into America anymore,' he said.

'Maybe they'll send me to Guantanamo Bay.'

That Friday afternoon I rode the bus to Multan, six hours south and west of Lahore. Multan was famous for its several large and venerable Sufi shrines. I was curious to see these, but I also just wanted to get out of town again, and on the bus from Peshawar to Rawalpindi I had met someone who invited me to visit.

This was a young Pathan named Israr ul Haq. I told him I wanted to visit Multan, and he invited me to stay with him in his student hostel at Nishter Medical College. Israr was fair like a Pathan but otherwise didn't fit the mould; he was small and delicate, with a baby face, and had a fastidious little pencil moustache. He wore an elegant and tidy shalwar kameez. He was in his early twenties but looked about 13.

I phoned him from the Daewoo station in Multan, and half an hour later Israr and his friend Zeb arrived on Zeb's motorbike. I had ridden around Lahore a lot on motorbikes, with Shakoor and with my student Usman, but I hadn't yet ridden three adults to a motorbike.

'The number plate on this bike is broken,' said Israr, over his shoulder as we rode. He was in the middle; Zeb was driving. 'Second thing is, there are three of us riding on it, which is very illegal. Third thing is that we just went through a red light. Fourth, the registration of the bike does not belong to us.'

Zeb said something I didn't catch.

'He said, "In Pakistan, he who obeys the rules, suffers,"' Israr told me. 'Everybody is very much excited. I've been telling them, "Ethan is coming! Ethan is coming!" How was your journey?'

'It was fine. There was a guy across the aisle who was annoying me. He asked if I was from the FBI.'

'You should have told him you were from the FBI,' said Israr. 'He would have left you alone.'

We joked and bantered on this theme.

'He'll be taking us to America,' Israr said to Zeb. 'As suspects. That way we'll see each and every place in America.'

Israr and Zeb were part of a gang of five final-year medical students – the others were Iqbal, Shahzad, and Umer – who had been fast friends ever since the beginning of their studies. Israr was the odd one out; the other four were Punjabis. Their hostel was a long two-story building around a large, bare courtyard, with no-frills rooms and communal bathrooms off an outdoor corridor on each floor. Umer gave up his room to me for the five days I stayed. I slept in a sleeping bag on a mat on the cement floor.

The five friends chipped in together to share the fee for cable television, contributing 30 rupees per month each. 'It's not much in pounds perhaps, but for students it's a lot,' said Israr. When we arrived, they were watching a movie starring Harrison Ford as the commander of a Russian submarine. The comedy *What Women Want*, starring Mel Gibson and Helen Hunt, came on next. We watched and talked for a while, then went out for fruit milkshakes at a little shop on the college grounds. We passed the female students' hostel. It was surrounded by a high wall topped with broken glass. 'For obvious reasons,' I suggested.

'For obvious reasons,' Israr agreed. 'But there are some girls who go out on dates. They make them shop for them – 1,000 rupees, 2,000 rupees. Then they give them one night. But I don't do such things, because my father says I should not, and I respect him.' But Israr did have a girlfriend, although the relationship seemed rather tortured and unsatisfactory. 'I proposed, but she said to me: "How can we get married? I am a Punjabi, and you are a Pathan. You will be speaking Pushtu all the time with your parents."'

Early the next morning they had an exam, in gynaecology. I slept in. Israr returned at 10.30 in high spirits. "I passed my test! I passed my test!" he cried. He had seen the teacher's mark on his desk.

These guys talked about sex and women a lot. They didn't like the idea of oral sex, though. 'The vagina has fourteen types of bacteria which can be harmful for the oral cavity,' Zeb told me. 'And the oral cavity also has several types of bacteria which can be harmful for the vagina.'

'Does studying gynaecology put you off thinking about sex?' I asked them.

'No,' said Umer, straight-faced. 'Gynaecology is part of our profession. When we are working, we are professional about each and every thing.'

'When we are free, we are devils!' said Israr. In a more serious tone, he added: 'We've got one problem in Pakistan, whether it's due to our Islamic reasons or what, but people don't share their sexual problems with each other. Unawareness and shyness are the two basic problems.'

'And there is no proper sex education,' said Umer.

'The point is, that the boy should be teached that sex is not a bad thing,' said Iqbal. 'But unprotected sex is a bad thing.'

'Only two AIDS cases are reported in Multan till now,' said Zeb. 'It means that there must be more than that.'

'But nowadays this is more due to multiple use of syringes, by these addicts,' said Shahzad.

On Sunday 14 December, Israr, Umer and Zeb took me out to see the shrines. On the city bus Israr said, 'This is the first time in my life that I've been on a KB and standing up.'

'The first time ever?'

'Yes.'

'Why is it so crowded today?'

'Because it is Sunday. And many weddings in Pakistan and Punjab take place on Sundays. They used to be on Fridays, but then they changed the holiday because of stock exchanges and international markets. So you see all the ladies have been to the makeup house and they are on their way to some wedding.'

Most of the women and children got off at one stop and we sat down. On the back of the seat in front of me was something scribbled in Urdu.

'Do you know what that says?' asked Zeb. He was sitting behind me.

'No.'

'It says, "Nawaz Sharif, our great leader, I salute you." You see, everywhere there is politics.'

'You see these people?' said Umer. 'They are addicts.'

'How can you tell?'

'Because they are speaking very badly. There are many of them here. If you go to these shrines, you see them there.'

'Why there?'

'Because police cannot get them in those holy places. Also, they have no homes.'

Later in my visit, they showed me around the teaching hospital attached to Nishter Medical College, including the freezers where dead bodies earmarked for dissection were kept. On our way to the freezers we passed a professor showing the muscles in an old man's dissected neck to a group of students. The police picked the bodies up off the streets and gave them to the hospital, and most of them were heroin addicts. Heroin addiction was a severe and growing problem in Pakistan. Most Pakistanis said this was because of the Afghan war of the 1980s and poppy cultivation in Afghanistan, but some also noted that Z.A. Bhutto's prohibition of alcohol had made many turn to heroin. The hospital kept the bodies frozen and dissected them if they were still unclaimed after three years, as they invariably were.

We saw a couple of shrines. 'This is where most of the Shias live,' Israr whispered as we walked towards one shrine through a neighbourhood of brick houses. 'You see' – he pointed up – 'they've got a black flag with a hand and a moon.' The shrines were beautiful large buildings, each housing the festooned tomb of a man revered in the Sufi tradition as a pir or saint. We had to pay a few rupees to check our shoes before going inside. Sufi tradition is suffused with Hindu practices and attitudes, in Pakistan as in Kashmir. Inside one shrine, a scruffy man with long black hair and an unkempt beard elbowed past me and repeatedly kissed the surface of a small alcove in the wall. This disgusted Israr.

'This is strictly against Islam,' he said. 'This is not fair in Islam. You cannot bend before anyone else.'

After a few minutes Israr, Umer and I went outside into the courtyard, where we found Zeb.

'I could not stay inside,' he said. 'They are just misguiding the people to make their own living.'

We walked around. 'This is the Haj complex,' said Israr. 'Haj means pilgrimage. It's the pilgrimage complex. When people go on Haj, they gather here and give them training.'

Further up the same road was a mess of bricks and broken concrete. 'This was a temple,' said Israr.

'Hindu temple?'

'Yes, Hindu temple. When Babri Masjid was destroyed in India, it was trashed by the Muslims.'

A man walking past had just told them this; they hadn't known. 'He was an old man. That's why we believe him,' Israr said.

Umer climbed up the hill of rubble.

'Do you see any Hindu stuff?' Israr called to him.

'No,' he said.

We all climbed to the top, where we could see that the dome was cracked and probably unsafe to walk on. 'You see, it's very near the Baha-uddin Zikrya shrine,' said Zeb.

'Oh,' I said, 'and that's a mosque –' I noticed small loudspeakers and minarets on a building adjacent to the temple.

Inside the temple were bits of coconut, clay bowls for holding ghee or clarified butter, and incense sticks. There were big cracks in the walls and ceiling. Loose bricks lay around the floor.

'So what do you think about Muslims destroying a temple like this?' I asked.

'I think this is not fair,' said Israr. 'This is just aggression, and aggression is not allowed in Islam.'

Zeb went into an alcove off one of the side walls. 'The Mummy returns!' he cried.

As we stood there inside the ruined temple, the call to prayer began sounding from two mosques nearby.

'It would have been nice if this temple had persisted,' said Israr. 'You could have come and taken some snaps of the great Hindu gods.' He said this with regret, but also with disdain.

'It's hard to believe these coconut shells and cups and incense sticks would have stayed here ever since '92,' I guessed.

'Maybe some Hindu worshippers still come here.'

'In secret?'

'In secret, definitely.'

'What if a Hindu worshipper came and worshipped not in secret but openly, in the daytime?'

'The people definitely wouldn't like it, but maybe they would spare his life,' Israr said. 'First time they might warn him and say, "Don't come here."'

'Would it be different for a Christian?'

'Definitely. Because the people have some sympathy for the Christians, but they don't have any sympathy for the Hindus.'

In the evening we went for dinner to a restaurant, Darbari Sajji House. On the way, four of us squashed into a motor rickshaw, we passed a Holiday Inn and a Kentucky Fried Chicken. 'Pizza Hut is under construction,' Zeb told me.

Over dinner we discussed Iraq, Salman Rushdie and other predictable topics. Just as we were polishing off the barbecued chicken, Umer showed me the screen of his mobile phone. It was a text message from Iqbal: 'SADDAM HUSSEIN CAPTURED TO DAY'. Excitedly, we hurried back to the hostel and turned on the television.

'I think it's fake,' Umer said. 'First of all they captured him alone, with no guards.'

'They told that there were 600 soldiers in the attack, and not one gun was fired,' said Iqbal.

'It took an army of 600 US soldiers to capture one Saddam Hussein,' said Umer. 'How can this be possible?'

'If he has handed himself over like this, then I think it's a shame,' said Israr. 'No, I think it is the real Saddam Hussein. But I think that soon as the war was over, they captured him and they've been holding him. This shows that if they can arrest Saddam, why can't they also arrest Osama bin Laden?'

'No, they won't make a fake Osama bin Laden,' said Umer. 'They will take him to some other country so they can attack that country.'

'They have secured the positions of Bush and Tony Blair,' said Israr. 'Because most of Americans will forget the deaths of their own soldiers now that they captured Saddam Hussein.'

'They are surrounding Iran,' said Umer. 'Next thing will be that Osama bin Laden is hiding in Iran, and that they will attack Iran. Only reason they are not attacking Iran is Iran is close to Russia, and it would be breaking their relations with Russia.'

'It's just like a movie,' said Israr. 'First making a person a hero, then making him a villain.'

'They will continue the resistance,' said Zeb.

'Interesting part of the story,' said Iqbal, 'is that he had two machine guns and one pistol in the hole. What is the use of that?'

'I think the war is starting now,' said Israr.

'This is the beginning of World War III,' said Umer.

'Ethan,' said Israr, 'you can imagine that you are getting this much anger from the educated people. Imagine the people in our society who are not educated. What do you suppose will be the effect on them? This just proves the fact that America is being ruled by the Jews.'

'What makes you think it proves that?' I asked.

'Why can't America interfere in Kashmir? Why can't they interfere in Palestine?'

'Why aren't they helping the Muslims there?' asked Umer.

'East Timor can be liberated in just three days,' said Zeb. 'Why can't Kashmir be liberated in 50 years? Why didn't anyone say anything about these killings in Gujarat?'

'I don't blame the Americans,' said Israr. 'I blame the Jews.'

'Don't interpret that we are against America,' Umer said to me. 'We would love to go there, higher studies. We are not against Americans. What they are doing is wrong.'

On the screen, Tony Blair gave a speech about working together to bring prosperity and freedom to Iraq. Then Major-General Ray Odierno said: 'Conditions for the Iraqi people get better every day.'

'What about the oil?' said Israr. 'Is that going to help the Iraqis or the Americans? *Badmash* is a term used for notorious people who impose their will on other people, like a dictator. This is what Bush is becoming.'

Amid all the excitement, we almost missed the day's other news: that a bomb had exploded on a bridge between Islamabad and Rawalpindi, just after Musharraf had passed over it in his motorcade.

'We people, educated people, we think that if Osama bin Laden was involved in the September 11, it was truly wrong,' said Iqbal. 'It was against Islam. There is a different scenario: that 5,000 Israelis did not show up in office that day.'

'Muslims were killed, Christians were killed, but not one single Jew was killed,' said Israr.

'Are you sure about that?' I asked.

'Yes, I'm sure. I read it in an article in a magazine.'

'I'm not sure about the American Jews,' said Iqbal. 'But I'm sure about the Israelis.'

Someone changed the channel to a soccer game, Arsenal v. Blackburn Rovers.

'Your son might be watching it,' said Umer, and I smiled at the thought. 'This is the key player, Henry.'

'I like the French because they are so straightforward,' said Israr. 'They said to the face of the Americans, "We are not going to send you our army."'

'If they said that they invaded Iraq not to get Saddam but to find the weapons of mass destruction,' said Umer, 'where are the weapons of mass destruction?'

'So that is the whole story,' said Israr. 'It's just a drama, a movie.'

'Perhaps *Rambo IV*,' said Umer.

'Or they could give a title: *We've Got Him*,' said Israr.

'Ladies and gentlemen,' said Umer dramatically, 'we've got him!'

'That was all planned,' said Israr. 'And it had to end like this. Because the Americans didn't have a good reason for staying out there. How could they kill so many of their own soldiers without any reason?'

Someone changed the channel again. George Galloway, a maverick member of the British Labour party, was saying: 'The proof will be in the pudding whether the resistance will continue or will collapse. And my prediction is that it will continue until the foreign armies leave Iraq.'

In unison, Israr and Umer cried: 'That's exactly what we've been saying!'

CHAPTER ELEVEN

MAN OF CRISIS

Back in Lahore, my students also gave me an earful.

'Sir, I think it's disrespectful to show people getting medical checkups on TV,' said Sadaf.

'I felt sorry for him,' said Ayela Deen.

'I felt sorry for him too,' said Zunera.

'Bush just needed popularity now because his popularity was going way down,' said Sadaf. 'Now after six months they're going to say we found Osama bin Laden too.'

'Sir,' said Zunera, 'if Saddam has done terrible things, what about Bush?'

'He's only got power, and nobody can say anything to him,' said Ayela.

'Bush is a very harsh person,' said Sadaf. 'He doesn't forgive anyone. He's really cruel. And how do we know that it's recent footage? It's just too shady. There's something wrong.'

'I think Americans are desperate now,' said Usman. 'That's why they have produced Saddam.'

On Christmas Day there was another attempt on Musharraf's life, this time two blasts at a petrol station in Rawalpindi, carefully timed to go off as his motorcade passed. The two assassination attempts brought into relief the brittleness of the country's stability. Musharraf was only the latest Pakistani leader to fail to square the circle. Civilian prime ministers had to come to terms with the army; military men had to go through the democratic motions; everyone was always unhappy with the results. The latest political shell game – indeed, the day's big news on 25 December, until the bomb blasts – was Musharraf's promise to step down as army chief at the end of 2004. But all sorts of things might have happened by then to render the point moot: Musharraf might have found an excuse to rescind his promise, or he might be dead. 'The attempt to legitimise a military government, this whole system that Musharraf has so carefully constructed for his own survival, will go the moment he goes,' Ahmed Rashid told me.

Musharraf had been a paratrooper, and no one could fault him for lacking nerve. 'No problem,' he told reporters after the first attempt on 14 December. 'I am used to such things.' But Pakistanis' expectations were always unrealistically high as well as contradictory, which was why they were always doomed to bitter disappointment. 'I don't think he has it in him to be a dictator,' Helga Ahmed's husband, Jamil, complained to me. 'You have to believe in something and you have to be ruthless. Hitler, whatever his bad qualities and however history may judge him, had it in him.'

'Do you think it's unfortunate for Pakistan that Musharraf doesn't have it in him to be a dictator?' I had asked.

'Yes, it is unfortunate,' he replied. 'One time I asked him how he planned to deal with the fundamentalists. He said, "These things are the result of poverty, illiteracy and overpopulation." I thought that was a very facile thing to say. You could say that about many things. He doesn't believe in anything. He's wishy-washy.'

Jamil's son Temur disliked Musharraf too, but for different reasons. When I told him my colleague Taimur-ul-Hassan felt Musharraf was better for the secular classes than Benazir had been, he said: 'He's not alone. There were a lot of people with liberal pretensions who said he's liberal, he had his picture taken with two poodles, he drinks, so we should support him. But at the end of the day he's still a dictator. It took a C-130 to get rid of our last dictator.'

The civilian political class was restive and bored. 'When the military is in charge, politics is not possible,' a man who had been a student politician and active in the Pakistan People's Party told me. He said he might go back into politics 'when Musharraf goes'. I asked when that might be.

'Ten years, 20 years.'

'He almost went a few days ago,' I said. 'He could go next week.'

'Yes.' It was the verbal equivalent of a shrug.

'It's just one man's friendship with the United States, and security of his job, and everyone is paying the price for it,' Raja Ashfaq Sarwar, who had been a minister under Nawaz Sharif, told me.

'What happens after he goes?' I asked.

'Americans should worry about this, not us.'

'He'll probably be succeeded by another liberal-ish general,' said a newspaper columnist in Karachi. 'But how many liberal generals are left?'

'Is he going to get killed eventually?' I asked Asad Rehman, Rashid Rehman's brother.

'Most probably,' he said. 'In this type of situation, no matter how much security you put around yourself, there's always going to be an element, maybe even within your own security apparatus. Look at Indira Gandhi's death.'

Military men were sanguine. Musharraf's death 'might make some difference outside,' said a retired major who showed up most days for tennis at the Gymkhana. 'But here, we're used to it. There's hardly ever been a transfer of power in a normal way. There would be confusion for a few days.'

I asked my favourite tennis friend, Mian Amjad, for a prediction. His answer was to remember the fall of Ayub Khan, Pakistan's first military dictator, who ruled from 1958 to 1969. 'I was in England, and there was great uncertainty about Ayub Khan and Bhutto and all of that,' he said. 'One of my friends asked me, "Will Ayub Khan remain president, with so many rallies going against him?" I said, "He has done so much for the country. He will be there for another ten years." When I came back, he was gone.'

I assigned my students to write about the assassination attempts, and we talked about them in class.

'If he dies, then what's going to happen?' asked Ayela Deen.

'The country will be in a chaos,' said Zainab.

'Sir, it's not such a big thing to say if Musharraf would die, but what about his family?' said Sadaf. 'Aren't they shit scared?'

'This country is already in a state of confusion, and the extremist parties are already against him,' said Ayela Deen. 'Once Musharraf conks off, do you think whoever takes his place would want to follow the same path?'

'I have a question,' said Amit, the Indian boy. 'Everybody is talking about army, army. What about the democracy?'

'It's a pseudo-democracy really,' said Ayela. 'This is not a democratic country.'

'Even America doesn't have a proper democratic system,' said Neelum.

'Democracy is an ideal,' said Ayla Hassan. 'Because it assures that everyone has equal rights, which is not possible. I think dictatorship is quite a good form of government.'

'Bhutto was strong,' said Neelum. 'But Sadaf is right: Benazir and Nawaz Sharif were not strong.'

'They were corrupt people,' said Ayela Deen. 'They just opened the loot and ran off.'

'I think there's nothing black or white,' said Ayla Hassan. 'I think there's a grey area in which we all have to live. I don't mind if the politicians are a little corrupt, as long as they do their duty.'

'I'm just astonished at his guts, the way he's staying out in the open,' said Sadaf. 'Nawaz Sharif would have gone underground.'

'Benazir used to wear a bulletproof jacket,' said Ayela Deen.

'Benazir knew that she was wrong, and she was a coward, basically,' said Zunera. 'There's no guilt in Musharraf's heart.'

'The worst is that he's a self-elected man,' said Ayela Deen. 'And if he conked off, there are all these people who would say, 'If he could be self-elected, why can't we?''

Like many members of Pakistan's elite class, Ayela had met Musharraf personally. 'At my cousin's wedding, he walked in with his wife,' she told me. 'He came over and he shook our hands, and he grabbed my cheek and he said, "You're very cute." He has no arrogance attached to him. He's open to any question you might ask him. My sister asked my uncle if she could ask him some questions. And he said, "No, he's at my son's wedding, and he doesn't have time." And Musharraf spoke up and said, "No, let the lady speak. I have time." And they spoke for like 45 minutes.'

In early January 2004, amid heavy security, a summit of the South Asian Association for Regional Cooperation was held in Islamabad. The summit ended with a hopeful feeling that a Prague Spring was in the air between Pakistan and India. Direct air links had been renewed on 1 January, and trains betweens Delhi and Lahore would start running again on 15 January. People hoped that a military ruler and a Hindu-nationalist prime minister might achieve what more liberal leaders, obliged to protect their domestic flanks, could not. My students remembered the last SAARC summit, in Kathmandu in November 2002, when Musharraf had ostentatiously shaken hands with Indian Prime Minister Vajpayee. 'It was a really long table,' said Ayla Hassan, 'and Musharraf was at one end and Vajpayee was at the other.

And Musharraf got up and walked all the way over to shake his hand.' There was even heady talk of a regional currency union. But Kashmir was the linchpin, and something Cecil Chaudhry had said to me in July 1999 came to mind: 'They never get anywhere. And they never will get anywhere. Because if they ever do come to any agreement, the million-dollar question is, will the Kashmiris accept that?'

Early on 15 January I went with my three male students to the train station to witness the Samjhota Express leave for Amritsar, across the border in India. None of the girls wanted to go. Neither did Shakoor. 'I no interest India,' he said. 'India bad country. I interest England.' But I bullied him into going because I thought he would enjoy it and because my students liked him. Besides Usman and Adnan there was Usman Azhar, or Big Usman as we called him.

We met at the station at seven. Usman pointed out a sign in Urdu. 'It is written that train will start from 15 January, 8 am. And you know the train is called Samjhota Express. And you know what samjhota means?'

'No, tell me,' I said.

'Agreement,' said Big Usman.

'It is an agreement,' agreed Usman. 'But like an agreement between husband and wife whose relations are not good.'

Multi-coloured tinsel hung from the side of the train, which was a standard green with yellow trim.

'But I think the train that used to go to India was of red colour,' said Usman. 'To specify that train they made it of red colour. But this time I think is just a makeshift arrangement.'

'Sir, be aware of pickpockets,' said Adnan.

'I've got my wallet in my front pocket,' I said.

'That's good.'

We went on the train, which was not crowded, and separately interviewed passengers. 'Are you going to Amritsar?' I asked a 25-year-old man named Aziz Mohammed.

'No, my grandfather and grandmother are going,' he said. 'But the problem is, we are from Karachi. We have to go for visa processing to Islamabad. Three times we have to go to Islamabad.' In 1995, the train I had ridden from Rawalpindi/Islamabad to Karachi had taken 30 hours in one direction. 'If there is embassy in Karachi, it would be easier for Karachi people. It would be good if you would convey this message.'

'Where is your family from?' I asked.

'India.'

'Where?'

'Hyderabad.'

'When did they come to Pakistan?'

'After separation of India and Pakistan. Nineteen fifty-four, I think. But it is good that India and Pakistan are compromising. Good in future. Really very nice. They have to appreciate, you know?'

'Why are your grandparents going by train and not bus?'

'Because it's the first day,' he said. 'For enjoyment, you might say. One more thing, buses are full until 25 February. Most of the people are preferring the train to the bus.'

'But why is the train empty?'

'It will be full, *inshallah*.'

The train pulled out at 8.05 and we met back up on the platform.

'Sir, I spent very nice time with Japanese boy,' said Adnan excitedly. 'He is coming from Japan on world tour. When I ask him about Vietnam, he said America is doing very wrong. And when I ask him about Israel, he said one side Muslim right, one side Israel right. Oh, and sir – he has no religion! When I asked him what was his religion, he said, "I have no religion."'

'What did you say to him?'

'I say, "Oh, it's good! One of my teachers has also no religion!"'

'I think our other students missed this opportunity,' said Usman.

'Yes, pretty lame,' I agreed.

'Because people give more information to girls. They just got 30 or 40 minutes of sleep, but they missed this whole event.'

'Sir,' said Adnan, 'when I told Usman Azhar, "Please you come with me and interview these people," he said, "No, you just go."'

'Do you think he's shy?'

'Yes. I think he has no ability to meet other people.'

It was true that Big Usman was quiet and awkward, but he chose serious topics to write about and had a remarkably mature understanding of world events. 'Musharraf says that if Pakistan is not friendly with Israel,' he once told me, 'then India will get advantages and Pakistan will get disadvantages. And it is better to get advantages than disadvantages.'

Tea and sandwiches had been laid out for the press. We helped ourselves.

'I think this is good job,' said Adnan.

'Journalism?'

'Yes. You learn things, meet people, see some sort of new things.'

Afterwards, Shakoor said to me: 'Sir, train station very much enjoy. And I going to India. Passport, visa after Eid I get. Then I go India. My grandfather was Indian. Smuggler. Small smuggler. Only clothes, not drugs. And good man.'

'You're going to miss this club,' Sajjad Gul said to me at tennis one day in January.

'You bet I'm going to miss it,' I said. 'I'll be back, *inshallah*.'

Tennis had been a wonderful part of my life in Lahore, but it ended on a sour note. A big, standoffish man who had recently returned from the US walked off court when I asked to join him and Omar Qayyum knocking up, until a fourth could be found for doubles. He told Omar in Urdu, in my presence, that he preferred to practice his ground strokes with Tariq. Maybe he disliked me because I had missed a few overheads one day as his doubles partner. I had been deferential to the club and tolerant of the members' quirks, because I was grateful and a guest. But to be snubbed so overtly was just too insulting and creepy. I had intended to host a tea for the gents on a Sunday before I left. Instead, I abruptly withdrew.

This was not my place, not my world – and it was helpful to be reminded of that. 'You always commit yourself firmly up front, then you step back and assess – that's your m.o.,' a friend had once said to me. It was true, and I had done it again. It was time for me to step back, not just from the Gymkhana but from Pakistan. 'Well, it's time to move on to the next thing,' my father had told me years earlier, at the end of a visit to Haiti. It was advice always worth referring back to. I had lost 20 pounds and become very fit; I had improved my backhand. And I had fond memories: of Mian-sahib saying, 'Irfan told me that you started playing tennis only three years ago. And for that you play remarkably well'; of Butt-sahib, the philosopher of tennis: 'Thing is to sweat. And another thing is that it's refuge from the nightmare. You're so involved, you forget everything.'

I had a few pieces of unfinished business. I sat down one evening with Asad Rehman. With his older brother Rashid, Najam Sethi and Ahmed Rashid, Asad had been involved in the almost forgotten insurgency in the remote province of Balochistan in the 1970s. The connections among the four men, and the tight-knit quality of the Pakistani elite generally, had been underscored for me earlier in January, when a businessman named Arif Abid had taken me to a party at the swanky Sindh Club in Karachi to celebrate the wedding of his friend Azhar Karim. It turned out that Sethi, Ahmed Rashid and Rashid Rehman all were longtime friends with Azhar Karim, and all three had flown from Lahore for the party.

'What are you doing here?' Ahmed Rashid asked me in a jolly tone, affecting surprise.

'Actually, I'm with the CIA,' I told him.

That was one of several whisky-soaked parties I had attended in swift succession over five blurry days in Karachi. As we drove back late that night to his house, Arif had said to me: 'You get a kind of culture shock, the next morning when you wake up and have to deal with the nitty-gritty of Pakistan again.'

Asad Rehman was writing a book about the Balochistan insurgency. 'I don't want that bit of history to disappear unrecorded,' he said. 'Even if my analysis is totally wrong or history proves me wrong, as long as the actual events get recorded, that's the important thing. And when it comes to people who died, their memories must be kept alive for the sake of history itself.'

There was a drought in Balochistan in the early 1970s, and controversy over federal control versus provincial autonomy. This was during and just after the Bangladesh War, and Z.A. Bhutto 'was a man who could not stand opposition from any quarter,' as Asad pointed out. The four young men from Lahore's privileged classes were radicalised. Of the four, Asad was the only one who saw combat.

'Having shared the experience of people who were living a life that was barely keeping their body and soul together,' he said, 'eking out a livelihood from little pieces of land on the sides of mountains, torn clothes – you see that, and you come suddenly back to this, and you see the affluence, and you think, Why? Why is there this difference? Except for Ahmed, both Najam and my brother have not even been to the mountains. Ahmed was there, in the mountains, for six–seven years. But he was very much protected, because unfortunately his eyesight was not very good, and his hearing was not very good, and he's flat-footed.'

'Needless to say, I think, you were never one of the people who thought of Bhutto as a great champion of the masses?' I asked.

'No.'

'Some people still today think of him as that.'

'Yes, but they are beginning to be disillusioned. There is no longer as much force in their arguments. He's no longer the national hero that he was in the late 1970s.'

I also spoke to Hina Jilani, the lawyer who with her sister, Asma Jehangir, did courageous work on behalf of women and religious minorities. Asma had defended and protected Salamat Masih, the Christian teenager whose death sentence under the blasphemy law had been overturned by the Lahore High Court the day before I arrived in the country in February 1995, and who as a result had had to flee into exile in Germany. Taimur-ul-Hassan called the two sisters 'the most brave, competent and dedicated people, who have been able to make an impact on human rights in Pakistan. These are my views based on working with them closely. Very, very inspiring people.'

'One thing that I cannot tolerate is injustice,' Hina told me. 'I fortunately still have the capacity to be outraged when there is injustice. My father was a politician, and he was always in the opposition because he was always protecting some principle or other. I have been targeted personally. My sister has been targeted personally. My family was held hostage for two hours, in this house. We feel that at least, if everybody keeps quiet, then who is going to take up these issues? That helps you get over the fear.'

I asked how long she and Asma had been fighting for human rights.

'About 25 years,' she said.

'Have things improved?'

'In some ways, yes. Take the example of women's issues. When we started, women's issues were not a political issue. Now, every party has to speak about women's rights, whether they believe in them or not.'

Her long experience in her own country and internationally had given Hina a perspective on recent events in the United States. She had been at UN headquarters in New York on 11 September 2001. 'Mary Robinson and I were walking down the corridor, and we saw that on the screen,' she remembered. 'People were so terrified. And Mary and I asked, "Why is there this level of fear?" And we realised these people have never had to deal with this sort of thing. We deal with it every day. We pick up bodies from the street. Americans were in shock. But for God's sake, let them come out of it.'

In November 2001 she had spoken at the Kennedy School of Government at Harvard. 'In my speech, which was on related topics, I said that this will impact on human rights. If you react, and you do it in an unjust way, you will make room for more resentment, and ultimately the people of America will suffer for it. And when I stopped speaking people got up, and some of them applauded, and they said, "Thank you for taking up this issue," because nobody was talking about it. Two years later I was in New York, and I attended two conferences focused on this theme: human rights and terrorism. At least three panels. So people are now talking about it. For me that's a hopeful sign.'

Back in December, my friend Zahyd Hamead had invited me to speak to his English-language classes at the Islamic University in Islamabad. His students had asked me predictable but thoughtful questions about Kashmir, 11 September, Iraq, Palestine and the Western media. Near the end of the last class, an earnest, bearded young fellow had raised his hand. 'I have a question,' he said. 'Who created us, and for what purpose?'

The very awkwardness of such a question can be fruitful, if the goal is to find common ground and reinforce mutual respect. Respect implies difference and distance.

I answered that our purpose is to learn. 'I'm not likely to become a Muslim,' I added, just to stir things up.

'Why not?' the student asked.

'Well, I don't believe Jesus was the uniquely divine son of God,' I conceded. 'So you've got me one step toward accepting Islam. Keep working on me.'

In early February, I returned to Islamabad to see Zahyd again. He told me he had asked his students: 'What did you think of your interaction with Ethan?'

'Sir, is he a good American?' they had asked him.

He had responded Socratically: 'There are 290 million Americans. Not all of them are like Bush. Now let me ask you something: There are 1 billion Muslims in the world. Can you tell me that they're all good?'

Zahyd was in his forties, of partly Turkish origin, had grown up in England, had lived in Iran and in the US state of Iowa. 'When we go to these eat-all-you-can type places in Iowa, I've seen some of the biggest backsides,' he said. He was enterprising and engaged, with a depth and breadth of experience that gave him a critical perspective on Pakistan as well as on the West, tempered by a native sympathy. He took me to see Rawal Lake outside Islamabad, where he used to enjoy rafting.

'I have never seen it like this,' he said. The shore was crowded with young men playing loud music and taxi drivers washing their cars. 'I mean, this is diabolical. Oh, and they've cut down all the bloody trees. Great! And when they do go anywhere there's only two things they can do: stand and listen to jukeboxes in their cars, or do barbecues. This used to be a lovely place. Five years ago, when Zeeba and I and the boys came here, there used to be barely four or five people here. And I brought one of those inflatable rafts from England. We used to go out on the lake.'

He pointed out a shantytown on a far shore of the lake. 'That's an illegal settlement,' he said. 'So you can imagine the sewage. Apparently they're from Sindh, from Karachi. They got driven out of Karachi and they had nowhere to go, so they ended up here.'

'I think Islamabad won't be recognisable ten or twenty years from now,' I said.

'Oh, I think sooner than that. See that land over there? All those houses? All those houses belong to Abdul Qadeer Khan. It's the same old story: people getting too greedy and then ending up disgraced.'

A.Q. Khan was the Pakistani nuclear scientist who had recently been exposed for having sold nuclear secrets to Libya, Iran and North Korea.

'These are all the aimless, jobless youths,' I remarked.

'Yeah, and what lies ahead? And they're producing more and more. The worst part of it is, they think this is really cool. This is Pakistan in a nutshell. You had this dream of a president, of a new capital, ecological and all, and you get this.'

Zahyd's mood reinforced my own. I had recently wasted a lot of emotional energy dealing with Pakistan International Airlines and with the bureaucrats of my own university, who had misplaced my return ticket to London and then suggested that I should have to pay for a new one and wait fourteen months to be reimbursed. The result was that I was feeling disgusted and appalled by Pakistan.

'I think I'm going to say some harsh things about this country,' I said.

'I don't think anybody's written a book about this country without saying harsh things,' said Zahyd.

We met up with his former student Hassan Iqbal, an earnestly well-read Pakistani of 24 who had grown up in Saudi Arabia, whom

I had met in December. 'I've been living only five years in Pakistan, and I've learned so much,' Hassan told me. 'From being a Wahhabi, I've become a Sufi. It was coming to Pakistan and seeing the reality here, the oppressed people, that changed my aggression into some positive thing. I had been living in Saudi for 18 years in a high middle-class lifestyle. If I had gone to America, I might have ended up just as some engineer, probably getting kicked out after 11 September, going for marriage with some white woman. Coming here provided me with a vital identification. Now at least I think I'm thinking as a human being.'

On 5 December, at dinner with me and Zahyd, Hassan had claimed to have heard from a contact inside the ISI – the Pakistani intelligence service – that the US had already captured Saddam Hussein. Nine days later, in Multan, I had learned of Saddam's capture.

'But things have not changed,' Hassan said now. 'The situation is still the same since the capture of Saddam Hussein. It's like Renaissance in Muslim world, this war, actually. This war has really been a blessing in disguise for the Muslim world. The logjam has broken. It's more like that French Revolution in France, that opened up the gates of Europe.'

'But you know how the French Revolution ended?' I asked him. Zahyd laughed.

'Yes,' said Hassan. 'With Napoleon. I'm coming to that.'

We talked about the US election campaign. 'Lieberman's out,' I said.

'He's not American himself. He's a member of Knesset.'

I mentioned John Kerry.

'But he is not good for Pakistan.'

'Because he's part Jewish?'

'No, these Democrats in general.'

'Because Republicans are more likely to appreciate a rogue state than the Democrats,' suggested Zahyd.

We discussed the A.Q. Khan nuclear proliferation scandal. 'All those countries are in the axis of evil,' Hassan pointed out.

'This is really significant, I think,' said Zahyd. 'I personally think Pakistan's goose is cooked. They're going to dismantle Pakistan without firing a shot. He is a national hero. He could have anything for the taking in Pakistan. Why would he sell nuclear materials to North Korea and Iran? They offered him probably billions.'

'Events are moving so quickly and rapidly that you can't keep up,' said Hassan.

I stayed several nights with Hassan's family in Rawalpindi, just down the road from Islamabad. It was winter, and their house was unheated; it took most of each morning for my toes to thaw out. But I enjoyed his parents' company, and Hassan showed me around the city's markets on his motorbike. He showed me his many books and carefully labelled and organised files of press clippings.

'Have you actually read all these articles?' I asked.

'Yes,' he said. 'Nowadays you have to know each and every subject. You cannot be a journalist if you don't know economics, you cannot be a diplomat if you don't know economics, you cannot be an economist if you don't know anthropology of society.'

He had the Encarta encyclopedia on his computer. We had both been trying to remember who the President of the United States had been at the time of the Mexican War. He thought it was Knox; I told him there hadn't been a President Knox. We searched the entries on Encarta until we figured out that it was James Knox Polk. 'For 30 rupees I got the software,' he said. 'And I keep updating it. This is the world of knowledge.'

'Hassan, I'm really impressed with how curious and intellectually enthusiastic you are,' I said.

'Well, my brother says, "Do you want to be a clerk, or do you want to have a lucrative job?"' he said. '"Do you want to earn forty–fifty thousand your whole life, or do you want to earn six, seven figures?"'

Hassan's father invited me into the TV room. 'Come in,' he said. 'We are watching his speech. He is saying that European countries are more involved than Pakistan.' Musharraf was on the screen, in a room full of reporters, wearing a camouflage uniform and a nametag that said 'Pervez'. He was talking about A.Q. Khan.

'Is Pakistan important, or is the hero important?' he said in English. 'Pakistan is important.' And, in Urdu: 'I will never save the hero at the cost of Pakistan.'

A Reuters reporter asked whether he would allow UN inspectors into Pakistan.

'This is an independent nation,' said Musharraf. 'Nobody comes inside and checks our things. We check them ourselves. There are Europeans involved. Have you gone and asked them that the same thing should be done there also?'

'The good thing about Ethan is that he's against his own establishment,' Hassan told his parents.

'Last two weeks there was a wedding,' said Hassan's mother. 'Qadeer Khan was there. I was so anxious to go and meet him.'

A.Q. Khan's hero status meant that Musharraf had to handle the whole thing with great delicacy. 'Qadeer Khan is a hero for the whole Muslim world,' Nusrat had told me. 'Bush is blackmailing Musharraf.' My student Usman expressed widespread sentiments when he said: 'Even if he smuggled the technology to Islamic countries, I don't think it's bad. Because Islamic world needs to be a bit more stronger.'

'Do you think this is a major crisis for Musharraf?' I asked Hassan.

'Oh yes,' he said. 'He is the man of crisis.'

'Every year he has crisis,' his mother remarked cheerfully. 'Two years before, Taliban crisis. Then last year, Iraq crisis. Now this Qadeer Khan crisis.'

CHAPTER TWELVE

THE HARDEST ROAD
TO TRUTH

Near the end of my stay in Pakistan, I had a conversation with a man in late middle age who had migrated there from India as a young man. He had failed – or refused – to feel at home in Pakistan.

'I had to make a choice whether I was going to stay in England and merge myself into that society,' he told me. 'And I chose not to, because I didn't want to give up my identity. The one place where I could have – where I thought I could have been at ease with my past and live in the society, and it's impossible now anyway – was the United States. And the curious thing is that I'm an outsider in this society also. I interact very little in this society, as you might have noticed.'

It was a sense of having reached a dead end in his hometown in India, plus a desire to be near family who were already in Pakistan, that led to his decision to migrate. It had nothing to do with politics or a commitment to the country, he said. 'It was purely circum-stances beyond one's control.'

'You were sort of a victim of history, weren't you?' I said.

'I wouldn't put it as strongly as that,' he said. 'One was sort of caught in the swings of history, and one didn't have the wherewithal to meet it on one's own terms.'

'In what way? What wherewithal didn't you have?'

'Oh, in every way. Financial, material, intellectual. And in fact in many ways it was a contradiction. Because I was already an agnostic, I wasn't sympathetic to the creation of this country. And I literally had to kill a large part of myself in switching over.'

'In what way?'

'You see, I don't accept their point of view. But I don't want to argue with them. In a way you could say I used the country, because I came here without believing in it. So I thought that the honest thing to do was to remain outside the mainstream.

'This was a country that was formed on a negativist principle. In fact, you could say that it took the opposite course of what a country should take, because instead of enlarging its people's view, it diminished it. And the reason it can't look at itself in the mirror is because of that. There you are, people living side by side for twelve hundred years, a thousand years, ever since the Muslims came here. Probably 2,000, because most of them were converts anyway. Then suddenly overnight they decide to go their separate ways.

'The Brits used it and exacerbated it, you know. No two ways about that. You lived in Southeast Asia. You must have been to Malaysia, you must have been to Singapore. There, colonialism was more benign. And it was left in a more benign manner. Here, it was left in a rush and in the crudest possible manner. And all the emphasis was on saving face, you know. One of the sad side effects of Partition is that instead of studying the immediate past in terms of the colonisation of the country, and what it had done to people and the society and the economy, it concentrated on justifying its own coming into being, which was in a way sidestepping most of current history.

'I'm really the last person who should be talking about Pakistan,' he added.

'I disagree,' I said.

'No, no,' he said. 'Because both on a personal level and on an intellectual level, it has hurt. It divided one's family, it destroyed what had been one's home for generations, and it polarised opinions so that no fruitful dialogue is possible. Look at it this way: instead of Pakistan becoming more like India, meaning more secular and democratic, actually India is becoming more like Pakistan. What is that? Is it that poison spreads? Or is it just the times? Because last time I went to India, I didn't feel very comfortable. It had become so overtly Hindu, you know. Ten years back I used to sort of hanker to read Indian publications, and the internet wasn't there. Now, the way things have gone there, I don't have any interest.'

'Because you're not a true believer in this country, I think you've got a more interesting angle on things than many people here do,' I suggested.

'Okay, but it doesn't do any good,' he insisted. 'To me, life is interesting when you go out that door and you look at what you can add to your life to make it more rich, more splendid. And one doesn't see that anymore. It's pure survival, looking after number one.'

He was eloquent but ill at ease, and getting more so the longer we talked. I pressed him to say more. We were drinking beer, in private of course.

'Look,' he said. 'This is a vast, vast area, you know. I mean what we're talking about, not geographically, which it is also. It takes really deep thinking, and one suppresses it, because one has to get on with one's life. I think a hundred years from now, this will be a forgotten time in history. It hasn't achieved anything. Maybe it could achieve something if Vajpayee and Musharraf can make some rapprochement. But even that would be only a beginning.'

Like many people, he found my sometimes obsessive scribbling of notes off-putting. We discussed the relative advantages of taking notes versus using a tape recorder. I told him I preferred taking notes, because a tape recorder made people self-conscious and was time-consuming for me.

'Everything has pluses and minuses,' he allowed. 'There are no absolutes in life. In that sense the Hindus really got it right. It's the only natural religion, and it's based more on observation. The monotheisms are based on an imposition that has conceit running right through it.'

By the third beer, we had widened our vista to the world at large.

'Ethan, I accept the point that there is a totalitarianism in Islam,' he said. 'There is that. Islam's contention that the Quran is the last message, and that that is the be-all and end-all, is really going to be the battlefield, in my view. Look at it this way: the Jews say they're the chosen people. Islam says it's the final message. The Christians rule the roost. Where does the answer lie?'

'Um …'

'It's a facetious question. The answer actually doesn't lie in any of them.'

Some Pakistanis thought I was with the CIA. What would Americans think when I told them – or when they saw in my passport, as I entered the country – that I had been to Pakistan? Paranoia is one of several traits Americans and Pakistanis share.

'I wonder what they'll do to me when I go back to the States,' I said.

'Look, don't misunderstand me, but I really don't think they'll do much,' he said. 'They'll probably just ask you to tell them everything you've learned about Pakistan, living here for five months.' This was deflating, but it evoked a happy memory of Ed Pettit in Bangkok, saying: 'I wanted to be arrested or interrogated, and I never could be. You can't ever be busted in the US when you want to be.'

'Okay, there's this guy Padilla,' said my friend. 'But the cases like him you can count on one hand. Lindh is a different case altogether.' This was John Walker Lindh, the infamous 'American Taliban'.

'Because he took up arms,' I said.

'Because he took up arms. As sad a story as that is, it's a different story. I mean, that poor guy, they'll probably release him in ten years or something, but his life is finished. He's a guy who would have been happy if he had been born in the time of hippies and flower power and all of that. He was born in an upper-middle-class family, and he felt that affluence was an end in itself, that truth had nothing to do with it. And he chose the hardest road to truth.

'This knife-edge we live on today is because everyone sees the successes, nobody sees the failures. Nobody is willing to see the failures. And for every success, there are hundreds of failures. And television plays such a big part in it: when you're sitting every night in front of the TV, and it's spewing out this stuff, and you get the sense that this is the centre of things, this is where it's at. You don't know how many ways I prefer living here to living in the West. At least you're not being bombarded with ads. There's no pressure to keep up. To be upper middle class in Pakistan is to be more independent than in 99 per cent of places today, as long as you can keep away from the mythology. The way I see it, all sides are crazy.'

'So as an individual, what should the response be?'

'As an individual, I think the response is to isolate yourself. But as a society – let's say it's a melting pot. The various elements in that melting pot have to combine. That's the only hope I see. I really think the world can't take opposing ideologies much longer. And what the West needs to realise is that the ideology that's doing the most damage is not Islam, it's Zionism. It was all going very well when the American economy was going well, and the world was following in America's footsteps.'

'Do you mean in the '90s?'

'Before that. All through the '60s, '70s, '80s. And now that the confrontation [with the Soviet Union] is no longer there and

American leadership should be accepted even more emphatically, it's a manifestation of Bush's failure that he's asserting it through war rather than through any other means.'

At the tail end of this long and intense conversation, which I scribbled down furiously until my wrist ached, my friend asked that I not publish his name. Dismayed, I remonstrated with him to change his mind. He refused.

'I've made my compromises with this society,' he said, 'and I'm not willing to expose myself in that way.'

'I'm going out on a limb writing this book,' I said.

'You don't have to come back to Pakistan,' he pointed out.

'But I do have to go back to the States,' I said. 'Or not.'

As I write this final chapter I find in my notebooks encounters and dialogue, whole conversations, that I wish I could include. When I was in Pakistan, I panicked that I would have too little material. When I sat down to write, it astonished me to find that I had far more than could fit in a book of 80,000 words. Even so, my notebooks contain only traces of all I experienced and encountered, which in turn is a thin and arbitrary slice of all that was going on. It's like the way newspapers pile up, unread despite best intentions: too much happening, too much to read and know, too much effort to make the connections, too little attention to spare.

A published book is the residue of a writer's failure to do what he initially set out to do. If the story I've told is a bit rough around the edges, then so has been my experience, and so is Pakistan. I witnessed a moment in history in a particular place: the action and passion of my time. All I can do is to record faithfully what I've witnessed; I speak only for myself. I have to trust that some of my words will take on overtones as time passes and events fall into place in the longer perspective, and that I've executed my charge. 'Why are you here?' Mian Amjad asked me. 'Why are you in

Pakistan? Why are we sitting down talking like this? I've been a member of Gymkhana for so long; I've never sat down like this. Everybody has been given an assignment. And you look at this assignment, and you see that there is a pattern also.'

My initial discovery of that part of the world had been heavily mediated through a youthful obsession with another writer who had travelled there. A decade on I was no longer youthful or worshipful. I had earned my own chops. I had begun as a disciple and a literary tourist; I had become a mature practitioner.

V.S. Naipaul had been to Lahore more than once, had even famously met his second wife there. But such tittle-tattle no longer interested me as it had done ten years earlier in Kashmir. I didn't ask many people in Lahore for Naipaul anecdotes, nor did I bother to reread *Among the Believers*. Salima Hashmi, a prominent artist and a dean at Beaconhouse National University, had met Naipaul. 'I thought *A House for Mr Biswas* was his best book,' she told me. 'But I also thought that if I passed such a comment I would stall the dinner party.' The evening I spoke with Ahmed Rashid in his office, he stepped out for a few minutes. Browsing his books, I opened his hardback copy of *Sir Vidia's Shadow* and found it inscribed for him by Paul Theroux, intriguingly, 'with gratitude for your wise counsel.' Ahmed had hosted Naipaul in the mid-1990s while he was in Lahore researching his book *Beyond Belief*, had introduced him to his second wife – and had fallen out with him. He wasn't alone. Naipaul, Rashid Rehman told me, 'has a lot of ex-friends in Pakistan.'

So I was well over that infatuation, which was an achievement. And I had lived through a decade's worth of encounters with Pakistan, in two senses: I had experienced them, and I had survived, alive and well. My memories come into focus on particular moments: Haji, in Srinagar, squatting and happily arranging and smoking his hubble-bubble; beardies hoisting Ayatollah Khomeini posters and burning an American flag on the Mall in Lahore, on my first day in

Pakistan in 1995; Tariq praying, his baseball cap turned backwards, near the grass courts; my hapless but loyal friend Shakoor running out of petrol taking me to the airport for my flight to Karachi, and having to ask another motorcyclist to tow us to a pump.

My fondest memories are of my students, above all Usman, who had such a deft angle of vision and such admirable ambition. 'Actually, I don't want to have love marriage,' he told me. 'I want to have marriage which my father will like. I think my father will choose the right girl for me.'

'Does the father usually choose, or does the mother choose?' I asked.

'Depends who is stronger. Depends who is in charge of the home gummint. My home gummint is run by my father. Finance ministry is my mother.'

I was also especially fond of Zunera Khalid, who at first seemed such an unpromising and callow rich girl, only 19 when our semester started, but who blossomed so impressively through hard work and hard personal experiences, while remaining so ingenuously charming. 'Sir, how do you develop a habit of reading books like this, about Taliban and stuff like this?' she asked me. 'I can only read love stories.'

'A book should be interesting,' I told her.

'Sir, when I was young I could never read *Jane Eyre*, *Pride and Prejudice*, *Little Women*, books like this.'

'Why not?'

'I don't know. Too many big words. And Charles Dickens also. My teachers always used to suggest me and my classfellows to read such books during our vacations. And I never could because, sir, they're boring!'

And pious Neelum, who said, 'Before coming to this university, I didn't even know what was going on in Pakistan. Now I feel I can discuss each and every thing that's currently happening in the world with the elder members of my family.' Neelum told us how she had spent New Year's Eve. 'First of all, I called all my friends and wished them Happy New Year,' she said. 'Then I spent my New Year's night in a very special way.'

'Praying?' asked Ayla Hassan.

'Yeah, praying. Until two am I prayed for everyone: all my teachers, all my classfellows. And I recited surahs from the Quran. I experienced something different this December 31st. Most New Year's, after watching movies, I would wake up in the morning feeling that I've wasted a lot of my time – it was useless. But for the very first time I woke up feeling nice, and I got a very good sleep, feeling I had done something very good. It was nice. I was happy.'

EPILOGUE IN ENGLAND

On 12 March 2004, en route to the local Chinese takeaway, I ran into my friend Syd at his front door.

'Isn't it terrible what's happened in Madrid?' he said. Syd and his middle-aged daughter, Annie, travelled often to Spain for holidays.

I agreed and added, 'I think it's Al Qaeda.'

Within a few days, the Spanish government's willingness to make political use of the bombings by accusing the Basque separatist group ETA looked not only shameful but pathetic.

'In a way you and I are "lucky",' said Syd, making inverted comma signs with his fingers, 'to be living through these times. Because there's been nothing like it. The First World War, the Second World War, Korea, Vietnam – they were wars. This is something different. But from a journo's point of view – it's terrible, but we're living through history. There's been nothing like it in my lifetime.'

'What do they want?' I asked, meaning the terrorists.

'They want to hit America because they feel, rightly enough, that the Palestinians are always losing out,' he said. 'And they want everyone to follow their fundamentalist Islam. And you know what that means: you won't be listening to Johnny Cash. And I sure as hell won't be listening to Sinatra.'

'You know, in Pakistan I met a lot of people who are not like that,' I said.

FURTHER READING

The first book any foreigner should read about Pakistan is the accessible thematic history *Pakistan: Eye of the Storm* by Owen Bennett Jones (Yale University Press, 2002; published in Pakistan by Vanguard Books). It includes a good summary of the Kashmir dispute, and the fascinating chapter on the 1999 coup is worth the book's price alone.

The second book to read, *Breaking the Curfew: A Political Journey through Pakistan* by Emma Duncan (Michael Joseph, 1989; available in paperback from Arrow), covers the transition from Zia ul Haq's military dictatorship to the civilian rule of the 1990s. It's now dated but is of substantial historical interest. Christina Lamb's *Waiting for Allah* (Hamish Hamilton, 1991) covers much of the same ground as Duncan and is also worth reading.

Jinnah of Pakistan and *Z.A. Bhutto of Pakistan*, both by Stanley Wolpert and published by Oxford University Press, are the standard biographies of Pakistan's two most important leaders. The academic historian Lawrence Ziring's latest book, *Pakistan: At the Crosscurrent of History* (Oxford: Oneworld Publications, 2004) has been recommended to me as concise and accessible to non-specialist readers.

Novels set in or concerned with Pakistan include the classic *Train to Pakistan* by Khushwant Singh and *Ice-Candy Man* by Bapsi Sidhwa, both of which depict the chaos and tragedy of the 1947 Partition. *Moth Smoke* by Mohsin Hamid portrays the latter-day denizens of Gulberg, Lahore's elite area. Accessible and enjoyable books of non-fiction on Pakistan include John Keay's two marvellous books on 19th-century explorers, *When Men and Mountains Meet* and *The Gilgit Game*, both published in paperback editions in Pakistan by Oxford University Press.

Anthony Davis of *Jane's Defence Weekly* and Ahmed Rashid of the *Far Eastern Economic Review* and *The Daily Telegraph* are two of the most authoritative journalists covering Afghanistan, Pakistan and the region. Ahmed Rashid's articles in *The New York Review of Books*, and his books *Taliban* and *Jihad* (both published by Yale University Press), are essential reading.

ACKNOWLEDGEMENTS

Isa Daudpota and Siva Vaidhyanathan separately suggested I use the occasion of my semester teaching at Beaconhouse National University to write a book. I might or might not have thought to do so unprompted, so thanks first to them.

During my stay there between September 2003 and February 2004, many people in Pakistan were extremely and spontaneously generous to me with their time, contacts, encouragement and other support. Thanks especially to Navid Shahzad, Salima Hashmi and Taimur-ul-Hassan at BNU; Ahmed Rashid and Zarina Sadik in Lahore; Rashid Rehman for sponsoring my guest membership at the Lahore Gymkhana Tennis Club; Helga and Jamil Ahmed and the Minallah family, Zahyd Hamead and Mardie Troth in Islamabad; Arif Abid and Beena Sarwar in Karachi; and Arif's brother Nasir Abid, whom I've had the honour to call a friend since 1994.

Abdul Shakoor and Nusrat were delightful company and went out of their way to be helpful and kind to me. Without them, the Beaconhouse guesthouse would have been just a place to crash. Thanks to them, it was a home to me for five months.

Najam Sethi has encouraged my interest in Pakistan and helped me develop and hone my understanding of a complex country in perpetual flux (not to say perpetual crisis), ever since I first looked him up in 1995. Thanks also to Jugnu Mohsin and Jude Heaton at *The Friday Times*. Ejaz Haider has been wonderfully encouraging and gave me space for initial airings of some of this book's stories and ideas in my weekly column for *Daily Times*, Pakistan's best English-language newspaper. Thanks also to Andrew Badenoch for commissioning me to contribute to the Observer Foreign News Service while in Pakistan.

Scott Anger and Ayaz Gul were hospitable and helpful during my visits to Pakistan in 1999. I remember them fondly.

Several friends and colleagues offered or agreed to read parts of the manuscript while I was writing it on a tight deadline in early 2004: Martin Brown, Sarah Cardey, Alex Dunne, Mark Gillett, Brendan Howley, Mary Kay Magistad, Ahmed Rashid, Nick Ryan. Tim Walker went above and beyond the call, and his razor-sharp editorial eye improved the early chapters a great deal. As any author must do, I take full responsibility for any factual or other errors that remain.

Sheena Dewan supported this book with an advance; after knowing her and admiring the growth and ambition of her small publishing house from afar for several years, I'm pleased now to be among her authors. Charlotte Cole commissioned this book and edited it with great sensitivity and tact. The publicist, Emily Bird, has been a pleasure to work with. Thanks also to Konstantin Binder and the rest of the staff at Vision.

Special thanks to Cindy Haralson for rescuing me at the last minute by drawing the map of Pakistan and Kashmir that appears at the front of this book.

My parents, Dayle and Judith Casey, have been unfailingly supportive for 39 years. My brother Aaron is an unstinting cheerleader, ally and friend. Lucy and Stefan have indulged my absenses and obsessions and sustain me in ways I couldn't possibly put into words.

ABOUT THE AUTHOR

Ethan Casey is the co-founder and editor-in-chief of the international online periodical BlueEar.com, editor or co-editor of three book-length collections of writings on global current events, notably *09/11 8:48 a.m.: Documenting America's Greatest Tragedy*, and co-author, with Michael Betzold, of *Queen of Diamonds: The Tiger Stadium Story* (1991). He has reported from Asia, Zimbabwe and Haiti for the *Financial Times*, *The Globe and Mail* of Toronto, the *South China Morning Post* of Hong Kong, the *Boston Globe* and other international publications.